Sheila Sullivan

Falling in Love

A History of Torment and Enchantment

MACMILLAN

First published 1999 by Macmillan
an imprint of Macmillan Publishers Ltd
25 Eccleston Place, London SW1W 9NF
Basingstoke and Oxford
www.macmillan.co.uk

Associated companies throughout the world

ISBN 0 333 75354 2

1 3 5 7 9 8 6 4 2

A CIP catalogue record for this book is available from
the British Library.

Phototypeset by Intype London Limited
Printed and bound in Great Britain by
Mackays of Chatham plc, Chatham, Kent

To my parents, all my family,
our past, present and future loves

Contents

Acknowledgements

I am deeply grateful to the many people who have helped me, both with their specialized knowledge and with invaluable general comments. Among various experts, I am indebted to Susan Reynolds and Oriel Sullivan for generous assistance, and to Rayner Unwin for skilful guidance in the making of a book. Peter Bayley, Deborah Kellaway, Catherine and Anthony Mulgan, Dieter and Florence Pevsner, Tess Sullivan and Jocelyn Smith have all greatly helped me (sometimes more than they knew) with thoughtful advice, comments and references. All errors and obstinacies of any kind are of course my own. I also owe a huge debt to Helen Kraemer, whose tireless labours on card indexes, notes and the bibliography have saved me uncountable hours.

I would also like to thank my agent, Christopher Sinclair-Stevenson, for his staunch support, and my editor, Tanya Stobbs, for her editorial skills, encouragement, and unfailing patience. Lastly, I want to praise and thank not only the British Library but the public library system, and in particular the undauntable staff of my own local library in Barnet.

Author's Note

The vocabulary both of literature and various academic disciplines has been a problem. Even if the effect is sometimes simplistic, I have struggled to avoid critico-socio-psycho-babble, which becomes a menace to all, except to workers within each particular field. For brevity, I have used 'love' to refer to sexual love, and to that early phase of being 'in love'; I use 'romantic' – a troublesome word, but unavoidable – not for the eighteenth- and nineteenth-century Romantic Movement, but for that individual, exalted, impassioned state which is character-istic of falling in love, and is the subject of this book; 'the lover' refers to either woman or man, and does not necessarily imply physical love; I have avoided the word 'desire', which now hovers between the normal senses of 'wish' and 'sexual longing', and the psychological use as 'drive' or 'demand'; 'beloved' is another uncomfortable word, but it has to serve to represent the loved one, for there seems to be no other; 'psychic' is used to refer to the psyche, and not to the supernatural; 'psychodynamic' refers to the processes, conflicts and influence of the unconscious; 'ethology' is the science of animal behaviour, and 'socio-biology' a theory of human behaviour based on evolutionary biology; 'patriarchy' I employ, rather loosely, to describe a general system of male domination.

Prologue

FALLING IN love is one of life's four great upheavals. We are born, we love, we have children, we die. Although only two are inevitable (for love and children do not come to everyone) all of them are events of power and danger. Of these four upheavals, my subject is falling in love and being 'in love' – that spellbound phenomenon which generally lasts from a few months to any period up to three years. Its later development and maturing, in marriage or otherwise, is outside the scope of this book, and so are all the other multifarious feelings described as 'love'. This is about *Eros*, not *Agape* nor *Caritas*; about sexual love, and not the love of God, or of family, or of friends. Yet even within these small boundaries, romantic love creates a dense configuration of emotion, sex, cognition and imaginative experience. Unlike those who despise it, I believe it is a worthwhile experience – yet it is no certain base for any future relationship, let alone marriage. Luck or fate may be with the lovers, and everything may turn out merry as a marriage-bell, but there is no guarantee whatever; falling in love is no way of getting to know someone.[1]

If there are ways in which these troubles could be relieved then love might turn out to be less wasteful. Even though we are so new to the human mind, and do not really know who we are, this ignorance should not stop us searching. For ignorance is bondage, and it is one of the themes of this book that knowledge, and especially self-knowledge, is a first step towards understanding and some kind of control. Before they can be exorcised, demons must be named, and hauled out where we can see them. Some thinkers find this is a naive belief, a scrag-end of the hopes of the eighteenth-century Enlightenment, but at the very least knowledge can reduce anxiety. While there is no spell, no prescription which will ensure that falling in love will have a happy ending, it does seem possible that its excesses and agonies could be made more manageable by some understanding of what is happening to us, and why. No one wants the passion for explanation to submerge the explanation of the passion, but I hope it may still be possible to analyse how love happens and how it feels, and to suggest reasons why it happens and feels as it does; to point out ways in which it might lead more often to happy and lasting relationships, instead of to disruption and despair; to show how we could live with it more consciously. Loss of innocence is the price we pay for rolling back the night, but new freedoms should emerge, and a new knowledge which might clarify the mysterious compulsive behaviours of love.

Theories about love flow into each other like running paint, but I have tried to separate the different streams, and to sort out the arguments about love's antiquity, its origins, its value, its future, and about the ways in which lovers relate to it and to each other. Full-blown love arrives in primary colours, and falling into it may seem all too simple — but there is nothing simple about it. Some three-quarters of this book describes and illustrates the history, nature and origins of falling in love; the two penultimate chapters survey the terrible distresses it can provoke, and the final chapter looks at possibilities for the future.

It is often claimed that the experience of romantic love is confined to the West, yet a recent survey of one hundred and sixty-eight widely scattered world cultures finds that eighty-seven per cent recognize in themselves the madness of love.[2] However, because of its immediate interest to us, and because evidence is easy to come by, I have confined myself to Western culture. This may seem parochial, but a survey of evidence from the rest of the world would need anthropological expertise in many volumes, and the mazes into which this much humbler work has led left me quite faint-hearted enough. So I must leave others to decide whether falling in love is a universal experience, or whether it is a purely western phenomenon. Because so much of our humanity is shared, I hope that what I have to say will also cover much of the experience of western minorities, both sexual and racial. But it will not cover all. Gay minorities, for instance, still have to struggle against an almost compulsory heterosexuality, and so will find the problems of gender, sex and love even more complex than for people still considered as the 'norm'.

In western culture we not only experience romantic sexual love, we ecstatically put ourselves and our futures at its mercy. Whether love is universal, or the cultural construct of different societies at different times; whether it is static or in transition; whether it is a force for life or for death; whether it is an attitude, an emotion, or merely a set of behaviours; whether it is a fraud, a tool for the sustaining of patriarchy and the suppression of women; whether it is a healthy response for troubled people in a troubled world, or an addiction bordering on the psychotic; whether its roots lie in infancy, or in the nascent state common to collective movements; whether it is as durable as flint or frail as a moth – we are besotted with it. Second only to our obsession with sex, love saturates our popular culture, in music, film, television, the press, advertising, the romantic novel. And as the comforts of traditional religion and stable domestic life recede, and all the old points of reference fade, we are left investing ever greater hopes in romantic love.

Along with science, this century has been shaped by ideologies;[3] but there are no fanaticisms in this book. The province of fanatics lies at the extremes, and extremes are beguilingly simple, but I have more respect for pluralities, for the assumption that there is rarely a single great 'truth', and that if anything is to be discovered all disciplines must be allowed to make shift together. 'Truth' is a magnetic notion, but what we actually live in is a mire of contradictions, and in order to find our way boundaries need to be fluid, disciplines co-ordinated and varied views given their chance. Somehow we have to hold in tension our longing for simplicity and our excitement in uncertainty – much less arresting than fanatical conviction. But conviction is frightening stuff, often providing a noble disguise for our ferocities and fears, lusts and greeds, and tending to appear (in love and in everything else) as celestial truth. Our frail consciousness bobs in the dark, on the drift of time, shining and vanishing and shining somewhere else. Because of this frailty, 'objectivity' is rightly under suspicion in most disciplines today; although the cognitive functions of the brain are awesome, steady rational thought is an ultimate impossibility, especially in the turmoil of love.[4] 'Truth' is in fact such an awkward commodity that all the great exploratory thinkers of the West, from Plato and Aristotle to Marx and Freud, are often inconsistent in their thinking, and only a carping mind could blame them.

There are various themes I shall often return to. For instance, I believe that the experience of falling in love in the West has been familiar for at least three thousand years; the *concept* of love has altered so deeply and so often it seems that love will not stay still, yet the aggregation of emotions called 'love' has hardly changed over that time. I follow William James, Peter Dronke, Irving Singer and others in denying the blandly accepted belief that romantic love did not evolve until the twelfth century, when it was created by the troubadours of France.[5] If romantic love implies the idealization and sexual adoration of its object, we can look at least as far back as Homer. What has changed, and changed vastly and often, is the attitude taken towards love's eruption in human affairs; it is these attitudes, and the behaviours they generate (not the emotions they are expressing), which are defined by the culture of each particular time. Many sociologists assert that 'human nature' is a myth, constructed and deconstructed by social change,[6] but I shall argue for a small, tough human core, which we recognize in the lives of people long ago, and around which we construct the mighty edifices of culture. Together with the urge for sex, a need for love may well be a part of that small, persistent centre.

Another of my recurring themes concerns the gender relations of romantic love. Because we are human beings first, and different sexes only second, both sexes share a vast proportion of the experience of love. One basic problem stems from our unthinking acceptance of the gender stereotypes, and before we can learn any more about love we need to consider whether these stereotypes are founded on intrinsic difference, or on social conditioning, or on a mixture of both. At least since the days of the early Hebrews and the classical Greeks, Western society has been dominated by men, and it is not aggressively feminist to argue that over the millennia women have been given a hard time. For the sake of happy and successful love (as well as for much else) this imbalance has to be rethought. However, although my sympathies are strongly with women, this is no radical feminist tract, for I recognize that not all women are wonderful and that men have genuine problems. We do

not need a 'separatist' feminist movement, nor a sex war
in which women and men line up as enemies; what we
need is a full recognition, by each, of the other sex's
needs and hopes and desires.[7] Both sexes have to share
the planet.

My enquiries and conclusions are based on evidence
from almost three thousand years of Western literature,
and on history, psychology, sociology and ethology, all
of which have their own contentious and contradictory
explanations of love; because of this wide range of subjects not every reader will be riveted by everything, but
I hope most will be riveted by something. Experts in all
these various disciplines will find my coverage simple,
but I hope it is not inaccurate. Of course, there are
innumerable problems, and some of them are more or
less insuperable; for instance, interpreting the writing of
the past is not easy, because we project our own present
back on to it, and it takes on new meanings in the light
of new events. But the past is always with us; nothing
makes sense to us without memory, and memory is
history. It would be arrogant, for instance, to ignore
Plato, because even two and a half millennia after he
died his words still flicker over us like distant lightning.
If we want to allay the often disastrous effects of falling
in love, we can do it only by understanding how we have
come to be the way we are. But the nature of acceptable
evidence changes over time, emphasizes change, and what
is thought suitable for publication changes wildly. There
have also been huge alterations in the vocabulary of love,

and this is only one of many ways in which our backward view is obstructed.

The enthusiasts for 'micro-history' make eager use of letters, diaries, memoirs, autobiographies, and I have also made use of a few letters and some passages from autobiography. But many of these sources have been over-plundered, and I have preferred to turn chiefly to imaginative writing, and sometimes to anonymous legend and myth. I have wanted not just to write *about* love but to illustrate (for those who may have forgotten) what love *feels* like; so instead of simply analysing I have made generous use of the words of creative writers, in the hope they will bring a vivid subject even more vivdly to life. Anyone who does not care for poetry or the novel or drama is not going to feel comfortable with this book.

Creative writers are skilful at searching out the particularities of experience and illuminating what we did not know we knew. They give us, not life, but an image of life, and of what we want to know about life – the construct of a fixed, concentrated world. The picture is not 'true', and it may be impossible in the way that a fairy tale is impossible, but it relates powerfully to our experience; the potency of what is 'virtual' rather than 'real' is often demonstrated in the kind of public outrage which has led to the bans placed on works such as *Madame Bovary*, *Ulysses*, and *Lady Chatterley's Lover*. For in creative writing life is never simply *presented* by a text; it is always *represented as* something.[8] Poets, novelists and playwrights long ago revealed much about human nature which the human sciences are only now systematizing.

Freud, for one, freely acknowledged that writers such as Shakespeare, Goethe and Dostoevsky already 'knew' what he had laboriously to uncover and organize, and he recommended those who wish to learn about women to 'turn to the poets.'[9] Although the nature of each period imprints itself on the creative imagination, the arts are not just reflections of social reality. Each reflects and alters the other, and the imaginative arts are as vital a part of their times as letters or journals or autobiography. Furthermore, more than any other kind of writing, poetry, the novel and drama concern themselves with love.

My passages are taken from English and American writing, and in translation from Greek and Latin, French, German, Italian, Spanish, Russian, Norwegian and Czech. Obviously translation adds another difficulty to interpretation, for any translation delivers the original through smoky glass, and most translators write to suit the literary fashion of their own times. One can only trust that the theme is delivered reasonably intact. Most of the writers I have selected are writing of heterosexual love, but for a homosexual or bisexual pair falling in love feels no different. Writing in the sixth century BC, the Greek poetess Sappho displayed no distinction of feeling or expression whether she was writing of her woman loves, or of the (probable) father of her daughter.[10] Similarly, Plato's writings on love, which almost all refer to homosexual pairs, could equally well be describing heterosexual experience. For huge amorphous subjects like sex and love, we put down markers to help us through the fog; but neither sex nor love is divisible into rigid heterosexual or homosexual segments, and both experiences drift in and out of our orderly frontiers. All in all, I think it must be obvious my subject is not a neat and linear one, but more like an untidy ball of wool in which one keeps passing the same places. And because of this a certain amount of repetition and cross-referencing has been unavoidable.

There are dire gaps in the literary evidence. For instance, after the fall of Rome in AD 410 and before about AD 1050, during the so-called Dark Ages, very little vernacular writing survived in Europe.[11] Another problem arises from the scarcity of writing, almost until this century, from the rural or urban working class, who had not the time, the education, or the financial support most writers need to write at all, let alone to write about love. Such writing is pitifully scarce, existing only in the work of scattered 'Peasant Poets' and in the rare isolated genius of a Robert Burns or a John Clare. Popular broadsheets and anonymous songs contain occasional love poetry, but their exuberance springs more from bawdiness than from love. And, as everyone knows, there is a desperate dearth of writing by women; the history of women is still deeply buried and, in spite of recent efforts to retrieve their voices, their work is still scant and until recently widely ignored. With a few glorious exceptions, we have almost no women's writing until the late sixteenth century, and even then much of it was probably written, or at least edited, by men. Through every century since, the amount of published work by women steadily increases, and I have used it where I could.

No one could look at literature today without reflecting on the ferocious wars of modern literary criticism. Some quarter of a century ago, the onslaught of French critical theory began a rout of both the old humanist approach, and of the New Criticism, and critical theory almost totally took over literary criticism. Whatever they have or have not done, both Structuralism and Poststructuralism fundamentally challenged our notion of 'reality', arguing that to a significant extent we create what we perceive. Delving deep into the underlying determinants of the text and the intense pressures at work on the author, they persuaded us into fresh ways of reading, revealing how much we are a function of the words at our disposal, and pointing to the difficulty of extracting permanent 'meaning', or establishing a definitive canon. It is a pity that in trying to free itself from the old accretions of power and privilege this heady revolution spawned such a lumpish jargon. One can only try not to be too intimidated. As far as this book is concerned, I am aware that extracting pieces for quotation disrupts and diminishes both the original text and the chosen words, and in a fluidity of meanings it can easily be misleading; I can only hope the reader will select, out of all possible interpretations, the one which illustrates my theme.

All scientific disciplines have lagged far behind literature in their attempt to explain the phenomenon of love, but love is now a fashionable study and recently most of the human sciences have begun to show an eager interest.[12] I shall often, for convenience, have to separate such categories as Nature, Nurture, biology, culture, cognition, psychology – but of course these are not true divisible entities, for their walls are porous and they interpenetrate. The most anyone should do is to lay emphasis on one or other category, for a researcher who insists that one single discipline represents the only truth is peering through blinkers. My own bias is towards psychology, many of whose schools (including those based on psychodynamic theory, learning theory, humanist, cognitive, behaviourist theories and evolutionary psychology) have their own views on love; and my preference is for a modern reinterpretation of the depth-psychologies established by Freud and Jung, and for the ramifying work of their descendants, with a leaning towards a feminist reconstruction. While every other relevant discourse vitally and energetically contributes, I hope to show it is the depth-psychologies which account most fully for the experience of falling in love.

Until very recently the subject has been neglected by sociologists, but this is now being vigorously remedied, and sociology is speaking up loud and clear. In general, radical sociologists take the view that 'love' as an unconscious psychic experience does not exist; that it is a social construct very rare in the world, and very recent in the West. In the ancient Nature–Nurture debate (which stretches back at least as far as the classical Greeks) the deepest divisions lie between the supporters of Nature, who emphasize evolutionary genetic inheritance and the innate human core; and the supporters of Nurture, who regard evolutionary inheritance as largely superseded by culture and learning.[13] But warfare is subsiding, and both camps are now attempting to establish the resonances between these two great influences on humanity.[14]

Much of the evidence on the sexual and behavioural aspects of love is provided by statistical studies and questionnaires. Since Alfred Kinsey's sympathetic reports on the sexual behaviour of human males and females, published in the sixties, and the slightly later studies of Masters and Johnson, such works have multiplied profusely. They are difficult to assess, because of their differing samples, methodologies and analyses, and because of the unreliability of responses to questionnaires. The 'average' on which they have to base their work often represents no one, and hides from sight all interesting variants and extremities. However, used with care, such studies are vital as general pointers.

In spite of its bitter problems, I have an optimistic belief in the power of love as a growing-point. Love cracks open the old moulds, breaks boundaries, re-orders time, challenges us to resolve inner conflicts, and exposes us to new risks which create new possibilities.[15] The myths of Eros spring from those urges which drive us towards relatedness, to warmth and happiness and creativity. Although love is often attacked and scorned,[16] and although it could perhaps change its nature at some future time, I hope to show that in the present state of our development it is not going to be magicked or rationalized away. For the time being at least, love's raptures and conflicts and agonies are embedded in the life of the West, and we must make what we can of them.

Wise, compassionate, learned, witty, perceptive, irrascible, and written in munificent prose, Robert Burton's 'Love-Melancholy', published in 1621, has been my distant lodestar.[17] Scribbling on in his Oxford study among his 'confused company of notes . . . as I doe ordinarily speake', Burton needled out the mind's anatomy, and even in the middle of scholarly disquisition he catches the heart unaware.

CHAPTER ONE

A First Look Round

FIRST, A look at that heady mutual ecstasy lovers have lived and died for, and will never forget. When a couple fall whole-heartedly in love they are thrown into a state of obsessive passion, and the normal daily range between small pleasures and small anxieties swells to encompass rapture and torment. Love offers golden hospitality, and while it holds sway it is fierce, compelling and anarchic, an energy system of tremendous power, in the service of which we mate, marry, divorce, remarry, betray, go mad, kill and die; 'I had rather contend with Bulls, Lions, Bears, and Giants, than with Love,' cried Burton.[1] This is the love which overturns the heart, draws together the sexual, the spiritual, the imaginative, and absorbs great tracts of the self. According to the French sage, Pascal, it challenges not only personal life but boundaries, rules, kinship, the institutions of society: 'This trifle, this thing so insignificant that we cannot define it, moves the earth, its potentates, its armies, the universe! Had Cleopatra's nose been a little shorter, the whole face of the world might have been changed.'[2]

Certain mammals and birds show preferences during

courtship, and certain primates, such as chimpanzees, show partialities which continue even when the female is not sexually receptive.[3] But only humankind exhibits anything like the full-blown symptoms of romantic love. Although not everyone believes that the process occurs at all, those who believe that *something* happens agree that sex is involved, that illusion predominates, that obsession is inevitable, that the degree of conscious control is not high – and that the time of glory is brief.

Sex presides over a huge kingdom. Whatever its true nature – whether it is the innate driving force of our lives, or a lesser activity almost entirely shaped by culture – its influence spreads far beyond the frontiers of love, which occupies only a small corner of the domain. But however small a corner, and whatever theoretical position one holds, sex-in-love is intensely important to most lovers – and demands chapters to itself. Obviously sex-in-love is not identifiable with simple desire, for in the love of which I am writing sex is deeply intertwined with the affections; as Forster's Maurice feels after his night with Alec: 'O for the night that was ending, for the sleep and the wakefulness, the toughness and tenderness mixed, the sweet temper, the safety in darkness.'[4]

Descriptions of love range between two distant poles, from those based on high-flown idealism to those rooted in earthy realism. To the high idealist, love is an experience of profound value, embracing trust, the affections, sexual passion, life itself; as her suitors found inscribed on Portia's casket, 'Who chooseth me must give and hazard all he hath.'[5] To the realist love is not so momentous; Shaw, for instance, pointed out that no one is occupied with love for more than a fraction of the time given to other occupations.[6] Other realists insist that there is no such thing as 'human nature', taking the view that all emotions, including what we call 'love', are culturally and historically specific, created and managed (in the West at least) to suit the needs of a patriarchal, capitalistic society.[7] Some agree with the seventeenth-century moralist, La Rochefoucauld, who believed that 'Some people would never have fallen in love if they had never heard of it',[8] and they point to the enormous power of the printed word, from the seventeenth century onwards, in spreading the notion of 'love' as a human experience no one should miss.[9] It is also argued that romantic love is an addiction verging on the pathological, or at best an irrational, immature experience with no values except those of self-interest. Others believe that we attach the grandiose label 'love' to what is no more than an acute physiological arousal, which embraces sexual feeling and includes any combination of loneliness, anger, guilt, anxiety, gratitude.[10] Stressing love as 'action', some see it not as a single, distinct phenomenon, but as a confused collection of behavioural events with nothing in common except that they occur in relation to one other person, and that probably about ninety per cent of the experience consists of sex.[11]

Certain recent research proposes that love should be rethought as a flowing 'pure' relationship, free of dependency, jealousy, regression and tyrannical gender relations;[12] new influences in our time should be able to transform it into an experience less excitable and infantile than traditional romantic love, which is now infrequent except among the young and insecure, and should be discarded.[13] But anyone who attempts to substitute obsession with more generalized feelings of sex and affection may well find those affections sliding treacherously into the turbulence of love. The practice of the pure, controlled 'confluent relation' seems (for the time being at least) an over-optimistic goal.

At least as far back as Homer love has been a mystery. Now, three millennia later, when it has become a fashionable academic study, thinkers in many disciplines have revolutionized our knowledge of ourselves – but new possibilities also mean new enigmas and new arguments. In his poem, 'In Sickness and in Health', Auden reflected that we have not done with perplexity yet:

> Rejoice. What talent for the makeshift thought
>   A living corpus out of odds and ends?
> What pedagogic patience taught
>   Preoccupied and savage elements
> To dance into a segregated charm?
> Who showed the whirlwind how to be an arm,
> And gardened from the wilderness of space
> The sensual properties of one dear face?

Defining love

The American 'Conference on Love and Attraction', held in 1982, proposed that love should be defined as 'a cognitive affective state characterized by intrusive and obsessive fantasizing concerning reciprocity of amorant feelings by the object of the amorance.' Once you have mastered the vocabulary, this definition seems reasonable, correctly including emotion, cognition, obsession and fantasy; but love could be defined, in simpler terms, as a state of intense emotional, sexual and cognitive arousal, obsessively concentrated on the beloved, and on the beloved's reciprocal feelings. In Toni Morrison's *Jazz*, Joe disapproves of the phrase 'falling in love', remarking to Dorcas: 'Don't ever think I fell for you, or fell over you. I didn't fall in love, I rose in it.' The first recorded use of 'falling in love', in a modern sense, is by the scholar Palsgrave in 1530, 'I shall fall in love with her',[14] and so the phrase has been serving us (however inaccurately) for over four and a half centuries.

The pursuit of love

Although it is fashionable today to describe love as a suspect ideological construct, many people still hunger for it, and it is pursued as ardently as ever. Few members of either sex are immune, and they look forward eagerly to an overwhelmingly wonderful experience, as advertised in all media throughout the Western world. Love is pursued in tenements and palaces, offices and farms, factories and fields, often simply because it is that magnetic stuff, 'love'. In Duras's *Emily L*, Emily writes to a young man that one should ' . . . set aside a place inside oneself

to wait, you never know, to wait for a love, perhaps for
a love without a person attached to it, but for that and
only that. For love.' As de Botton's narrator discovers, in
Essays in Love, the wish for love precedes the beloved,
and 'the need has invented its solution. The appearance
of the beloved is only the second stage of a prior (but
largely unconscious) need to love *someone* . . .'[15]

Reluctant to admit that romantic love can ever bring
real happiness, de Rougemont insisted that what we seek
from it is the branding of suffering.[16] More mundanely,
others see it pursued as a respectable cloak for sex; for
power or rebellion or revenge or money; or, as Don
Quixote understood, to acquire prestige – all that was
left for a fine knight to achieve was 'to find a lady to be
enamoured of.'[17] Love is pursued because it is a proper
occupation for the young; the peer group presses for it,
and adults long for it (within proper limits) for their
grown-up children. Ever since marriage for love began
to take root in the twelfth century,[18] love has often been
sought with only that end in view; Jane Austen's flightier
girls – Lydia Bennett, Isabella Thorpe, Louisa Musgrove
– are among myriads, then and now, whose chief purpose
in seeking love is to establish themselves in marital
security. Happy lovers are smiled on, social approval is
high, and in the mood caught by Ezra Pound the world
looks on benignly:

Nor is there anyone to whom lovers are not sacred at
    midnight
And in the Via Sciro.

If any man would be a lover he may walk on the Scythian
  coast,
No barbarism would go to the extent of doing him harm,
The moon will carry his candle, and the stars will point out
  the stumbles,
Cupid will carry lighted torches before him and keep mad
  dogs off his ankles.[19]

But not all pairs of lovers are so kindly regarded, for
social tolerance has its restraints. If one follows Eysenck's
trait-analysis, tolerance is generally confined to lovers of
two types only: the couple which is introverted, monogamous and family-oriented, and the couple which is
cheerfully extroverted, sensual and easy-going. On either
side of these approved norms, the sombre, guilt-ridden
couple on the one hand, and the over-sexed and violent
on the other, receive little public goodwill.[20] For general
social approval, it seems, recognizable affection must be
seen to be present.

As much as for any other reason, love is pursued for
solace, as escape from an over-ordered world of alienation
and loneliness, as a flight from boredom, and a comfort
for disappointment. In troubled times, when the old
social units are disintegrating, when religious faith is
declining and (for most people) an afterlife has become a
chimera, love presents itself as salvation, a hope round
which our lives can revolve, a magical comfort for our
losses.[21] However foolishly, in love we hope to find
our Eden, our Utopia, our lost Heaven.

Although over the centuries literature is brimful with

the sensations of love, for the time being most poets have
lost interest in describing it, and the proportion of love
poems in contemporary anthologies is minute.[22] In Amis's
The Rachel Papers, Charles Highway complains that ' . . .
young poets like myself are forever taunted by subjects
which it is no longer possible to write about in this
ironic age: evening skies, good looks, dew, anything at
all to do with love . . .'[23] As in 'In My Craft or Sullen
Art', Dylan Thomas was one of the last of this century's
major poets who dared to write of love, and for lovers:

> Not for the proud man apart
> From the raging moon I write
> On these spindrift pages
> Nor for the towering dead
> With their nightingales and psalms
> But for the lovers, their arms
> Round the griefs of the ages,
> Who pay no praise or wages
> Nor heed my craft or art.

Love is wayward

Everyone knows that in the normal course of events love
does not behave to order, and often arrives with a feckless
disregard for convenience or resistance or command; it
will not be summoned, cannot be measured, cannot be
put away for a more suitable time. The wise and mighty,
the magi themselves, are not immune; once he had met
the enchantress Nimue, the magician Merlin became

'assotted uppon hir, that he myght nat be from hir . . . And allwayes he lay aboute to have hir maydynhede, and she was ever passynge wery of him.'[24] Love lies in wait even for its sceptics, who may find themselves, to their astonishment, in love – as Stevi Jackson discovered, 'Even Sociologists Fall in Love.'[25]

In the first early wavering, choice is still open, progress towards love may be accepted or denied and a prompt exit will evade it, but once the lovers have reached a certain fusion there is little hope of escape. Unless some highly unpleasant revelation occurs, when love can drop stone dead, no amount of interference or rational discourse will prevent it burgeoning. If love, beyond this point, is unavoidable, the converse is also true and it cannot, in ordinary circumstances, be deliberately created. Nevertheless, as I shall describe later, there are hidden and specific reasons for falling in love, and also means by which a state of love can sometimes be engendered. But in general, and to all appearances, love strikes out of an innocent sky.

Variety and range

'Love's limits are ample and great, and a spacious walk it hath . . .'[26] As Burton understood, love arrives for different people at different times, in multifarious forms and by a maze of paths. It may drift in as a wandering wraith, it may rush in on a fever of exaltation; it may creep in unexpectedly through uneasy or bantering relationships; it may suddenly erupt after years of familiarity with its object; it may seep in through religious experience and waft into being in a spiritual swoon, or burst over the heads of the lovers with ferocious danger; or, as for Benedick in *Much Ado about Nothing*, it may arrive in bewildered wonder; 'I do love nothing in the world so well as you; is not that strange?'[27] Love and sex may first appear as separate impulses, either as sexual attraction with love arising in its wake, or as deep affection into which sexual feelings slowly infiltrate.

Attempts have been made to dissect love into specific categories and to build 'love profiles' on them. Sternberg defines eight varieties, the eighth of which combines his three essentials of intimacy, passion and commitment.[28] In another such list, *Eros* relates to physical and sexual feeling; *Agape* to forgiveness and self-sacrifice; *Storge* to caring and friendship; *Mania* to euphoria and emotion; *Ludus* to competition and exploration; *Pragma* to caution and deliberation.[29] Although most loves combine qualities from various of these divisions, writers have been particularly drawn to *Eros* and *Mania*, those heroic, rebellious loves which sweep all before them, in a wild flight from responsibility and reason; Paris and Helen, Antony and Cleopatra, Heathcliff and Cathy. Such 'great' love makes a compelling story and is often dreamed of as enviable, but depth-psychologists look at it with much suspicion, finding that the immense transference of ego suggests an inadequacy in the lover and threatens stability. Likewise, the undying devotion of a rejected or unrequited lover does not point to psychic health. Such a love is heart-rending for the lover to endure, and for others to watch, yet sitting like patience on a monument is a poor recipe for recovery[30] and the better survival strategy is to run. But if there is some hope (and especially if there are obstacles in the way), love may win through, for it feeds, to a certain point, on denial and repression, and on fantasies that cannot be fulfilled.[31]

Once it has come, love may stay quietly, approaching the category of *Storge*. To those who take a realist's view of life, and do not expect too much, this steady, sustaining love may be perfectly adequate. Jane Austen took a particular interest in love which comes slowly, grows slowly, often survives despair, and eventually has its reward; Elinor Dashwood's love for Edward, Fanny Price's for Edmund, Anne Elliot's for Wentworth all share these qualities.[32] Such a love may be painfully shy and slow, with both lovers unable to believe in its reality and desperately uncertain how to proceed. The love of Lucy Snowe and Paul Emmanuel, in Brontë's *Villette*, traces a course so twisted it is agonizing to the diffident Lucy and tormenting to Paul, until at long last he can say, 'Lucy, take my love. One day share my life. Be my dearest, first on earth.'[33] This is a love which tends to arouse more respect than excitement in the observer, but it is moving too, for love that survives pain and separation makes an impressive spectacle, in life as in story. Orpheus, who descended into Hades to rescue his wife Persephone, and Penelope, who waited twenty years for the return of Odysseus, provide two of the great prototypes of faithful love, and their descendants abound in literature.[34]

Another love, approaching *Agape*, is 'holy' and 'perfect', as it was for Phoebe in *As You Like It*, and for Flaubert's Madame Bovary, who at confession thrills to, 'The metaphors of affianced lover, husband, divine wooer and eternal marriage, which . . . moved her heart with an unexpected sweetness.'[35] Sometimes such love is so nobly loving that the welfare of the beloved comes before everything, as it did for Helen of Kirconnel:

> I wish I were where Helen lies,
> Night and day on me she cries
> O that I were where Helen lies
> On fair Kirconnel lea!
>
> Cursed be the heart that thought the thought
> And cursed the hand that fired the shot,
> When in my arms burd Helen dropt,
> And died to succour me! . . .[36]

But love can also be experienced as *Ludus*, beaming like a daisy, the simple and festive joy most people long for, celebrated endlessly in music and lyric. Or it may exist half underground, expressed in teasing and witty abuse, as for Shakespeare's Beatrice and Benedick, in 'a kind of merry war'.[37] It may come lighter still, a game in which neither lover is engulfed but both are amused and satisfied; such a merry-go-round of light-o'-loves represents a hope, rarely fulfilled, that love can be truly carefree. Schnitzler's *La Ronde*, in which everyone in turn loves everyone else, has many forebears, including a

blithe poem by the Greek Moschus, from the second
century BC:

> Pan loved his neighbour Echo; Echo loved
> A gamesome Satyr; he, by her unmoved,
> Loved only Lyde; thus through Echo, Pan,
> Lyde, and Satyr, Love his circle ran.[38]

It is doubtful whether these circling amours qualify as
'love', but some sort of special attraction is operating,
and all such stories make an ironic comment on the
unpredictability of love.

The scale on which love is lived is as various as the
ways in which it arrives. It may involve a profound
restructuring of being, a death and a resurrection, or only
a modest adjustment; it may be absorbing and creative,
or an anxious experience to be kept firmly in its place.
Just as love will affect the lover's personality, so will that
personality have a significant effect on the experience of
love. Although he found marked differences in the sexual
needs and behaviours of women and men, Eysenck is
clear that difference is more applicable to personality
than to biology. We are human beings first, women and
men second, and the diversity of our love is shared to a
high degree.[39]

It is very rare that love, once it is truly over, will
ever revive again with the same partner. However, when
its course has been interrupted rather than ended, and
gone underground, surviving time and other loves, a
resurrection does sometimes occur long afterwards. This

is yet another variety, one which has vanished and much later proves itself alive. When Peter and Rhiannon meet again, in Amis's *The Old Devils*, long after their love affair in youth, they find themselves in love all over again, and he is able to tell her that all through time and forgetfulness he has always loved her.[40]

In a shadowy corner lurk the strange, intense loves sometimes experienced by children. These passions may be of child for child, or of child for adult, and they are uncannily reminiscent of romantic adult love. In Thomas Hardy's *Life*, he described how as a small boy his feeling for Julia Augusta Martin, the lady of Kingstone Maurward, 'was almost that of a lover'[41] and a century later Betjeman described in 'Beside the Seaside' the heartbreak of a schoolgirl whose 'rejection' by her schoolmaster scarred her entire future. These eerie experiences point two ways, back into the world of infancy and on into adult sexual love, and they obviously hint at psychodynamic explanations.

The antiquity of love

Whether this spellbound experience has been with us for millennia, or for only a few hundred years, is a highly contentious question. Opposing the widely held view of de Rougemont, C. S. Lewis, Lawrence Stone and many others, I believe that falling in love, as we experience it and recognize it in others, has flourished for at least three thousand years, and therefore for over two millennia

before it is supposed to have been 'created' by the troubadours of twelfth-century France. To some people this may
seem obvious, but the views of Lewis and de Rougemont
have now prevailed for half a century.

As Peter Dronke has comprehensively shown, falling
in love has marked the life of Western humanity at least
as far back as the civilizations of the Egyptians in the
second millennium BC, and of the Greeks in the first.[42]
The oldest of all known collections of love-songs, written
on papyrus in Egypt about 1300 BC, displays the sensations of the modern lover in every important particular;
one begins 'More lovely than all other womanhood . . .'
and another 'My darling – my beloved – whose love
empowers me . . .'[43] For over three thousand years we
find these records of passion, infatuation, suffering, joy,
all charged with the authentic sensations of romantic
love. Only the most bizarre definition of love could cut
out the experience of Sappho, Achilles and Patroklos,
Paris and Helen, Amor and Psyche, Daphnis and Chloë,
all of whose loves were celebrated in classical times.
Tremulous worship, dependence, salvation and erotic
rapture shine as brightly there as in the lines of any
nineteenth-century Romantic poet.

As far back as the evidence stretches, something we
can only call falling in love has been a matter of desperate
import. Whatever the true causes of the Trojan War,
Homer presented it as a direct consequence of the love
of a Trojan prince, Paris, for a Greek queen, Helen.
Throughout the *Iliad* and the *Odyssey* no other explanation
is put forward, and when the veteran Trojan soldiers

assemble by the gates of Troy, 'like cicadas, which settle on a tree in the woods . . .' they acknowledge that war undertaken for a woman as beautiful as Helen is no shame.[44] The legendary love stories of ancient Greece (which would have been recited centuries before they were written down), describing the loves of Eros and Psyche, Echo and Narcissus, Troilus and Cressida, Acis and Galatea, Dido and Aeneas, are all recognizable to us as immediate, familiar experience.

Even through the mist of translation, a few random samples should be enough to show the antiquity and persistence of love. The poetess, Sappho, who (probably) lived on Lesbos in the sixth century BC and was later venerated by Plato as 'the Tenth Muse', seems to have written love poetry to both women and men. Apart from one poem, her work survives only in fragments (and some may not be hers), yet it is a marvel of skill, and it surely proves that obsessive and committed love existed in the sixth century BC, and that the experience of loving is common to homosexual, bisexual and heterosexual lovers. In Elizabeth Taylor's novel, *Palladian*, the young governess, Cassandra, listens to Sappho's poetry read aloud to her: 'The words seemed to have been brought up, glittering, dripping from the sea, encrusted still by something crystalline, the fragments and phrases like broken but unscattered necklaces, the chipped-off pieces of coral, of porphyry, of chrysolyte.'[45] In all her surviving lines on love, Sappho treats it with veneration:

> Some say that an army of cavalry
> Others that infantry
> And others that a fleet of ships
> Is what is most desirable
> On this dark earth
> But for me it is whatever
> Inspires one's passionate love . . .[46]

Later, in the third century BC, the Greek poet Theocritus described the one-eyed Polyphemus, suffering his unrequited passion for Galatea:

> O whitest Galatea, can it be
> That thou shouldst spurn me off who love thee so? . . .
> I know to sing, as there is none
> Of all the Cyclops can – a song of thee,
> Sweet apple of my soul, on love's fair tree . . .[47]

Two centuries later, another Greek poet, Meleager, addressed the ships which sailed between him and his beloved:

> O gentle ships that skim the seas
> And cleave the strait where Helle fell,
> Catch in your sails the northern breeze
> And speed to Cos where she doth dwell,
> My love, and see you greet her well.[48]

There was no lack of interest in love among the poets of Rome. Catullus, for one, wrote of it prodigiously, often with ironic tenderness, and the lovers' haunting theme of time was as well known to him as to all lovers since:

My sweetest Lesbia, let us live and love,
And though the sager sort our deeds reprove,
Let us not weigh them. Heaven's great lamps do dive
Into their west, and straight again revive,
But, soon as once set is our little light,
Then must we sleep one ever-during night . . .[49]

In the *Aeneid*, Catullus's contemporary, Virgil, described the widowed Dido's meeting with the hero, Aeneas:

But she who Love had long since swallowed down,
Melts with hid fire; her wound doth inward weep:
The man's much worth, his nation's much renown
Runs in her mind: his looks and words are deep
Fixt in her breast: care weans her eyes from sleep.[50]

The gimlet eye of the Roman poet, Ovid, took note of all the quirks and pains and ecstasies of love, as well as of simple lust;[51] and his near contemporary, Propertius, rejected by his beloved, bitterly imagined her life in the hereafter:

When thou must home to shades of underground . . .
Then wilt thou speak of banqueting delights,
Of masks and revels which sweet youth did make,
Of tourneys and great challenges of knights,
And all these triumphs for thy beauties' sake:
When thou hast told these honours done to thee
Then tell, O tell, how thou didst murder me.[52]

And the Roman poet, Petronius, foreshadowed the fascination felt by the nineteenth-century Romantics for the process of lovers' 'merging':

Ah God, that night when we two clung
So close, our hungry lips
Transfused each into each our hovering souls,
Mortality's eclipse![53]

A handful of works written in Greek, between the last century BC and the third century AD, have a claim to be called the first novels of the Western world.[54] All of them are tales of love, describing initial passion, trial and separation, and final joyful reunion. Longus's *Daphnis and Chloë*, for instance, concerns itself with the pining and turbulence still entirely characteristic of love; Chloë 'did not know what was wrong with her . . . but she felt sick at heart, and she could not control her eyes, and she was always talking about Daphnis . . . One moment she would be laughing, the next she would be crying . . .'[55] It is also worth looking at the Icelandic sagas, and the few remaining morsels of Anglo-Saxon verse, written down between the seventh and twelfth centuries, many of them replete with devotion and longing and loss, entirely recognizable by any lover of a later age.[56]

It is surely clear that these small scraps, lifted from the huge corpus of classical and post-classical love literature, describe feelings wholly familiar to twentieth-century lovers. In spite of the distortions of translation, these are not passages describing sexual obsession but passages describing sexual love, the love which much later came to be known as 'romantic', the love which Homer's Paris describes as one of 'golden Aphrodite's lovely gifts . . . the glorious gifts that come of the gods' own giving.'[57]

Changing attitudes

It is not the experience of falling in love but our attitudes to it which have changed, and changed and changed again; the admiration of the classical Greeks for homosexual love, for instance, provides a dramatic contrast to the Christian abhorrence which followed later, and our own revolt from middle-class Victorian puritanism is almost as great a change. Sometimes the male role has been totally dominant, sometimes the woman has been idealized, sometimes the emphasis has been on spirituality, sometimes on sex. At various times love has been seen as a divine delirium of the gods; as the crazed creation of potions and witchcraft; as a tiresome disease. These constantly changing emphases and interpretations make it seem that over the millennia the sensations of love have constantly transmuted from one experience into another. But this is not so. What changed, and changed profoundly, at innumerable points in time, was the degree of interest taken in different aspects of love, the values accorded it, the proper behaviour associated with it. While that core of emotion, obsession and bedazzlement, which we now call romantic love, has scarcely altered throughout western history, the aura draped around it has changed all the colours of the rainbow. What the Ancients and their successors *thought* about love is often mysterious to us; what they *felt* is entirely familiar.

Of course, no society has ever been homogenous enough to share all its convictions, about love or anything else, and there will always be both collective and individual beliefs;[58] but for varying reasons certain shifts become the social norm, and come to represent, in a general way, the character of that time. Instead of rushing through the entire history of shifting attitudes to love, I will look at just three Western literary movements which challenged their societies' stereotypes of love, and both altered and reflected, for some people, contemporary attitudes to love and sex. Although they did nothing to change the heart of love, the twelfth-century troubadours, the eighteenth-century followers of the cult of 'Sensibility', and the nineteenth-century Romantics, all saw it as something ennobling, worthy of investigation and even veneration; all of them made some effort to heal the old Platonic–Hebraic–Christian rift of body and spirit, to soften the harsh outlines of the male and to give women a degree of respect unusual for the time. Each was interested in different ways of looking at love in a life.

A great wonder has been made of Courtly Love. But as Dronke has demonstrated, it did not burst new-minted on the world from the castles of Provence, for its antecedents stretched back to classical Greece, to Egypt, and to Mozarabic Spain. It was far from being a consistent 'school', for alongside the idealism of Ventadour ran the subversive bawdy of Macrabu, alongside its cult of secrecy ran its public expression in verse, and scholars have never agreed on its 'code' of adultery because a single view did not exist. However, from the Provençal poets' cult of *'fin'amors'*, in a flowering of lyric verse, *something* interesting did emerge; in their celebration of devoted, idealistic 'Courtly' love they turned a new, rapt attention inward, to individual experience.[59] What was happening was not a transformation of the nature and experience of love, but the rise of a new fascination with the old familiar emotions, and the proper behaviours associated with them. Love came to be seen as an event of real worth, an experience central to living, rising from within rather than by the imposition of destiny. A new absorption in the numinous, transcendent aspects of love arose from its ancient involvement with deities, and from the first medieval fading of religious experience.[60] Taking a fresh look at old passions, sweetening the imagination, creating the seed of the 'gentleman', these poets also conferred a new personal dignity on the high-born, powerful women at the heart of their poetry. (At about this time, two immensely powerful Queens replaced two of the four Kings in the game of chess.)[61] Courtly Love gave some release to the feminine aspect of men, encouraging sensitivity and helping to humanize the old crudity of sex and dominance. In a bold attempt to heal the ancient rift between sinful sex and holy love, many of these poets elevated sex as a joyful, innocent expression of the love of woman and the love of God, and began to shift their interest from the Holy Virgin to the idealized earthly woman as a new road to divinity.

What they did was not to *invent* love but to reorder and reinterpret old feelings and beliefs; their idealization of women had its roots in Middle Eastern poetry,[62] and their fascination with the numinous re-created the magical part played by gods and goddesses in the love stories of the ancient world. What had developed was a new, delving interest in the nature and significance of being in love.

The southern troubadours, the northern trouveres, the German minnesingers, and the few women troubaritz were sparse and scattered, yet the towering poets who came hard on their heels – Dante and Petrarch and Chaucer – eagerly absorbed their influence (Chaucer a little later – for everything arrived late in the north). It was these writers who began the long task of establishing the new notion of marriage for love. Although it is widely assumed that such marriages rarely occurred until the mid-eighteenth century,[63] recent work has shown that love was accepted as an important ingredient of marriage as early as the thirteenth century; in 1215, for example, Pope Alexander III decreed that marriage was valid 'through the free consent of the spouses', and the permission of parents was no longer required.[64] This law become a new lovers' charter – a charter of which Margery Paston and the bailiff Richard Calle availed themselves in 1469, to the fury of her well-to-do Norfolk family.[65]

The next period ranges from the late seventeenth century to the late eighteenth, when alongside sterner, older traditions a new cult of 'Sensibility' arose, first on the continent and then in England. Various writers again began to advocate a softer attitude, a new respect for gentleness, a new emphasis on the *coeur sensible* and on the value of the emotions, expressed in words, deeds and tears. As in the realm of Courtly Love, a man was encouraged to exhibit some of the 'feminine' qualities rejected by the patristic gender-role. The new cult deeply affected writers of the calibre of Goethe, Richardson and Sterne, and later amused Jane Austen, whose Marianne, all passion and tears, is as easy to mock as the antics of Mackenzie's *Man of Feeling* and Brooke's *A Fool of Quality.* Yet the movement was touching in its earnest wish for goodness, for the free expression of emotion and for the tinge of dignity it gave to women. This is the period in which Lawrence Stone places his 'affective individualism', the first acceptance of the close, affectionate nuclear family, based on free choice and the domestication of love;[66] and this is another moment when romantic love once again intruded on religious values, and for some people began to carry our hopes of heaven.

The third of the periods in which love attempted to shake off the traditional shibboleths spanned the late eighteenth and early nineteenth centuries, and is celebrated as the Romantic Movement – of which we still remain the tattered offspring. Like their forerunners in the cult of Sensibility, the Romantics revered emotion; in 1817 Keats wrote to his friend Bailey, 'I am certain of nothing but the holiness of the heart's affection . . .' and in the same letter called for 'a Life of Sensations rather than of Thoughts!'[67] Shelley was the Romantic high-priest of idealized, sexual love, elevating it into a creative experience of metaphysical sanctity; eroticism shimmers through his work, and that of Keats, and many of their brotherhood. Like the poets of Courtly Love before them, the Romantics denied the sinfulness of sex and believed the sins of the flesh were nothing compared with the sins of the spirit. Together with his fellows, Shelley found both earthly and holy rapture in the fusion of love, as he expressed in 'Love's Philosophy':

> Nothing in the world is single;
> All things by a law divine
> In one spirit meet and mingle.
> Why not I with thine?

Sex-in-love was to be the redeemer of humanity, transforming sensuality, and leading to transcendence and intimations of eternity. Fervently denying the received standards of morals and art, the Romantics constructed a new, personal morality, in love and all else, unfettered by the rational values of the eighteenth-century Enlightenment. Their fascination with the notion of lovers' 'merging' can be traced back to Plato,[68] and the powerful alliance they forged between love and nature only re-emphasized and transfigured the part played by nature in the classical pastoral 'novels', and in Anglo-Saxon poetry.

Certain of their number, such as Byron, delighted in the darker side of love, in incest, sin, melancholy, death. In John Bayley's engaging phrase, the Romantics recreated 'the old tragic darkness', with couples such as Brontë's Heathcliff and Cathy replacing Tristram and Iseult in the experience of love, separation, agony and death.[69] Their fascination with love-and-death intensified the interest once shown by Homer, by Virgil, by the Anglo-Saxon and Icelandic poets of the early Middle Ages. For love, it seems, borrows an authority from death. When the life-giving energy of *Eros* is alloyed with the destructive drive of *Thanatos*, the alliance creates the allure of the celebrated *liebestod*. In such epiphanies of high romance, death offers freedom in a present which is for ever, a resurrection in eternal unity, and (perhaps above all) protects love from fading into disillusion.[70] For de Rougemont, this blending of love and death is the core of romantic love, and in order to be 'romantic' love must be fatal and doomed, filled with passion and pain, and culminating in death and transfiguration.[71] As Shakespeare's Mark Antony murmurs as he sweeps towards it, there to be joined by Cleopatra –

> ... I will be
> A bridegroom in my death, and run into't
> As to a lover's bed.[72]

Lovers enmeshed in love and death drift through the centuries – Orpheus and Euridyce, Paolo and Francesca, Tristram and Iseult, Romeo and Juliet, Antony and Cleopatra, culminating in the full grandeur of *liebestod* in Wagner's cycle of *The Ring*. Even in our own anti-romantic times death and love often still ride together;

when Norah's lover leaves her, in Barnes's *Nightwood*, 'Norah knew now that there was no way but death. In death Robin would belong to her . . . and with the torment and catastrophe, thoughts of resurrection, the second duel.'[73] But there are new attitudes about; it is suggested that our twentieth-century inability to cope with death is corrupting the creative view of sex-in-love into a process of guilt and violence.[74]

It is tempting to be carried away by the glowing splendour of *liebestod* and to imagine that only this can be true romantic love. Yet it is not only death that makes love 'romantic'; death merely adds a further resonance to the obsessed sexual devotion we call romantic love. It is part of our native ambivalence also to long for happy endings, and to enjoy stories of the innumerable lovers who are driven by the brilliant, unifying, life-giving Eros. Shakespeare's Rosalind and Orlando, Fielding's Tom Jones and Sophia, Tolstoy's Kitty and Levin, Forster's George and Lucy – all of them find romantic love and *live*.[75]

Feeling and thinking

Obviously the heady experiences of love are deeply emotional. While sex can function on a very low emotional content, as a matter of physiology, falling in love cannot. Love is a potent producer of various neuro-chemicals, including adrenalin, and the surge of these creates a complex euphoria beyond any other known to us – not more profound, not more permanent, but the most dazzling.[76] As I have said, some sociologists propose that emotion is a purely cultural and linguistic construct, specific to each society and each period, with no presocial root,[77] yet the simple fact that we have some basic understanding of stories and histories from all cultures of all known periods suggests that certain emotions are common to most human beings, and that humanity shares some kind of common emotional core, however small. It is true that a variety of less basic emotions are obviously socially conditioned, and therefore not immutable, and it is very clear that the *expression* of all emotions is largely governed by culture, but it is unreasonable to reduce all emotional life to no more than its social aspects – important though these are.[78] The basic emotions – anger, fear, joy among them – are primitive, heady, intractable survivors, probably innate, even universal, and can be distinguished from emotions which are clearly adaptive and sensitive to cultural change. Unlike our cognitive processes, which function chiefly from the cortex (or 'new' brain), emotions mainly originate in the 'mid' and the 'old' brain – the inner parts which we have inherited from our evolution through the animal kingdom. The 'old' brain does not generate new emotions at the galloping rate the 'new' brain generates new ideas, for the primitive emotions are much less susceptible than thought to change. The profound feelings involved in love are not easily altered; it is not they but our attitudes towards them which constantly change. It is possible that one day the aggregate of emotions we call love will alter or disappear, but for three millennia at least its obsessive, sexual exaltation has recognizably survived.

The connection between strong emotion and physical bodily symptoms ('visceral arousal') has always been obvious to lovers, and 'The Song of Solomon' puts it bluntly; 'My beloved put in his hand by the hole of the door, and my bowels were moved for him.'[79] There have been many contending theories attempting to explain emotion, each jostling the other aside,[80] but many researchers would probably at least agree that different emotions are experienced from the same visceral disturbance; the cortex labels them according to their context, and to its previous store of knowledge.[81] In the case of love, or simple sexual attraction, the genital organs will provide the cortex with an instant clue as to what its interpretation should be, but a beating heart, panting breath, trembling, sickness, tears, may all be experienced as love or terror or anger or joy. This overlapping gives rise to one of love's more devastating demons, which shifts one emotion bewilderingly into another, love to hate or hate to love.[82] In his small, searing poem 'The Vixen Woman', Harold Monro conveys the horror:

> The vixen woman
> Long gone away,
> Came to haunt me
> Yesterday
>
> I sit and faint
> Through year on year.

Was it yesterday
I thought her dear?

Is hate then love?
Can love be hate?
Can they both rule
In equal state? . . .

Her whom I loved
I loathe today:
The vixen woman
Who came my way.

In full spate, sex, love, hate, fear, anger are very difficult to subdue, alter, or socialize; 'When the prick stands up,' cries Roth's Portnoy, 'the brains are as good as dead!'[83] If there is no happy outcome to love, the lover is left in a physiological turmoil, in which adrenalin plays a destructive part, leading to the kind of psychosomatic distress which occasionally ends in breakdown and suicide. That omnivorous man of the Renaissance, Sir Francis Bacon, did not care for the emotions, which he considered troublesome and messy: ' . . . the mind in its own nature would be temperate and staid, if the affections, as winds, did not put it in tumult and perturbation.'[84]

Like other primates (with whom we share a very high proportion of our genetic material), we show preference, we feel anger and pleasure and lust and fear, and an urge for the company of our own kind; yet it is obvious that vast tracts of our behaviour and culture are not like theirs at all, and this distance is due largely to the 'new' brain, our human cortex. The cortex is the chief seat of our fiendish cleverness, of our creative conceptual thought, of the overwhelming power of language. But we have to be wary of simplistic divisions. For all its majesty, the cortex is not an absolute monarch but the co-ordinator, mediator and intimate companion of the 'old' and the 'mid' brain. Whatever model of the brain you favour – a switchboard, a vast building, a pattern of modules – the various parts of the organ resonate together, and every time we choose to consider them separately we have to remember that they do not *function* separately. Emotions are more than a simple expression of primitive energies, for they are influenced by the cortical 'new' brain, just as they in return influence the cortex, and become deeply involved in the formation of attitudes, beliefs and motivations. Other than by the unproved paths of prayer, or other paranormal experience, there is no way into the mind except through the senses, and 'cognition' provides the means by which the brain arranges the stream of sensory signals into an order it can interpret and make use of. Cognition includes such vital processes as thinking, perception, language, memory, reasoning, judgement, imagination, and it is our high degree of cognitive development which makes us human rather than animal. Much respect has been paid through the centuries, and especially in recent years, to the part played by cognition in the act of falling in love; throughout his regal volumes on love Irving Singer emphasizes its role, and especially the part played by the marvels of the imagination.[85] Operating on the vast store of experience built up in the brain, the imagination enables us to envisage what is not present, reconciles opposites, reduces confusion into order, concentrates diversity from all corners of the lover's life, and centres obsessive attention on the loved one.

It has often been noticed how events of high emotion etch themselves on the memory.[86] Drab normality does not provoke either emotion or recollection; but surprise, interruption, ambiguity, paradox — these startle and arouse. And what is more startling and arousing than falling and being in love? In William Trevor's *Lovers of their Time*, Norman remembers long after it was over the decade of the Sixties, which

> ... trailed behind it the marvels of his love affair with Marie ... Their walk to the Great Western Royal, the drinks they could not afford in the hotel bar, their studied nonchalance as they made their way separately upstairs, seemed to Norman to be a fantasy that had miraculously become real. The second-floor bathroom belonged in it perfectly, the bathroom full of whispers and caressing ... he would recall the delicately veined marble and the great brass taps, and the bath that was big enough for two. And now and again he heard what appeared to be the strum of distant music, and the voices of the Beatles celebrating a bathroom love, as they had celebrated Eleanor Rigby and other people of that time.

One of the strangest of all acts of the imagination is to provoke love for an absent figure, never yet encountered in the flesh, and about whom only certain qualities are known. In her *Memoirs of Colonel Hutchinson*, written in the mid-seventeenth century, Lucy Hutchinson described how her future husband was so in love with her before they ever met that when he heard (falsely) she had been married he 'turned pale as ashes, and felt a fainting fit to seize his spirits.'[87] Sometimes a writer's work is all that is needed to provoke love; before they ever met, Benvenuta fell in love with the German poet Rilke; Isabella Burton with the explorer, Sir Richard Burton; and Elizabeth Smart with the poet, George Barker.[88] As to fiction, in *A World of Love*, Elizabeth Bowen tells the story of a girl who falls in love, through his letters, with a man long since dead. Both actual and imaginative experience can stir the brain in exactly the same way.

Startling evidence of the imagination also occurs when the sudden sight, or touch, or sound, or smell of someone *thought* to be the beloved produces an electrifying effect in the lover. When the realization dawns that this was not, after all, the beloved, sensation abruptly dies. Lovers who have been deceived by darkness can enjoy ecstatic happiness with the one they suppose to be the beloved; Elaine deceived and almost ruined Sir Lancelot, and in Lodge's *Small World* Persse McGarrigle rapturously believes, in the darkness, that Lily is his beloved Angelica.[89] There could hardly be stronger proof of the interplay of cognition and feeling.

Nature and Nurture

To learn more about love we need to know whether all its hectic activity is innate in our human structure, or whether we create and learn it, as we learn so much else. The Nature versus Nurture debate is at least as old as the Greeks, and it has appeared under many synonyms, including 'innate' versus 'learning', but I shall stay with the traditional labels of Nature and Nurture, which are old-fashioned but vivid and concise.

Supporters of Nature argue that our genetic inheritance is of prime importance; most of what we feel, do, think, believe, is inherited and 'natural', an intrinsic part of us. We are born not made. Their opponents, the supporters of Nurture, argue that we are largely created by the culture – the Nurture – into which we are born; in Burton's beguiling words, we arrive 'naked to the world's mercy'.[90] Culture immediately begins its immense work on every newborn baby; usually without realizing what is happening, we are taught, we are modelled, we learn from the society that lies about us. That ardent champion of Nurture, B. F. Skinner, in his novel, *Walden Two*, describes how Frazier, the founder of the model community of Walden, sets out to prove that he and his small society have the power to change human nature as required.

These arguments veer into every corner of human life, and debate on their merits has provoked seething rage. Defenders of Nature argue that their opponents' faith in the 'new' brain, and its ability to override the 'old', labels them as cultural determinists, who have failed to study their evolutionary biology, and that their confidence in humanity's power to reorder itself condemns them as naive idealogues. The advocates of Nurture see their adversaries as politically suspect, the upholders of patriarchy, class, property, inheritance, the oppression of women, and the unequal distribution of wealth. It is all too easy, they argue, to pass off what are in fact social constructs as if they were 'natural' inherent phenomena; myths, wrote Roland Barthes, 'lose the memory that they once were made' and thus a myth 'transforms history into nature.'[91]

To support totally either Nature or Nurture, to the exclusion of the other, is to peer with only one eye, and at last the crude attempt to apportion a percentage of genetic inheritance against a percentage of cultural adaptation is giving way to the belief that what matters most is the interpenetration between the two. The reduction of all explanations either to biology ('Nature') or to culture ('Nurture') is being radically altered by those who argue that our genetic inheritance resonates unceasingly with our environment, and that each profoundly influences the other. The new evolutionary psychology proposes that the neural complex which is our brain, and gives rise to human nature in all its physical, psychological, cultural and imaginative variety, was (and is) shaped by natural selection, adapting and readapting over aeons to solve the problems of our ancestors; our variations in behaviour and personality are caused more or less equally by genetic inheritance and by the cultural adaptations we have the skill to invent and the learning to adopt.[92] Our genetic and cultural evolution has provided us with brains of such subtle power that we are able to break away, at least in part, from primitive compulsion, to exercise judgement and will-power, and to create societies which are only partially founded on the 'selfish' gene and are capable of moral and imaginative adaptation.[93]

If we are to hope for any form of control over the excitable phenomenon of love, we need to know how all these pressures oscillate together. Upholders of Nature argue that love is a natural event that simply happens because we are human; we are not taught it, we do not learn it, it is there as a fact of life. Upholders of Nurture, however, take the view that falling in love is a behaviour we have created and learned, and we experience it according to the cultural demands of our time.[94] We love because that is what we are taught to expect, and from our society we acquire a 'love-script', a pattern which directs us how to feel and behave in love.[95] Those who look for an intermediate view argue that love is based on inescapable genetic needs, but profoundly adapted by culture. Nature affects Nurture, and Nurture affects Nature; we are both the creatures and the creators of our own existence. Speaking in *The Winter's Tale* on the art of grafting plants, Polixenes neatly concludes:

> . . . This is an art
> Which does mend nature, change it rather, but
> The art itself is nature.[96]

CHAPTER TWO

The Symptoms of Happy Love

WHAT DOES it feel like to be head-over-heels in love and whole-heartedly loved in return? I will look later at the belief that love is a curse, or that all a lover experiences is sex dressed up in flummery, and I shall also look at the heartache, the delusions and the treacheries which so often blast it. But happiness first.

Although at first glance the symptoms of love seem chaotic, it is possible to separate various elements. As I have said, every age has its own modes of expression, its own inhibitions and freedoms, its own notion of how lovers should think and behave — in fact, its own socially constructed norms, which let us know whether we are permitted to cry, faint, speak frankly, or be demure and silent, and all of these modes and customs will be described in the writing of the time. If my descriptions seem over-ripe with literary illustration, this is because writing on love has been so prolific and irresistible.

Immoderation

Moderation is not in the nature of love. In Winterson's *The Passion*, Vilanelle cries out, 'With this feeling inside, with this wild love that threatens, what safe places might there be? Where do you store gunpowder?'[1] Lovers are driven by terror, by joy, by laughter, by tears, finding themselves whirled up into the skies, then dropped in the abyss. In Brown's view, 'The agent becomes a patient, and is overcome by desire for the object: that is, does not critically examine, or intervene in, the process of seeking it. The process is non-rational.'[2] As Ezra Pound described it, nothing is normal, nothing is steady:

> Fool who would set a term to love's madness,
> For the sun shall drive with black horses,
> > earth shall bring wheat from barley,
> The flood shall move toward the fountain
> ere love know moderations.[3]

Sometimes the senses are not turbulent but stunned, as they were for Turgenev's Vladimir, sitting 'as if under a spell. What I felt was so new, so sweet. I sat quite still, hardly looking around, and breathing very slowly. Only from time to time I laughed silently at some memory, or grew cold at the thought that I was in love – it was here – this was love.'[4]

Both women and men in love will find themselves in a state of sexual upheaval, when longing for the beloved can become a desperation:

Western wind, when will thou blow,
The small rain down can rain?
Christ, if my love were in my arms
And I in my bed again![5]

Although frank description of sex has been proscribed for long periods in polite literature, in our own time there is no equivocation. In *Lolita*, his once-notorious novel of the late 1950s, Nabokov delivers the quaking intensity of sex-in-love: 'All at once we were madly, clumsily, shamelessly, agonizingly in love with each other; hopelessly, I should add, because that frenzy of mutual possession might have been assuaged only by our actually imbibing and assimilating every particle of each other's soul and flesh . . .'[6] Obviously the erogenous zones receive the most rapt attention, but to lovers the entire body is a source of erotic delight.

Joy and omnipotence

'Perfect love', wrote William Hazlitt, 'reposes on the subject of its choice, like the halycon on the wave; and the air of heaven is around it.'[7] There are very few raptures like the raptures of happy love. It glows through Western literature as far back as the Hebrews and the Greeks, and the shine it brings to the world is almost too common-place to dwell on. For Roland Barthes, every meeting is a celebration: 'The Festivity is what is waited for, what is expected. What I expect of the promised presence is an unheard-of totality of pleasures, a banquet; . . .'[8] The neuro-physiological changes which accompany love provoke a brilliant sharpening of the senses, brighter eyes, a surge of energy and a sunny conviction of well-being.

On the back of this exultation rides omnipotence, charging the lover with godlike powers. Once enamoured, wrote Burton, the lover 'will go, run, ride many a mile to meet her, day and night, in a very dark night, endure scorching heat, cold, wait in frost and snow, rain, tempests, till his teeth chatter in his head . . . he will swim through an Ocean, ride post over the Alps, Apennines, or Pyranean hills, fire, flood, whirlpools, though it rain daggers with their points downwards . . .'[9] In the welter of books Patrick Brontë laid before his children, did Anne find this breathless passage of Burton's? For this is exactly what Gilbert Markham does, in *The Tenant of Wildfell Hall*, when in his desperation at Helen's (supposed) marriage he runs 'across the country, just as a bird might fly – over pastureland and fallow, and stubble, and lane, clearing hedges and ditches, and hurdles. . . .'[10] This exalted state of mind inures the lover to all discomforts of the body, as Tolstoy's Levin finds when he realizes Kitty loves him: 'He had not eaten for a whole day, had not slept for two nights, had been exposed to the cold for several hours with scarcely any clothes on, and felt not only fresher and sounder than ever, but completely independent of his body.'[11]

Love injects a charge not only of physical energy but of high courage and even timid lovers find themselves as bold as Jane Austen's Edward, who refuses to marry the girl his father demands: ' . . . I scorn to marry her in compliance with your Wishes. No! Never shall it be said that I obliged my Father.'[12] There is a long history of women emboldened to dress up as boys to accompany their loves on dangerous journeys, and only with difficulty did John Donne prevent his adorer from following him overseas as a page.[13] As Nin's Djuna proclaims in *The Four-Chambered Heart*, 'Ali Baba protects the lovers! Gives them the luck of bandits . . . Love runs free and reckless . . .'[14] De Botton's narrator perceives how both lover and beloved feel certain of their reality, of their worth, of being loved for what they *are*: 'Without love, we lose the ability to possess a proper identity, within love, there is a constant confirmation of self.'[15] This surge of energy is often accompanied by a release of creative imagination, when the lover turns eagerly to the making of poetry, music, painting. The results may be dreadful, but sometimes the beloved does indeed become the true and animating Muse, to whom we owe peerless love poetry from Sappho to the present day.

Admiration and awe

Lovers bestow admiration on each other and this can soar to heights only a lover could believe in – and only the most naive observer could accept. In *Sartor Resartus*, Carlyle's Herr Teufeldrockh describes how to the young lover 'all women were holy, were heavenly . . . all Soul and Form.'[16] In the late twentieth century this is not a fashionable state of mind, yet a warm admiration, even veneration, is still a normal ingredient of love – and is likely to be very much greater than the beloved's due.[17] Nevertheless, this bestowing of admiration is one of the creative gifts of love, and sometimes the beloved is inspired into fulfilling these extravagant expectations.

'Helen, thy beauty is to me / Like those Nicean barks of yore . . .'[18] As it was for Poe, admiration of woman's beauty has been an endless inspiration to male writers, and the theme runs on through the centuries, too abundant and too familiar to need illustrating. Either because of the dearth of women writers, or for more obscure psychological reasons, there is far less literary evidence of women's admiration for male beauty, although it is familiar enough in classical mythology; Silene is enraptured by Endymion, Aphrodite by Adonis, Venus by Mars. Although these stories were probably composed by men, women's admiration certainly plays its part in falling in love, and a good-looking man receives his due of attention; in a recent novel of light romance the heroine, Elodie, sees a stranger emerging from the sea, whose beauty might be that of a classical Greek: 'Thick dark hair was plastered in spiky curls to a deep forehead. High cheekbones and an aquiline nose gave his features a chiselled appearance only slightly softened by the ironic smile lifting one corner of his wide mouth.'[19]

As when Levin sees Kitty on the ice, the emotions inspired by love charge the image of the beloved with a brilliance which separates it from its mundane surroundings; 'There was nothing particularly striking about her garments or her pose, but for Levin she seemed to stand out from the rest as a rose among nettles. Her presence brightened all about her. She was like a smile shedding radiance all around.'[20] Love not only endows the beloved with this particularity but it enhances all other qualities, and the gazing lover, like Florizel in *The Winter's Tale*, finds graces never noticed before:

> . . . when you do dance, I wish you
> A wave o' th' sea, that you might ever do
> Nothing but that; move still, still so,
> And own no other function: each your doing
> So singular in each particular,
> Crowns what you are doing in the present deeds,
> That all your acts are queens.[21]

If the qualities seen by the bemused lover seem nothing much to the rest of the world, that is in the nature of romantic love, for the image of the beloved owes much more to the lover's fantasy than to reality.[22] Nevertheless the lover will battle angrily to defend it, for an attack on the beloved is an attack on the lover and for both their sakes it must be repulsed. Dissecting this touching absurdity, in *Zuleika Dobson*, Beerbohm describes how, 'No man really in love can forgive another for not sharing his ardour. His jealousy for himself when his beloved prefers another man is hardly a stronger passion than his jealousy for her when she is not preferred to all other women.'[23]

One love for ever

To the Hebrew writer of 'The Song of Solomon', 'love is strong as death'.[24] The whole-hearted lover is convinced that love is for always and, as Emily Dickinson described in 'Choice', the beloved is the only possible one:

> Of all the souls that stand create
> I have elected one.
> When sense from spirit flies away
> And subterfuge is done;
>
> When that which is and that which was
> Apart, intrinsic, stand,
> And this brief tragedy of flesh
> Is shifted like a sand;
>
> When figures show their royal front
> And mists are carved away, –
> Behold the atom I preferred
> To all the lists of clay!

To the lovers, love is now and always, and time has no authority. Writers and their readers have always been moved by stories of lifelong love, the conqueror of time and mutability: nearly three thousand years ago bards and writers described the long love of Penelope and Odysseus; in the Middle Ages, of Lancelot for Guinevere; in the nineteenth century, of Dobbin for Amelia in Thackeray's *Vanity Fair*; today, the fifty years' devotion of Fiorentino to Fermina, in García Marquéz's *Love in the Time of Cholera*. No one needs reminding how often poets have celebrated belief in this eternal future, and in 'My love is like a red, red rose' Burns does it with such simplicity it surely must be true:

> Till a' the seas gang dry, my dear,
> And the rocks melt wi' the sun:
> And I will luve thee still, my dear,
> While the sands o' life shall run.

A sense of personal renewal is intrinsic to love, marking an undoing and a remaking; at Dante's first sight of Beatrice, 'Incipit Vita Nuova'. The metaphor of rebirth reappears constantly, implying that all previous dross, all past disappointments are scoured away, leaving the inner self young and shining, as once it was:

> I was born here a second time, to learn
> Slowly like a child, by heart and touch,
> Till your life's web and furnishing
> Grows older in me than my cradle. . . .
> I have drunk forgetfulness
> Of former worlds . . .[25]

For E. J. Scovell, touching the nerve of this metamorphosis, the world before love becomes prehistory.

Made new, a lover feels transformed into a better person – perhaps a partaker in a spiritual journey, or merely the purveyor of a general benevolence, with a conviction that love is good for the character. In Plato's *Symposium*, the host Agathon praises love as the giver of goodwill, good humour and affection,[26] and two and a half thousand years later A. E. Housman noted the (temporary) improvement wrought by love in a Shropshire lad;

> Oh, when I was in love with you
> Then I was clean and brave,
> And all around the wonder grew
> How well I did behave.
>
> And now the fancy passes by,
> And nothing will remain,
> And miles around they'll say that I
> Am quite myself again.[27]

Home and destiny

The lover is home at last. As de Botton's narrator fervently believed, when he met Chloë, ' . . . all the rest had been compromise and self-deception . . . I recognized in her the woman I had been clumsily seeking all my life . . .'[28] Love seems to the lover a dispensation of the gods. Only the hand of destiny could have arranged the meeting, and the impression of a directing destiny is strengthened even further because such meetings so often seem haphazard. Brooding on his abrupt and overwhelming love, in *The Black Prince*, Murdoch's Pearson declares: 'My love for Julian must have been figured before the world began. Surely it was lovers who discovered astrology. Nothing less than the great chamber of the stars could be large and steady enough to be context, origin, and guarantee of something so eternal. I realized now that my whole life had been determinedly travelling towards this moment.'[29]

This apparent act of destiny may present itself as a universal truth, or the voice of the god of love, or even of God himself. At the banquet in the *Symposium*, Aristophanes proposed that once there were three sexes, female, male and hermaphrodite, each of them with four legs, four arms, two heads, etc. When Zeus split each in half, the half-woman would seek her severed half (creating a lesbian couple), and the half-man would seek *his* severed half (creating a male homosexual couple); and then, when one of a pair died, the remaining half might seek a partner of the opposite sex (creating a heterosexual couple), all in re-perfected union.[30] This is an eerie but fruitful metaphor, for its image of two becoming one embraces both the human longing for union and the lover's sense of destiny.

Love offers hearth and haven. Although she scarcely knows him, Colette's Claudine has no doubt that Renaud is her only home: ' "At one moment, I lifted my head to him. His intelligent eyes looked down into mine and I smiled at him with all my heart. I have seen that man exactly five times; I have known him all my life . . ." She leant her head against him . . . with the blissful security of someone who had at last reached the end of a long journey.'[31] Implicit in this sense of homecoming is the giving and receiving of absolute trust. So much is offered in love – the self, the future – that trust is an absolute necessity. Fear of abandoning the self to the beloved can be profound, but a lover who is afraid to trust is not, in the end, going to be able to love. The childhood home is where trust begins, and if this was never so then happiness in adult love may run a troubled course.[32]

Allied with this sense of homecoming is the uncanny conviction that the beloved has been known before, and that love is not a new experience but the recognition of an old one, as Dante Gabriel Rossetti described it in 'Sudden Light':

> I have been here before
>   But when or how I cannot tell:
> I know the grass beyond the door,
>   The sweet keen smell,
> The sighing sound, the lights around the shore.
>
> You have been mine before, –
>   How long ago I may not know:
> But just when at the swallow's soar
>   Your neck turned so,
> Some veil did fall, – I knew it all of yore . . .

Either we are back with Aristophanes, and the belief that love is a recogniton on earth between beings once divided – or we are looking at the psychodynamic view of love and its roots in infancy.[33]

Togetherness

The sense of togetherness can be so strong that lovers create the illusion of a separate world, which only they inhabit. Snowed up in the silent dangerous countryside at Varykino, Lara and Zhivago create this world apart: 'Outside, the frosty winter night was pale blue. To see it better, Yury stepped into the cold dark room next door and looked out of the window . . . The splendour of the frosty night was inexpressible. Yury's heart was at peace. He came back into the warm, well-lit room and began to write.'[34] The rapt concentration that lovers bestow on each other creates a golden bauble, and those outside the charmed circle sense a togetherness so intimate it excludes everyone beyond. Their understanding feels so deep that nothing either does seems alien, and both feel suspended together in another place.

Even when they are apart, lovers still feel together, and their absorption in each other disrupts all other activity; in 'The Good Morrow' John Donne asked, 'I wonder by my troth, what thou, and I / Did, till we lov'd?' Each seethes with curiosity about the other, all must be discovered, stories of horror and joy dug out which had never been told before. Their intense intimacy embraces their bodies, their imaginations, their intellects, their habits, their pasts. Some lovers are delighted to be baffled by each other, but others feel they need to know the other's very core. This concept of the 'core' is of great interest to many writers on love, some of whom feel there can be no true love unless the 'core' is discovered.[35] This is what Birkin longs to discern, when in Lawrence's *Women in Love* he cries out to Ursula, 'I want to find you, where you don't know your own existence, the you that your common self denies utterly.'[36] Others assert that although people are a mystery, with their own 'otherness', no one possesses anything which might be called a core, spirit or soul.[37]

The confident lover never feels finally bereft or lonely, for even in the painful absence of the beloved that person is always there, making two against the world. Yet an actual parting, however temporary, will feel as raw as the wound described in Amy Lowell's 'The Taxi':

When I go away from you
The world beats dead
Like a slackened drum.
I call out for you against the jutted stars
And shout into the ridges of the wind . . .
Why should I leave you
To wound myself upon the sharp edges of the night?

Any couple happy in love feel a deep, protective gentleness towards each other. They long to be giving and they are in a state in which giving is easy, for in love the boundaries between giving and receiving blur. The wish to care for the other's needs, from simple matters of warmth and food and the swapping of clothes, to the demands of sexual and imaginative companionship, is deeply felt and often highly idealistic. There is a longing for unselfish sharing, with none of the shifty calculations of output and reward common in ordinary life. As in Burns's poem, the lover puts the welfare of the beloved above all selfish needs:

> O wert thou in the cauld blast
> On yonder lea, on yonder lea,
> My plaidie to the angry airt
> I'd shelter thee, I'd shelter thee.
>
> Or did misfortune's bitter storms
> Around thee blaw, around thee blaw,
> Thy bield should be my bosom, [shelter]
> To share it a', to share it a' . . .

And the beloved is filled with gratitude – gratitude for care, for happiness, for companionship, above all gratitude for being loved.

Such loving togetherness centres on one particular person, and the centuries have worked no alteration on the obsessiveness of love. As this fifteenth-century Irish poet understood, the love into which we fall is exclusive;

Slender graceful girl, be no longer inconstant to me; admit
    me,
soft slender one, to your bed, let us stretch our bodies side
    by side.
As I have given up, O smooth side, every woman in Ireland
    for your sake,
do you give up every man for me . . .[38]

T. L. Peacock is only one of many writers who have amused themselves with the idea of being in love with two people at once; in *Nightmare Abbey* Scythrop is questioned by his long-suffering father:

> ' "Will you have Miss Toobad?"
> "Yes."
> "And renounce Marionetta?"
> "No."
> "But you must renounce one."
> "I cannot."
> "And you cannot have both. What is to be done?"
> "I must shoot myself."
> "Don't talk so, Scythrop. Be rational, my dear
>   Scythrop." '[39]

No one need believe in these doubly enchanted suitors, because if they think they are in love with two, they are in love with neither. Of course it is commonplace – and a source of much trouble – to 'love' one person and be '*in* love' with another, but the kind of love into which we fall is obsessively concentrated, and those who truly fall in love fall for one beloved only. One love blocks out the possibility of another, for in order to fall the emotions must be open and unbonded.[40] If they are damaged, or already captured, falling in love will fail altogether, or occur in such an attenuated form the experience cannot be described as 'in love'.

Once the heart is set, the lover will listen to no warnings, no advice. In Malory's 'The Tale of Sir Gareth', Lyonette and Sir Gareth will have only each other; ' " . . . if I may nat have hym, [she says] I promyse you I woll never have none. For . . . wote you well he is my fyrste love, and he shall be the laste . . ." "That is trouthe," seyde sir Gareth, "and I have nat you and welde you as my wyff, there shall never lady nother jantyllwoman rejoyse me." '

To anyone but the beloved, obsessed lovers often seem plain rude – a point which has been noted by various writers since the time of Plato. In the *Phaedrus*, Socrates observes of a lover that ' . . . the conventions of civilized behaviour, on whose observance he used to pride himself, he now scorns'.[41] In Austen's *Pride and Prejudice*, Bingley becomes neglectful of his social duties once he has met Jane Bennett, and Elizabeth comments to her aunt on his inattention to all other young ladies: ' "Is not incivility the very essence of love?" '[42] A century and a half later, in *Cold Comfort Farm*, Flora Poste observes that it is 'Curious how Love destroys every vestige of that politeness which the human race, in its years of evolution, has so painfully acquired'.[43]

Pursuit of the beloved's haunts is one of the most crazed of love's obsessive symptoms. Whether there is any hope of meeting or not, the lover will feel compelled to look for a chance encounter, or merely to be where the beloved has walked. Pining for a glimpse of Dora, David Copperfield 'walked miles upon miles daily in the hope of seeing her . . . I walked about the streets where the best shops for ladies were. I haunted the Bazaar like an unquiet spirit, I fagged through the park again and again, long after I was quite knocked up.'[44]

Merging and the oceanic

'She is myself. What am I to do?' asks Nora of her love in *Nightwood*.[45] From this point we move into the more esoteric realms of love, not experienced by all lovers. But for some, togetherness may slip into the experience described as 'merging', a profound sensation of identity, interpenetrating both partners and leading to a sense of fusion which seems to transcend the self, and feels as undeniable as sun and moon. In Freud's view, the sensation of merging arises because in love the boundary between ego and object almost dissolves, and the lover feels that 'I' and 'you' are the same,[46] as they seemed in infancy, between infant and mother. The starkest of all cries of unity must be Cathy's, in *Wuthering Heights*, when she declares of Heathcliff, ' " . . . he's more myself than I am . . . If all else perished, and he remained, I should still continue to be; and, if all else remained, and he were annihilated, the Universe would then be a mighty stranger.'[47] To those who find that love creates a gain in identity, and not a loss, this 'merging' seems incomprehensible, even repellent, it does to Lawrence's Birkin, in *Women in Love*: 'Fusion, fusion, this horrible fusion of two beings, which every woman and most men insisted on . . .'[48] What Birkin longs for is 'the paradisal entry into pure, single being . . . taking precedence over love and desire for union . . . even while it loves and yields.'[49] Singer resolves his scepticism of 'merging' by turning to the notion of love as magic, which violates the laws of nature and changes the world, and so perhaps 'may well symbolise the radical transformations that love can actually institute.' Love, he argues, works a transformation so profound that it truly transcends the self's perception of reality.[50]

The 'oceanic' sensation expands from the sense of merging, reaching beyond the beloved, beyond the self, and into the wider world of nature and even the universe. This is the sleepy rapture of Robert Graves's witching poem:

> She tells her love while half-asleep,
>   In the dark hours,
>   With half-words whispered low:
> As Earth stirs in her winter sleep
>   And puts out grass and flowers
>   Despite the snow,
>   Despite the falling snow.

These oceanic effects act as catalysts for the ecstatic experience known as 'Adamic', described by Laski in *Ecstasy* as a mystical, joyful renewing, in which the raptures of the lover and those of the religious mystic become almost indistinguishable. The orgasms so obviously experienced by Margery Kempe ('a flame of fire, wondrous hot and delectable') and St Teresa of Avila (speared by her Lord with 'a point of fire') were, in Laski's view, not merely physical but a vital part of the mystical experience of Adamic ecstasy, tenderly evoked by Auden:

> Soul and body have no bounds:
> To lovers as they lie upon

> Her tolerant enchanted slope
> In their ordinary swoon,
> Grave the vision Venus sends
> Of supernatural sympathy,
> Universal love and hope . . .[51]

This ethereal light drifts into the realm of myth. In Nin's *The Four-Chambered Heart*, when Djuna and Rango are living on their boat on the Seine,

> 'He carried her down the trap-door into the freezing room damp with winter fog. She stood shivering while he made the fire, with an intensity into which he poured his desire to warm her, so that it no longer seemed like an ordinary stove smoking . . . or Rango an ordinary man lighting wood with damp newspapers, but like some Valkyrian hero lighting a fire in a Black Forest. Thus love and desire restored to small actions their large dimensions, and renewed in one winter night in Paris the full stature of the myth.'[52]

Paradox and magic

Bewildered, in *The Passion*, by her feelings for her new love, Winterson's Vilanelle muses on the 'Hopeless heart that thrives on paradox; that longs for the beloved and is secretly relieved when the beloved is not there. That gnaws away at the night-time hours desperate for a sign and appears at breakfast so self-composed. That longs for certainty, fidelity, compassion, and plays roulette with anything precious.'[53]

The symptoms of love can be so bewildering that only paradox seems able to compass them. A conviction of intense individuality may coexist with the sense of oneness and 'merging'; the beloved may appear both real and yet ideal, unique yet universal. Just as lovers seem to be one yet two, so (as Barthes describes) they both know and do not know each other: 'I believe I know the other better than anyone and triumphantly assert my knowledge to the other . . . ; and on the other hand, I am often struck by the obvious fact that the other is impenetrable, intractable, not to be found . . . I know what I do not know.'[54]

The challenges of paradox slip easily into the embrace of magic, with its long history of interfusion with love, in numinous awe and enchantment. Revealing the collapse of reason in love, the tales of *Eros* are filled with events which apparently only magic can explain; tales of capture by elf, fairy queen, mermaid, the returning ghosts of lovers, and by the transformation of beasts into humans through the power of love. Sometimes such stories express the difficult passage from child to adult, and describe how humans, once translated into beasts by witchcraft, are transformed back into human shape by love. Sometimes it is the girl who is the agent of change, as in 'Beauty and the Beast' and 'The Frog Prince', in which her courage and affection transform the beast into a figure of adult male love; sometimes it is young men who are given the credit for initiating women's adulthood, as in 'The Sleeping Beauty' and 'Cinderella'. Such legends and fairy-tales touch the nerve of human fears and longings, providing a simple route by which the unconscious reaches the daylight.[55]

Sea nymphs, mermaids and mermen haunt their human loves, and sometimes destroy them. For love is not only strange, it is full of danger. In the realm of magic and faerie, love is pagan, alien, far distant from the love of God; witchcraft haunts it, spells decide the fate and the sexual prowess of lovers, and virtuous love does not always win through. Potions and magic drinks are commonplace, as in the legend of Tristram and Iseult, or in the ministrations of Puck's juice in *A Midsummer Night's Dream*. Mirrors appear frequently; in *The Faerie Queene*, Britomart first sees and loves Artegall in a magic mirror, just as the Lady of Shalott falls in love with the image of Sir Lancelot in the mirror in her room.[56] Sometimes love is so compelling it draws the dead lover's ghost back from the grave, as it drew Margaret to Clerk Saunders:

> 'My mouth it is full cold, Marg'ret;
> It has the smell now of the ground;
> And if I kiss thy comely mouth
> Thy days of life will not be lang' . . .
>
> 'Is there ony room at your head, Saunders?
> Is there ony room at your feet?
> Or ony room at your side, Saunders
> Where fain, fain I wad sleep?'

'There's nae room at my head, Marg'ret,
There's nae room at my feet;
My bed it is fu' lowly now,
Amang the hungry worms I sleep.

Cauld mould is my covering now,
But and my winding-sheet;
The dew it falls nae sooner down
Than my resting-place is weet . . .'[57]

The Wavering of Boundaries

The frontiers of the self are always more fluid than we like to acknowledge, and in love this wavering may become almost a dissolution, when masks dance and swop; as D. G. Rossetti described in 'The Kiss', lovers find themselves merging into mother, father, child, spirit, god:

I was a child beneath her touch – a man
When breast and breast we clung, even I and she –
A spirit when her spirit looked through me –
A god when all our life-breath met to fan
Our life-blood, till love's emulous ardours ran
Fire within fire, desire in deity.

As in White's *The Beautiful Room is Empty*, sex and gender meander through the relations of Maria and the young man, Bunny, slipping constantly under the pressure of love.[58] Colette's Claudine shrieks at the dismayed, middle-aged Renaud: ' "Oh! why don't you want me, at least for your daughter? I ought to have been your daughter, your friend, your wife . . ." '[59] A shift from adult to child is a common sign of lovers' intimacy, when they cast off the chains of adulthood, return to their genderless, asexual infancy, and in a cosy world of escape call each other by the infant names with which the Valentine columns of newspapers overflow. The squirming embarrassment of the world outside their love is of no account to them, for they are oblivious enough to think their private communication is invisible. This wandering of boundaries helps to make falling in love an experience of bewildering totality, in which the entire being becomes involved, physically, emotionally and imaginatively, as it did for Goethe's Werther, in love with Charlotte; 'Good God! was there a single force in my soul which remained unutilized? Could I not, when with her, unfold that entire power of feeling with which my heart embraces all nature?'[60]

Humour

Romantic love can be very dense and solemn – but humour is never far away, and lovers are greatly given to laughing. As the mind runs agog with new lights and linkages it explodes into the laughter which both expresses and creates well-being. Laughter is a healer,[61] and even though humour is often based on anxiety and guilt, nothing lightens the intensities of love like more humour. Jokes derived from sex and love – the most fruitful single sources of humour in recorded history – provoke us to smile, snigger, purr, and fall about laughing.

Laughter is usually created by discrepancy between expectation and performance, by displacing the norm and creating disjunction. As William Hazlitt noticed in the last century, 'Man is the only animal that laughs and weeps; for he is the only animal that is struck with the difference between what things are and what they ought to be.'[62] In the fraught exploits of sex and love, anarchic urges and social manners are constantly askew, setting up a target for deflation, and in *Zuleika Dobson* Beerbohm deflates with his nib again and again: ' "The iron has entered into my soul [groans the Duke]. I droop. I stumble. Blood flows from me. I quiver and curse. I writhe. The sun mocks me. The moon titters in my face. Tomorrow I die." '[63]

Because so much of it rises from the mazy underworld of sex and excretion, the humour of sex and love can be uneasy and even cruel – yet it is often frothy and untroubling too. Addressing his 'darling, precious, beautiful tart', the Roman poet, Catullus, cries:

> . . . Quick, this minute,
> Now, if you're in the giving mood;
> For lying here, full of good food,
> I feel a second hunger poke
> Up through my tunic and my cloak.[64]

As to sex in the vernacular, the twentieth-century 'Ballad of Eskimo Nell' tells it baldly:

. . . The women knew his playful ways
Way down on the Rio Grande,
So forty whores tore down their drawers
At Deadeye Dick's command.

Now forty arses and forty cunts
You'll find if you use your wits,
And if you're quick at arithmetic,
Signifies eighty tits.

Now eighty tits is a goodly sight
To a man with a mighty stand;
It may be rare in Berkeley Square
But not on the Rio Grande . . .[65]

The ludicrous discrepancy between the dream of sex and its actual performance provides one of the most famous humiliations in literature, inflicted on Sterne's Walter Shandy as he sets about the conception of his future son, Tristram: '*Pray, my dear*, quoth my mother, *have you not forgot to wind up the clock?—Good G—!* cried my father, making an exclamation, but taking care to moderate his voice at the same time,—*Did ever woman, since the creation of the world, interrupt a man with such a silly question?*'[66] Even to D. H. Lawrence, deep into the solemnity of sex, the act seemed blackly absurd: 'Yes, this was love, this ridiculous bouncing of the buttocks, and the wilting of the poor insignificant, moist penis. This was the divine love!'[67]

Wit deals in words, farce deals in chaotic events. And (as every theatre director knows) of all the sources of farce, sex and love are supreme. When, in Nin's *The Four-*

Chambered Heart, Sabina meets Rango, 'We got into an elevator and he began to kiss me. . . . First floor, second floor, and he still kissing me, third floor, fourth floor, and when the elevator came to a standstill it was too late . . . I pressed the button wildly and went on kissing as the elevator came down . . . he pressed the button and we went up and down, up and down, madly, while people kept ringing for the elevator.'[68] The trim shape of the limerick is perfect for sexual wit:

> There was a young student of John's
> Who attempted to fondle the swans.
>   Whereupon said the porter,
>   'O pray take my daughter,
> The birds are reserved for the dons.'[69]

And sex is the inspiration for one of the neatest scraps of wit in the English novel, when Fielding wrote of his hero, *Jonathan Wild*, ' . . . he in a few minutes ravished this fair creature, or at least would have ravished her, if she had not, by a timely compliance, prevented him.'[70]

CHAPTER THREE

Sex By and Large

‌ᴄ⬥⬦⬥ᴄ

Sᴏᴍᴇ ᴋɪɴᴅ of sexual passion must be embedded in the experience of a couple in love, for if it is absent they are not (by any reasonable definition) 'in love'; and so some understanding of sex is essential to an understanding of love. Even in the most idealistic of romantic loves the sexual element cannot be completely transcended, for when this is so we have the sexless loving-kindness of Christ or St Francis, the love described not as *Eros* but as *Agape* or *Caritas*. But although romantic love needs sex to define it, the experience cannot be *only* sexual, for when personal affection is bleakly absent the obesssion cannot be described as love.[1] In this and the following chapter I shall look at sex in its happier aspects, and defer its tormenting and disruptive effects until later.

Heterosexual sex obviously embraces the biological aspects of being female or male, and is fundamental to most life on earth. Evolution is driven almost entirely by sex, and most of the animal kingdom snuffles around it with insatiable curiosity. It would be hard to exaggerate the sexual energy behind evolution, or the variety of attitudes, behaviours and appearances it generates. Sexual pleasure is the most intense of all the pleasures of human-kind, and sex has always been pursued not just for reproduction but for its raptures; Chaunticleer, Chaucer's farmyard cock, served Venus 'more for delyte than world to multiplye'.[2] Our sexual behaviour is less influenced by hormones, less automatic and more affected by past experience than in any other member of the animal kingdom. Although all forms of sexual arousal are physio-logically much the same, any two experiences are very rarely felt to be identical, because the mighty human cortex modifies the rigid innate behaviours we inherit in the 'old' brain, creates new skills and behaviours, and provokes imaginative sexual activity which explores and adapts and refines. As it was for Chaunticleer, repro-duction is only a fractional part of sex. The psyche is a frail thing and sexual activity, filled with pleasure and overall sensuousness, offers a route to comfort and confi-dence. At its happiest, sexuality includes a pungent amalgam of excitement, pleasure, danger, exploration and recreation; it strengthens bonding, affection and co-operation; it provides security, defines relationships and contributes a glow of self-esteem. Sex in humans is not a raw genital drive, but a complex psycho-sexual experience.

Is sexual behaviour intrinsic or learned?

If we make an imperfect but useful distinction between 'sex' as referring to biological activity, and 'sexuality' as referring to all that accompanies and surrounds it, the traditional school of Nature holds that 'sex' is an unchanging biological drive, and that 'sexuality' incorporates the submissive woman and the dominant man. Seen as an anarchic, 'natural' function, sex is in conflict with culture rather than a part of it. The school of Nurture, on the other hand, dismisses the idea that we have a 'natural', unchanging sex drive, arguing instead that sexuality is largely a social construct, a component of social relations, learned through the 'sexual script' of each succeeding society.[3] Because the nature of sex is malleable and contradictory, its status and activities vary widely in different cultures, at different times, and apart from the most basic forms of sexual intercourse there is no abiding norm, nor any fixed 'instinctive' pattern; for instance, the sunny acceptance of homosexuality by the classical Greeks, who saw it as a love far surpassing the vulgar love of women, was replaced in a few centuries by Christian abhorrence.

All this suggests that the human species does have to learn a great deal of its sexual behaviour. As Uncle Toby nervously approached the Widow Wadman, in Sterne's *Tristram Shandy*, Corporal Trim bade him 'never fear'. But, writes Tristram, 'Now my uncle did fear; and grievously too: he knew not . . . so much as the right end of a Woman from the wrong . . . – '[4] And the anonymous

Victorian ballad makes blatantly plain the fact that human sex requires instruction:

> . . . Father was in the corner
> Explaining to the groom
> The vagina not the rectum
> Was the entrance to the womb.

No one needs to be reminded of the changes in sexual attitudes and behaviour over the last few decades, during which a gulf has opened up between women over forty, who grew up under the old codes and were often virgins when they married, and the next generation whose behaviour has been moulded and learned in a far more permissive society. Not only are there differences in individual sexual attitudes and behaviours within one period, but also between social classes, involving fidelity, masturbation, the resort to prostitutes, the kind of sex practised, and many other distinctions;[5] forty-five years after Kinsey, Wellings's survey found that although these differences are much weakened they still exist.

As usual in these debates, arguments from both Nature and Nurture have something to contribute; it seems reasonable to accept the argument from Nature for a basic fundamental urge in all creatures, including humans, to engage in sex; and on behalf of Nurture, to agree that much of human sexuality is learned, and highly susceptible to cultural change and fashion. Our bonds, in sex, in love, and all else, are embedded in the reciprocal relationships between physiological, psychological and social structures.[6]

Since about the middle of the the twentieth century we have become more and more openly engrossed by sex, and in recent years the body has become a magnetic site of academic activity. But for over two centuries its sexual aspects had already been a favourite subject for analysis, and we cannot be sure that our interest is any greater than that of our forebears – only that at this end of this century we have given ourselves permission to be openly active and openly fascinated. In spite of certain enduring taboos and social controls, sex for pleasure is now per-formed exuberantly, even in Catholic and puritanical lands, and is probably written and joked about more than ever before in history. Sex as pornography proliferates in clubs, in private, in magazines, on satellite sex channels and on the Internet. As Byatt's Maud says to Roland, in *Possession*, ' "I was thinking last night – about what you said about our generation and sex. We see it everywhere. As you say. We are very knowing." '[7]

Not only do our leniencies change from one time to another, our concepts of proper 'feminine' and 'masculine' styles change also, for not everyone is entirely female or male, physically or psychologically, and the borders between heterosexual, bisexual and homosexual waver and slither.[8] Alfred Kinsey's sexual scale graded those who are wholly heterosexual as 0 and those who are wholly homosexual at 6, with degrees of bisexuality in between.[9] This is not always a popular assertion, for we find it safer to be categorized, and sexual indeterminacy is often seen as threatening.

Sex surveys

In spite of greatly improved methods, and new computer technology, surveys are still awkward instruments. The samples chosen are crucial, and on some grounds someone is certain to object to them. On such an intimate subject as sex, the replies of interviewees are often affected by reticence or boastfulness, or the wish to provide a 'correct' answer; and because our practices and our theoretical standards are so often at odds the results will be partial and ambiguous. And all surveys are reflexive, influencing behaviour as well as revealing it. However, if we tread warily, a soundly based survey will provide working material – and there is no other way of finding out how people in general think and behave.

Various massive studies have emerged over the last fifty years, and made their originators household names. Since the middle of this century the work of Kinsey, Masters and Johnson, and Hite, has sold around the world, and further surveys have been legion.[10] In the 1940s, Kinsey established sex as a respectable study. His aim was to be as scientific as he could, and concentrate on the objective measure of sexual behaviour, disentangled as far as possible from its emotional ties. He rejected the age-old tendency to accept the male as the norm, he refused to accept the concept of sexual 'perversion', and he startlingly demonstrated the gulf between conventional sexual attitudes and actual sexual practice. Beatrice Faust described his books as works of *caritas*, and although he has been fiercely attacked he has been just as fiercely defended.[11]

The work of Masters and Johnson in the 1960s was highly innovative, and because the authors measured the physiology of sexual acts in their laboratory it caused great scandal. They were well aware of the emotional aspects of sex, but believed that the physical basis had to be understood before the other components could be integrated. Perhaps their greatest gift to women was to establish the role of the clitoris, and finally to dispose of Freud's baleful insistence on the 'vaginal' orgasm. The updating of their work in 1994 re-emphasized the variety of sexual need and performance in both sexes, and found a new converging of female and male practice and experience.[12] Hite's impassioned *Hite Report* emerged, in 1976, as a cry of protest on behalf of women and their difficult, damaged sex lives – a cry continued a decade later in her *Women and Love*.[13] Wellings's *Sexual Behaviour in Britain*, which began its extensive survey in 1990, covered a sample of 18,876 women and men between the ages of sixteen and fifty-nine,[14] and in 1994 the authors of *Sex in America* published a massive survey of sexual behaviour and attitudes in the United States.[15]

In *The Female Eunuch*, Germaine Greer gathered up a resounding set of objections to the side effects of sex surveys, insisting that 'There is no substitute for excitement.' Surveys, she argues, tend to turn sex into something mechanical and official, until we find ourselves making love to organs and not to people.[16] No one could deny that we now live in a deluge of sexual information, some of which heightens rather than reduces anxiety, and Greer is right to insist that excitement is paramount — yet 'excitement' can be devastated by ignorance.

Physiology

Though very few are active, we are all to some degree bisexual,[17] and sexual physiology is very similar in both women and men. In both, the area of the hypothalamus, in the 'old' brain, plays a vital part in the regulation of bodily activities, such as eating, drinking, body temperature and sexual behaviour. In spite of first appearances, this similarity between women and men is not surprising, for only one pair of our forty-six chromosomes determines genetic sex, and sexual difference does not appear in the embryo until towards the end of the second month. Newly conceived, it has a built-in female bias, whose course is turned towards the male only by the presence of the Y chromosome in the father's sperm. Left to itself, the X chromosome in the ovum, fertilized by an X chromosome in the sperm, simply replicates itself as female. But if the male's Y chromosome does the fertilizing, it will generate the male hormones (in particular testosterone) which are largely responsible for turning the embryo into a male. (As I shall describe later, this is the first of the two occasions in his life when the male must separate himself from his female progenitor.)

Masters and Johnson established that breathing, heart rate, sweating and an increase in blood pressure are the same in both female and male orgasm. Defying the evidence of our eyes, the female and male sex organs are surprisingly similar in structure and function – in effect, embryological reversals of each other. At about seven or eight weeks the embryonic male gonads begin to differentiate from the same tissues which in the female are becoming the clitoris, vagina and labia. Both vagina and penis are roughly similar in size – an average of four inches for the vagina and five inches for the penis. Like the penis, the vagina secretes, engorges and pulsates, and in orgasm both contract every 0.8 seconds, for about ten seconds, after which the rate declines.[18] However, the feat of male ejaculation is the more complex, demanding such an elaborate interaction between the endocrine and nervous systems the wonder is it ever happens at all.

In an absorbing study of the shifting relations between sex and culture, Lacqueur finds two persistent historical views. The first, which held general sway until the eighteenth century, he describes as the 'one-sex' theory, which maintained that the woman was as fully sexed as the man, but an inside-out copy of him; ovaries were reversed testicles, the vagina an inside-out phallus. After the eighteenth century the 'two-sex' theory took root and the woman came to be seen as the *opposite* of the man, therefore sexless and incapable of orgasm.[19] In shadowy form this conviction persisted well into our own century.

The human female is the only female mammal whose sexual activity is not limited to periods of oestrus, or 'heat'. This development of the female menstrual cycle marked a huge evolutionary change, in providing the opportunity for almost constant sex, and the possibility of endless non-reproductive coupling. Like other primates, the human male also has no seasonal variation and can enjoy sex throughout the year. However, sexual arousal responds to novelty and slowly subsides in satiety; beyond a certain threshold the central nervous system acts to dampen down the effects of stimuli – the 'adaptation effect'. For both sexes, sexual activity declines as a couple's relationship lengthens – a fact which is often responsible for the end of relationships in which sex was paramount.

Is sex important?

There is vehement disagreement on the true place of sex in our lives. The Nurturist school, for instance, believes that its importance has been grossly inflated in western culture; Michel Foucault maintained that our absorption in sex dates back only to the late eighteenth century, when the new study of sex as a science encouraged an exaggerated view of it as a force of enormous power, and by means of medicine, the law and the Church created a new obsessive and oppressive authority, controlling bodies and their pleasures for political and social ends. Sex, he argued, is in no way a 'special' pre-existing biological entity, and if it could be freed of false aggrandizement it would take its proper place as just another of our everyday pleasures.[20] In his novel, *Walden Two*, B. F. Skinner attempts to show how our present sexual confusions could be abolished by correct social conditioning, and sex quietly integrated into daily life.

It must be said that sex is the only function of the autonomic nervous system which can be inhibited for life without physical harm. We must eat, drink, breathe and sleep, or we will die. But we can stay alive and even flourish without sex. It is because sex is not necessary to life that Maslow places it on only the third level of his hierarchy of human needs, less vital than food and security.[21] Alone of all creatures, humankind devises reasons for deliberately rejecting sexual activity. Because sex is acutely sensitive to psychological damage, the price of abstinence may be a debilitating neurosis – but it may not. It is obvious (in spite of spectacular lapses) that innumerable nuns, priests and monks have managed to live chaste and stable lives, and in every generation millions of ordinary women and men have lived without sexual activity, and often without desperate unhappiness either.

However, defenders of Nature take the view that sex has always been of high, innate significance, and many follow the sociobiologists in arguing that the human frame has evolved in ways that make sex ever more successful; because of a permanent upright stance humans can display a great variety of sexual signals, including expressive faces, swollen female breasts, obvious buttocks and the opportunity (shared only with whales) for face-to-face sex[22] — all of which has greatly contributed to the flagrant success of the human species. Supporters of Nature also point out that at least since the Stone Age sex and procreation have engrossed humanity, and innumerable museums and private collections contain ancient artefacts of exuberant sexual parts, vaginal or phallic; the 'Venus of Willendorf', for instance, dating from about 30,000 BC, is little more than a fat ball of sexual and pregnant organs.[23] Indicating the innate intensity of our interest, the copious vocabulary of human sex covers a huge range of attitudes and practices: coitus and copulating, fornicating and debauching, screwing and fucking, having it off, making love. And in many European languages even the most mundane everyday objects are given gender. For upholders of Nature, sex is intrinsic, determined by biology, understood without learning, and different sexual customs in different periods are only shifting shadows on the surface of a monolithic structure.

Those who believe in the innate importance of sex step out from widely differing ideologies: from that of the fourth-century St Jerome, for instance, and of the twentieth-century Freud. To Jerome, and other early Fathers of the Church, sex loomed dark and ominous, a beast to be starved and beaten; all sexual matters were sinful, and virginity and chastity were extravagantly exalted.[24] Camille Paglia joins forcefully with all who see sex as daemonic and dangerous: 'Sex is the point of contact between man and nature, where morality and good intentions fall to primitive urges. I call it an intersection. This intersection is the uncanny crossroads of Hecate, where all things return in the night. Eroticism is a realm stalked by ghosts. It is the place beyond the pale, both cursed and enchanted.'[25] No one needs to be reminded of the emphasis placed on sex by Freud. For him sex was the driving force of the psyche, inspiring a vast range of activities from reproduction through pleasure, love, work, creativity and all urges to survival. What he found destructive was the guilty repression of excess sexual energy, which in a healthy psyche should be transformed, or 'sublimated', into some kind of creative activity, such as work or art. While he regretted the punitive sexual repression of his own early twentieth-century Vienna, he believed that sexual pleasure must be somehow sublimated if civilization is to survive, and the popular notion that he advocated free, guiltless, promiscuous sex is confuted time and again in his work, as when he declares that his treatment liberated sexuality precisely so that sex should *not* dominate, and could be suppressed without undue harm.[26] Few thinkers have suffered more from those who have never read him. True, his huge range of work, throughout a long life, is littered with contradictions, confusions, dead ends, obstinacies, and other human frailties; yet he was an awesome explorer of the uncharted human map, in the mind's buried past. His wavering journeys were guided by deep analysis, and by the study of dreams, hypnotism, madness, art, literature and infant play, by means of which he delved into terror and joy, sex and love. When Freud died, Auden wrote 'In Memory of Sigmund Freud': '. . . sad is Eros, builder of cities, / And weeping anarchic Aphrodite.'

Although Freud's one-time disciple, Carl Jung, thought Freud was too committed to his sexual theory (and broke with him largely because of it), he also saw the sexual impulse as a vital part of our psychic selves. For him, sex was more than a mere physical drive or an amorphous instinct, it was a numinous, creative power in psychic life, far more deeply concerned with pleasure and bonding than with procreation, and with an influence extending from infancy to old age.[27] The widely branching psychodynamic school, which grew from these and other founding fathers, sees sexuality as a primary structure bound into our beings, and far more diffuse than mere genitality and biological drive. Many modern interpreters of Freud – the 'neo-Freudians' – reorder his original concepts, but for them the phallus remains the supreme signifier (or symbol), and sex remains central to our experience. The Wellings survey found that for both women and men the first full sexual experience was deeply memorable, suggesting that for most people sex is highly significant.[28]

Sex is anarchic stuff and Freud was troubled by its relation to society, believing that the erotic instincts are hard to mould and that sex cannot be easily reconciled with the demands of culture.[29] Greer (unusually) appears to agree with him, in finding sex so anarchic that it cannot survive the civilizing process without becoming neutral and mechanical.[30] From time to time the guardians of law and religion make a heavy effort to regulate it, but they are never entirely successful, and the history of sex is probably marked more by resistence than by co-operation.[31] The long, unwavering history of bastardy suggests that general sexual activity was never much inhibited,[32] and John Hale notes that in Europe in the sixteenth century neighbours were accusing one in seven in their local communities of fornication, adultery, buggery, incest, bestiality or bigamy.[33] Religious and pagan feelings have always coexisted, and the freedom permitted on Mayday, Christmas and other festivals was full-bloodedly enjoyed.[34] In the vivid, aberrant world of the late-medieval Border ballads, fornication is wrong only when it is discovered, or leads to pregnancy or death; no moral restraints inhibit Clerk Saunders and May Margaret, or the Demon Lover and his beloved.[35] They love, they lie together, and if the consequence is mutilation or burning or death, then so be it. Left to itself, as Graves wryly describes in 'Down Wanton', sex is wholly amoral, taking no heed of ethics, status, colour or creed:

> Down, wanton, down! Have you no shame
> That at the whisper of Love's name,
> Or Beauty's, presto! up you raise
> Your angry head and stand at gaze?
>
> Poor bombard-captain, sworn to reach
> The ravelin and effect a breach —

Indifferent what you storm or why,
So be that in the breach you die!. . . .

Will many-gifted Beauty come
Bowing to your bald rule of thumb
Or Love swear loyalty to your crown?
Begone, have done! Down, wanton, down!

To a couple in love, the world is ripe with ancient sexual symbols, and the imagination is warmly receptive to them. In his early work, Freud found the world of dreams bristling with sex: pits, bottles and suchlike represented the vagina; rooms and cupboards, the uterus; mouths and gates, the vaginal orifice. The spurting of semen appears in fountains and watering-cans; sticks, knives and guns stand in for the penis,[36] and no doubt (as Marge Piercy has it) so do radishes:

> Sometimes happy in bed I think
> of black radishes, round, hefty,
> full of juice and hot within,
> just like our love.[37]

Later in his life, Freud modified his views on sexual symbolism,[38] but his earlier work had already given rise to a century of mirth. In Gibbons's *Cold Comfort Farm*, Mr Mybug finds the woods and downs of Sussex burgeoning with sex: 'The stems reminded Mr Mybug of phallic symbols and the buds made Mr Mybug think of nipples and virgins . . . there were few occasions when he was not reminded of a pair of large breasts by the distant hills.'[39] Women's bodies have always provided delicious poetic landscapes, the contours of their breasts, buttocks and bellies inviting comparison with the lines of the earth. In *Tropic of Cancer*, Henry Miller finds the earth 'not an arid plateau of health and comfort, but a great sprawling female with velvet torso that swells and heaves with ocean billows; . . . all of her, from her generous breasts to her gleaming thighs, blazes with furious ardour.'[40] The symbolism of receiving and entering, of earth and rain, lock and key, persists over the centuries, even to the cheerful blatancy of 'male' and 'female' electric plugs. As everyone knows, advertisers make full use of the charge which flashes from sexual imagery. Sex sells films and books and newspapers, and almost anything it touches; semi-naked girls, cars, cigarettes, horses, guitars, the moon, presented in association with the object to be sold, make us buy and buy. In the terse four lines of 'Fire and Ice', Robert Frost suggested the cataclysmic possibilities of the sexual impulse:

> Some say the world will end in fire,
> Some say in ice.
> From what I've tasted of desire
> I hold with those who favour fire . . .

It is very clear that our sexual attitudes and behaviours are profoundly affected by the societies we live in. None the less, sex is grounded in the body, and those who find it innately significant seem to have the best of the argument. Our enthusiasm through millennia suggests that whatever towering cultural structures we build into it and over it, we should not underestimate its smouldering presence in our lives.

Sex and love

Paradise is full of snakes, and one biblical snake seems hardly enough to account for all the problems of carnal knowledge. For at least three millennia the relationship between sex and love has proved a troublesome problem for the West, and endless theories, philosophies and metaphors have attempted to explain it. Plato's solution was to devise an elegant structure of ascent from body to spirit, progressing from sex to soul, from the earthly to the divine. He did not invent this split, but through his visionary prose it has dogged us ever since, bedevilling centuries of thought on the nature of our beings, and on the nature of love. He and his Neoplatonist successors, from the early centuries of Christianity through to the Renaissance and onwards, continued to insist on this cleft between the earthy body and the iridescent soul. Over the centuries many efforts have been made to heal this dualism, with the most determined effort in the second half of our own century, when the revelations of psychology, advances in physiology, a slackening fear of divine disapproval and a new fascination with the role of the body are all helping to dissolve it.

Sex and love drift in and out of each other's territories, and their foggy frontiers cannot be rigidly staked out.

However, it is possible to distinguish sex-in-love from what used to be called 'lust'. The biblical overtones of this word are uncomfortable, but it helps to distinguish between general sexual drive, which has little or nothing to do with affection, and the intimate, personal sex involved in love. Insofar as they can be teased apart, sex includes the pleasurable and reproductive functions, while love embraces inventive eroticism and a torrent of other feelings, including variants on anxiety and loneliness, joy and content. Describing his new and astonishing sensations with his lover, Roth's Portnoy cries, 'What am I trying to communicate? Just that we began to feel something. Feel *feeling*! And without any diminishing of sexual appetite!'[41] Although lust does not contain love, love contains lust.

As it was for White's male lovers, in *The Beautiful Room is Empty*, the coalescing of love and sex creates rapture and peace: 'Kisses that with other men were only empty forms now filled with content. Sexual acts served as shades of meaning, a darkening or heightening of the voice.'[42] Sex-in-love has always had a crucial part to play in human creativity, dishevelling our humdrum conscious life, stirring the unconscious into fantasy and dream[43], and (as in Dylan Thomas's 'A Winter's Tale') creating a sense of 'merging' and transcendence, on the frontiers of consciousness:

. . . the bird lay bedded
In a choir of wings, as though she slept or died,
And the wings glided wide and he was hymned and wedded,

And through the thighs of the engulfing bride,
The woman breasted and the heaven headed

Bird, he was brought low,
Burning in the bride-bed of love, in the whirl-
Pool at the wanting centre, in the folds
Of paradise, in the spun bud of the world.
And she rose with him flowering in her melting snow.

However, not everyone sees sex as all delight and rapture. A few have preferred to live, as it were, in retirement from sex, not only for ideological reasons but in order to avoid the messy inelegance of the whole arrangement. The seventeenth-century physician, Sir Thomas Browne, felt that, 'I could be content that we might procreate like trees, without conjuction, or that there were any way to perpetuate the World without this trivial and vulgar way of union: it is the foolishest act a wise man commits in all his life . . .'[44]

Do sex and love have different roots?

Some argue that sex is a biological reproductive drive common to all species, while love is a separate, cultural development; their roots are therefore distinct, and become tangled at their peril. Although both drives may be directed on to the same object, the conjunction of love and sex (it is argued) is no more 'natural' than their separation, and sex and love are as different in origin as in character. There is a trend in our own times to follow these precepts, and to see sex as even more enjoyable when it is divorced from love. Posner, for one, proposes that we should aim for an 'economic' theory of sexuality, directed to secular and utilitarian ends, and cleared of ignorance, ideology and prejudice;[45] and in similar vein, Giddens argues that sex should be interpreted as 'plastic', leading to exploration and pleasure, and to 'pure' relationships based on a cost–benefit system.[46] Then each lover is equally in control, free of the confusions of gender, role and personal emotion.[47] In his awestruck poem, on 'Eros', Robert Bridges brooded on the enigma and found that for all his beauty Eros, the god of love, is in truth the god of sex:

> . . . For in thy face is nought to find,
> Only thy soft unchristened smile,
> That shadows neither love nor guile,
> But shameless will and power immense,
> In secret sensuous innocence . . .

The opposing school of thought argues that love is innately integrated with sex, both of them growing together from a common root at the core of the psyche, and that what we call 'love' is in fact a turning aside, a 'goal-inhibited' form of the sexual urge, by which sex is partially redirected into the set of emotions known as love; in Freud's belief, the nucleus of what we mean by love consists of sexual love with sexual union as its aim.[48] This process could be interpreted as a purely selfish trick of the body to procure sex, but this is not how it seemed to Freud. As represented in Bettelheim's translation, Freud describes the transformation from sex to love as a genuine metamorphosis into a creative passion of intimacy and caring, full of the beauty of Eros and the soul of Psyche,[49] and fit to stand at the heart of a civilized society. 'Lust, thro' some strainers well refin'd, / Is gentle love, and charms all womankind.'[50] A century and a half before Freud, Alexander Pope might have been paraphrasing his thought.

The tangled relations of sex and love are neatly described by Jessica, in Jong's *Serenissima*:

> The tight rosebud between my thighs, furled for so many celibate months, wants nothing more than to explode, but my mind races ahead as minds will. Perhaps when animals mate it is all a matter of blood and nerves, scents and synapses, vessels filling and vessels emptying . . .; but humans love within the context of that great convention 'Love', that well-worn metaphor 'Love', that gaudy tapestry 'Love' woven through the ages by the poets and artists, dyed in our nerves, imprinted on our brains, accompanied by sweet familiar music.[51]

The age-long intertwining of love and sex suggests they spring from a common source, with sex as the mainstream, driving all living creation, and sex-in-love as a side channel, carving a bed for itself off the main current.

CHAPTER FOUR

Sex, Women and Men

~~~~~~~~~~~~~~~

Women

A T DIFFERENT times men have thought of women as lustful, then as cold, then as lustful again.[1] In myth and legend female sexuality is often insatiable, as it was in Lilith, the Sirens, Jezebel, Herodias, the female vampires, all of whom harried men for sex, threatening and engulfing them. In a time like our own, which still usually assumes that men's sexual urges are stronger than women's, it is useful to remember that there have also been opposite assumptions; almost two millennia ago, for instance, the Fathers of the early Church fulminated against the voracious lust of women.[2] But not everyone feared and hated it. Chaucer, for one, found it a source of frequent glee, and has his Wife of Bath declare of her husbands:

> As help me God, I laughe whan I thynke
> How pitously a-nyghte I made hem swynke [work]![3]

In the early seventeenth century the gossip John Aubrey recorded that Sir Francis Bacon's widow married her gentleman-usher, 'whom she made deafe and blind with too much of Venus',[4] and a century later in 'Gie the Lass her Fairing' Robert Burns openly revelled in the amorousness of women:

> Come nidge me, Tam, come nudge me, Tam,
> Come nidge me o'er the nyvel!
> Come lowse and lug your battering ram
> And thrash him at my gyvel!

In the nineteenth century came the Victorian *un-sexing* of women. If women were endowed with sex at all (it was argued), this was not an autonomous function but something stimulated by the male, whose sexual energy was to be satisfied, curbed and directed by the woman. While love was often regarded as pure and almost holy, sex was bestial. William Acton was a compassionate doctor, but he is most celebrated as the physician who thought it 'a vile aspersion' that females have sexual feelings.[5] Even Krafft-Ebing, who did so much to dispel Victorian inhibitions about sex, believed that as long as women were physically and mentally normal, and properly educated, 'they had little sexual desire'.[6] History had been here before, particularly in the creation of the pure and sexless Virgin, but now this purity was to be spread among all women, just as the Fathers of the early Church had wished. The old Madonna–Whore division reappeared in the chill propriety of the bourgeoisie and in stark contrast with the sexual pleasures of sections of the working classes, where

Acton found that female sexual activity was by no means in abeyance, and was celebrated in the kind of crude doggerel verse which culminated in the twentieth-century 'Ballad of Eskimo Nell':

> She lay a while with a subtle smile
> And then her grip grew keener,
> And with a sigh she sucked him dry
> With the ease of a vacuum cleaner . . .
>
> He slid to the floor and knew no more,
> His passion extinct and dead.
> He didn't shout as his tool slipped out
> Though tis said she'd stripped the thread.[7]

My Secret Life, an anonymous and unpublished diary of eleven volumes by a 'Victorian Gentleman', completed about 1890, described more than forty years spent in the secret low life of Victorian England and included what middle-class writers such as Dickens, Reade, Thackeray, Hardy were compelled to leave out of their novels. This explicit account of visits to London prostitutes gives ample proof that not all Victorian women had lost the power of sexual enjoyment,[8] and that those who had suffered its loss were the tragic victims of respectable parents, who smothered sex for their growing daughters in a caul of fear.

It is sad that Freud, who threw light into so many dark corners, was unsatisfactory on women and less interested in their psychology than in men's; yet he believed women to be endowed with full libido, both sexual and aggressive, although this was deeply inhibited by social constraints very early in life.[9] However, in the public mind, women gradually became sexual beings again. Early in this century writers such as James Joyce and D. H. Lawrence described women as fully sexual, and in 1948 Kinsey revealed that after ten or fifteen years of marriage women often wanted more sex than their husbands could provide.[10] By the second half of our century women had been readmitted as sexual creatures; as Joy says to Bill, in John Osborne's *Inadmissible Evidence*, 'You see I want to have sex constantly, I mean I'm always wanting it, I always have.'[11] It seems probable that a woman's libido and her urge to promiscuity are basically no less than a man's, and that these may have evolved as strategies to aid and protect her, for multiple partners mean greater resources, an insurance against loss, and a wider genetic variety.[12]

What have women had to say about their own sexuality? Until recently, not very much, for they have almost always been hampered by the shackles of respectability, by a lack of creative outlets, and by all the ancient devices for keeping them in their place. But they have also been hampered, as they are still, by the meagre vocabulary of women's sex. Men's words are noisy and crude and voluminous, both for their own activities and parts, and for those of women; but the words that women might wish to use of themselves are scarcely there. Very little women's writing survives from the past on the intimate, physical aspects of their own sexuality, whether combined with love or not, but a few small scraps have been unearthed, beginning with Sappho in the sixth century BC, and proceeding intermittently onwards. In certain earlier writings one cannot always be sure whether the words are about sex or not, for the language is so coded, and the vocabularies of love and religion are so often intertwined. But certain mystical episodes, however genuinely spiritual, obviously also include the sensations of unrecognized orgasm; in the sixth century, for instance, St Teresa of Avila described mystical raptures which seem indistinguishable from those of sex.[13]

In the late seventeenth and early eighteenth centuries there was a liberal period when women's work was more freely published, even when it touched on sex. In Aphra Behn's poem, 'The Disappointment', woman's sexual pleasure is displayed as fully (in respectable literature) as at any time before this century:

> Her balmy lips encount'ring his,
> Their bodies, as their souls, are joined;
> Where both in transports unconfined
> Extend themselves upon the moss.
>
> Cloris half dead and breathless lay;
> Her soft eyes cast a humid light,
> Such as divides the day and night
> Or falling stars, whose fires decay . . .

As late as the middle of the nineteenth century, when respectability was closing in on the middle and literary classes, Christina Rossetti produced many painful, frozen poems, but she also wrote ardently of love. The luscious sensuality of 'Goblin Market' points directly to an erotic impulse, in the beauty and youth of Laura and Lizzie, the succulent fruits, the cramming in of the gleaming flesh and juices.[14]

After a long, scarcely broken silence, lasting through the later Victorian age and for much of this century, women's writing on their own sexual experience has moved from sparsity to an overwhelming abundance. Murdoch's A *Severed Head* and McCarthy's *The Group* are two novels from only one decade (the sixties) which examine how women behave when freed from the old sexual rules. Today there is no longer any shyness, no longer any shortage of information, and many novels and anthologies range through a copious variety of sexual feeling, from gentle to savage;[15] in her novel, *Mercy*, Dworkin details the experience of a woman with a young Greek lover: '. . . it was outside at night on the old stone, on rubble, on garbage, fast, exuberant, defiant, thrilled, rough, skirt pulled up and torn on the rocks, skin ripped on the rocks, semen dripping down my legs.'[16] But even now not all women's sex is so rumbustious. The fact that everything may now be said, in crudest detail, does not mean that it can no longer be gentle; in Grace Nichols's tender poem, 'I go to meet him', the writer moves shyly towards sexual intimacy:

> . . . my eyes
> make four
> with this man

there ain't
no reason
to laugh

but
I laughing
in confusion

his hands
soft his words
quick his lips
curling as in
prayer

I nod

I like this man . . .

Women have the unfair advantage of a sexual apparatus which does not need to do anything at all in order to engage in sex. As Jong's Isadora comments, in *Fear of Flying*, '*That* was the basic inequity which could never be righted: not that the male had a wonderful added attraction called a penis, but that the female had a wonderful all-weather cunt. Neither storm nor sleet nor dark of night could faze it. . . .'[17] However, for some a little or no sex is quite enough; Barbara Pym's exquisite Laura, in *The Sweet Dove Died*, is much in need of men's devotion, but nevertheless 'had never enjoyed *that* kind of thing', and is filled with relief when she is old enough to ignore it.[18]

Women's orgasm

Both clitoris and vagina are involved in orgasm together, but in coition the direct stimulus is provided almost entirely by the clitoris, which is as densely packed with nerves as the penis, and has the distinction of being the only organ in either female or male body with the sole function of producing pleasure. For over half a century Freud did much damage with his assertion that a woman could achieve 'mature' orgasm only by abandoning her clitoris and moving her attention to her vagina,[19] and one of the great achievements of Masters and Johnson was to overturn this unhelpful belief and return the clitoris to its proper function.

Spontaneous orgasm occurs, without the help of the clitoris, in dreams or fantasy or high sexual excitement. In Molly Bloom's last monologue in Joyce's *Ulysses*, when her mind wanders over the events of her life, she daydreams about her unsatisfied desires, and above all she remembers her long-ago meeting with Captain Grove: 'I felt something go through me like all needles my eyes were dancing . . . the excitement like a rose.'[20] Many investigators, from Kinsey on, have emphasized the pleasure women find in masturbation; fewer than half the women Kinsey interviewed came to orgasm with a partner, while ninety-five per cent achieved it in masturbation.[21] As Fleur Adcock reveals in 'Against Coupling', it is a sad fact that orgasm is often stimulated more easily by the woman herself than by a lover:

I write in praise of the solitary act:
of not feeling a trespassing tongue
forced into one's mouth, one's breath
smothered, nipples crushed against the
ribcage, and that metallic tingling
in the chin set off by a certain odd nerve:

. . . I advise you, then, to embrace it without
encumbrance. No need to set the scene,
dress up (or undress), make speeches.
Five minutes of solitude are
enough – in the bath, or to fill
that gap between the Sunday papers and lunch.

Masters and Johnson established that women's capacity for repeated orgasm is greater than men's, and
(although performance in both sexes declines with age)
orgasm in women generally survives longer than a man's
ability to achieve erection. Is orgasm absolutely necessary
to happy sexual life? The survey *Sex in America* statisti-
cally confirms that if there is love then perfect textbook
orgasm often matters very little.[22] Wellings's study in
the UK reveals that both men and women think the
man's orgasm is more important than the woman's, and
men think a woman's orgasm more important to women
than women do.[23] There are various unhappy problems
centred on women's orgasm, and I shall look at these
later.

Chastity and virginity

These words are often used interchangeably, but strictly 'virginity' applies to those who are sexually intact, and 'chastity' to the faithful partner. A woman's chastity remained the queen of virtues for centuries, and kept its crown well into our own times, but (except for its part in religious life) chastity has never been seriously required of a man. Most of the Greek goddesses were chaste, but the same could hardly be said of the gods.

Descriptions of sinning women are littered throughout history and literature, yet even for women chastity persisted as a shining ideal. It seems likely that it was once felt to be a definition of the personality, outlining a boundary and offering a 'unity of self'.[24] In her chastity a woman found she had something of value, which was actually respected, and even sometimes acknowledged to be hers. In the desperately unequal world of the past (far more terrible for most women than our own), chastity offered an escape from unwanted marriage, and sometimes the paradoxical freedom of life in a convent. If a woman was raped, her threat or act of suicide was thought to be morally justified, for if body and soul were one the body could not be assaulted with impunity. To the psychodynamic school the values put on chastity indicate a complex tangle of guilt, fear and inadequacy, but for sociobiologists the justification is entirely different; a male has to be certain that his mate's offspring carry his own genes, so she must be available to him alone. Marxists see the insistence on female chastity as another device for ensuring the subordination of women, and the proper descent of family wealth in a capitalist society.

These old ideals of virginity and chastity have held a power as fearsome as any of the beliefs which have governed human behaviour, and it is chilling to think of the tortures and martyrdoms that have been suffered in their name. To anyone born after the middle of this century their power is hard to credit, but they lasted so long, and at a level so deep, that to many people they seemed inalienable. But they were not. By the early years of this century, in Catholic Dublin, Joyce's Molly was already musing on adultery: 'if that's all the harm ever we did in this vale of tears God knows it's not much doesn't everybody only they hide it.'[25] The ardent concept was fading, and although it survived in religious and idealistic circles it was soon to be widely ignored or treated with sophisticated amusement, as in Elizabeth Taylor's *A Game of Hide and Seek*: 'Harriet's virginity they marvelled over a great deal. It seemed a privilege to have it under the same roof. They were always kindly enquiring after it, as if it were a sick relative.'[26] Ironically, the symbolism arising from invasion of the female body has returned in a new guise, not as concern for matters spiritual but as concern for the autonomy of women, which is seen to be violated by male penetration.[27]

For the first time in western history, women's sexual lives are breaking free. Of women born in the US after 1953, about fifty per cent have had more than one sexual partner, whereas of those born between 1933 and 1942 some eighty-four per cent had had only one.[28] With the coming of the Pill, the upheavals of feminism and a general ferment of social change, the symbolic aspects of a chaste and virgin body have almost drained away.[29] But not quite. Giddens notes that a boy's 'loss' of virginity is generally seen as a gain, whereas a girl is still thought to have surrendered something.[30] There are ripples indicating a return of virginity and chastity as immutable values, and in the United States, for instance, certain growing fundamentalist cults are making virginity once again compulsory, and calling for the severest penalties for adultery.[31]

Women's fantasy

Fantasy provides a way of releasing tension, dealing with the unobtainable and avoiding any crazed rush to action. No doubt women have always fantasized about men, as men have about women, but the prescription for the ideal male alters over the centuries. Although it is obviously now in flux, for generations the most popular image of the male lover was one generated by the nineteenth-century Romantic movement, represented by Austen's Darcy and Byron's Childe Harold, with Rochester and Heathcliff hard on their heels,[32] and such figures still loom over countless tales of popular romance – most of which is written by women. Then, and often now, this hero-man is an assorted combination of the saturnine, the authoritative and the paternal, cool yet passionate, tender yet strong, older than the heroine, and of an acceptable social rank. Although interest in romantic fiction seems to be declining,[33] the persistence of this male fantasy is remarkable, and millions of stories continue to be sold on his image. Even in highly sophisticated modern writing, as in Nin's *The Four-Chambered Heart*, the man may still be seen as a romantic, heroic figure: ' . . . a woman, as she sews, cooks, embraces, covers, warms, also dreams that the man taking her will be more than a man, will be the mythological figure of her dreams, the hero, the discoverer, the builder . . .'[34]

Apart from men, women's fantasy is traditionally thought to be of wind, waves, clouds and dreams of romance. But surveying it over eleven years, Nancy Friday found it labyrinthine, promiscuous, both sadistic and masochistic,[35] and ten years after Friday's work Leroy also found women's fantasies anarchic, cruel as well as tender.[36] Certain fantasies are deliberately chosen to assist with orgasm. De Beauvoir, Greer and other honest women researchers seem to agree (however reluctantly) that in love or out of it many women find themselves possessed by orgasmic fantasies of domination and rape, and admit to being perversely stimulated by what they consciously detest.[37] In *The Unbearable Lightness of Being*, Kundera's Sabina cannot endure a gentle lover, and she asks Franz why he never uses his strength on her. When he replies that love means the renouncing of strength, she realizes that he is noble – but useless to her as a lover.[38] There are certain celebrated male authors, such as Henry Miller, whose writing brims with the conviction that masochism is the gladly accepted lot of all women

— a view held by Van Nordern who, in *Tropic of Cancer*, says of the women he has had in his bed, 'I want to kick them out immediately . . . I do now and then. But that doesn't keep them away. They like it, in fact . . . There's something perverse about women . . . they're all masochists at heart.'[39]

The conviction that this is the inborn nature of all women is highly presumptuous. But some, following Freud, continue to argue that women are indeed innately masochistic, in fantasy and often in action; the male acts and penetrates, the female submits and receives. Some research indicates that in or around the hypothalamus in the female brain there are areas which regulate receptivity to mounting, and in the male brain there are similar areas which provoke it;[40] such passive–active behaviour represents ancient patterns, which we should accept without guilt or anger. But others see women's sexual behaviour as more deeply entangled with anatomical, psychological and cultural influences. Wherever male sex is built on strength and domination, as in any patriarchal society, woman's submission becomes necessary for accommodating male demand, and her sexuality becomes a site of oppression. Most women are brought up to feel they have no choice except to comply, and such gender inequality can disastrously interfere with love and desire, creating anxiety rather than pleasure. Possibly most women do have an intrinsic tendency towards sexual accommodation, and most men towards sexual demand, but the overlap is so wide that generalization is on shaky ground. If Leroy is right in asserting that masochistic fantasies occur less often in women who are still under thirty, it is possible that the breaking down of the old social structures of domination are already having a liberating effect.[41]

However, fantasies of sexual activity do not seem so dominating in the lives of women as of men. Half a century ago, Kinsey found that eighty-three per cent of men came to a climax in sexual dreams, compared with only thirty-seven per cent of women; thirty-seven per cent of men fantasized frequently about women, while only twenty-two per cent of women fantasized about men.[42] These figures are now hoary, and thirty years later a consistent theme of the Wellings 1994 UK survey is the ever-increasing convergence of female and male sexual fantasy and behaviour. Yet, for the time being at least, a modified form of these differences seems still to exist.

Women's response

It has been thought until recently that women do not respond to external sexual stimuli in the same way as men. Although thirty years ago Masters and Johnson found that the range of responses was greater in women, these did not include acute reaction to the kind of explicit erotic imagery which aroused men. However, this seems to be changing. When women are nowadays shown erotic pictures their reactions still *appear* more subdued than men's, yet physiological measurements show them to be just as excited.[43] Men's height, shoulders, buttocks, and of course faces provoke arousal, but this still tends to be more generalized and less genital than men's.[44]

Many male writers like to think that the naked penis provokes excitement and awe in women; in the eighteenth century, John Cleland's Fanny Hill describes 'the white veins, the supple softness of the shaft . . . carrying a head of the liveliest vermillion . . . such a breadth of animated ivory!'.[45] Flaccid, D. H. Lawrence supposed the penis to be a source of tenderness, as Lady Chatterley describes it: ' . . . when he's soft and little I feel my heart quite simply tied to him.'[46] But Sullerot points out that a woman rarely, if ever, describes it as a wondrous love object[47] and Leroy argues that it is often a positive deterrent.[48] Certainly Joyce's Molly had no time for it. For her the penis was 'that tremendous big red brute of a thing'; 'like iron or some kind of a thick crowbar'; 'sticking up at you like a hat-rack'.[49] Lawrence did his best to solemnize the mystery of erection, as when Lady Chatterley decorates Mellors's penis with flowers[50] — but it seems not all women think of the erect penis as a maypole to be decked. As a concept of masculinity and power, the significance of the phallus is immense, but its naked self — purple, one-eyed and absurdly hopeful — is not always a sexual thrill. And to women who have had alarming experiences in childhood, such as confrontation with a flasher, or worse, the erect penis can be a terrifying object.

Falling in Love

What do women in love want of sex?

All some women want of sex is pleasure, all some others
want is a baby, and there is obviously no necessary
relation between love, the enjoyment of sex and the
ability to reproduce. However, there is more to women's
sexuality than either babies or orgasm and many find
satisfaction in arousal which never reaches a climax.[51]
Writings collected in Chester's anthology, *Deep Down*,
point to the importance of mood and surroundings for
creating not only orgasm but the sensual, all-body
pleasure which women seem to seek, and Greer is
emphatic that clitoral frenzy is no more than a con-
tributor to women's pleasure, and that a general
gratification of the whole body is deeply desired.[52] Sex
needs to be generally eroticized, and liberated from its
focus on genitalia.[53]

Many researchers, from Kinsey onwards, have agreed
that in sexual relations, and particularly in love, most
women need intimacy, seek tenderness, and wish to form
some kind of personal relationship; in her *Women and
Love*, Hite found that women wanted sex with feeling,
with closeness and loving words.[54] Even though the
sexual revolution found this an antiquated attitude,
almost no woman in Hite's work wanted impersonal sex
more than occasionally, and in *Sex in America* eighty per
cent of women agreed.[55] A high proportion still seem
to prefer 'traditional' rather than 'recreational' sex, and
according to *Sex in America* the vast majority of them,
even now, feel a strong link between sex and love, and

declare that when they first had full sexual experience they were in love.[56] However, research also indicates that there are many women who find not only their fantasy but their sexual urges as roving and aggressive as any man's. Several recent women researchers and writers – Friday, Reyes, Perriam, Lunch among them – describe experiences in which women's sexual appetites are impersonal and sadistic, in an erotic style traditionally associated with men.[57] Musing on her lover, Kundera's Sabina finds that 'the more she thought about it, the more she longed to ravish his intelligence, defile his kind-heartedness, and violate his powerless strength'.[58] There is a wider variety in women's response than the usual generalizations assume.

Men

Because for millennia men were thought of as the accepted norm, and women as the aberration, it is only in the course of the last two centuries that men have had consciously to look at themselves as 'men' with a problem of 'masculinity'. Once it began, this interest has continued unabated, and grown into the relentless investigations of today, when innumerable studies, from Kinsey's on, have found that the male's primary interest is in unadorned sex, or what is known in the US as 'bathhouse' sex. *Sex in America* finds that fifty-four per cent of men think about sex at least once a day, compared with nineteen per cent of women;[59] in Roth's *Portnoy's*

Complaint, the young hero describes how 'In the middle of class I would raise a hand to be excused, rush down the corridor to the lavatory, and with ten or fifteen savage strikes, beat off standing up into a urinal.'[60] And his sperm would emerge, like all human sperm, at about twenty-eight miles per hour.[61]

In fact, there is no absolute compulsion for men to practise sex, and there is no question that men can be chaste or virginal if that is what they choose. It is a matter of culture and will-power. A man falling in love is unlikely to be troubled by thoughts of lifelong chastity, yet he still comes of a line in which male chastity has a part, and as a symbol of sacrifice it has shared something of the importance it once held in the lives of women. What greater sacrifice can a man offer to God than the desires of his body, and the comfort of a wife and family? However, no one could argue that virginity or chastity is easy, and our sex-centred age makes it, for most men, almost impossible. It is now generally believed that men seethe with sex, and many twentieth-century novels explore this unadorned male appetite to its extremities. In Henry Miller's two 'Tropic' books women appear almost exclusively as sexual objects, as 'cunts' and 'pelts', useful only as receptacles for the penis,[62] and in *The Rachel Papers*, Martin Amis's Charles is well aware that sex with Rachel is one thing, and his other sexual life quite another: ' . . . did I really want to show her the other side, my place? Dionysian bathroom sex: troop in, tug back the covers, go through the gaping routine, do everything either of you can conceivably think of doing,

again, lurch lick squat squirt squelch, again, until it's all
over, again. No.'[63] Charles felt a small charge of warmth
with Rachel, but neutral sex without intimacy was
simpler and less threatening.

Kinsey, and many others, have found that more men
than women tend to divide sex from love and look for
sexual attractiveness rather than a warmer, longer
relationship. Male sex (it is said) is more performance-
ridden, more promiscuous, more impersonal than
women's; Kundera's Tereza comes to her lover 'to make
her body unique, irreplaceable. But he had drawn an
equal sign between her and the rest of them: he kissed
them all alike, stroked them alike, and made no, absolutely no distinction between Tereza's body and the other
bodies.'[64] While love is home and family, sex is performance and competition. Because of their tendency to divide
women up into various personae, men seem able to
regard women as sexually charged fragments, devoid of
the personal.[65] Time and again male sex is described as
something done to an object, as in the cold-fingered wit
of E. E. Cummings's 'she being Brand':

> . . . i went right to it flooded-the-carburettor cranked her
>
> up, slipped the
> clutch (and then somehow got into reverse she
> kicked what
> the hell) next
> minute I was back in neutral tried and
>
> again slo-wly; bare,ly nudg. ing (my

lev-er Right-
oh and her gears being in
A1 shape passed
from low through
second-in-to-high like
greasedlightning) . . .

Most researchers have found that visual stimulus has a rapid effect on men. The stimulus may be blatant, as in an erotic picture or in real life, when the parts of a woman – face, buttocks, breasts, legs – can be instantly arousing, especially when displayed by girls and young women; but stimulus may also be mysterious, floating out of a cloud or a painting. Certain surveys suggest that on the whole men's sexual arousal is faster than women's, but others disagree.[66] However, it seems certain that many men are easily roused to sexual activity with any woman, however unappealing; the raucous laughter of women watching male strippers is a far cry from the glazed, yearning silence of men in a strip joint. Just as most men are more easily roused, they are more readily sated, needing a period of recovery before they can re-engage.

For some men, the simple act of sex seems momentarily to open the gates of death: 'I get so godamned mad at myself that I could kill myself . . . and in a way, that's what I do every time I have an orgasm. For one second I obliterate myself.' Henry Miller is describing *le petit mort*, an experience referred to again and again through the millennia.[67] During and just after climax, many men feel spent and consumed; the ego is dissipated, the rational mind is swamped, consciousness fades, and death is the nearest equivalent that presents itself. This loss of autonomy can be frightening, for men are trained to be in control and the fading of the rational self is an unnerving experience, as the SS Augustine and Thomas Aquinas both acknowledged.[68] But no doubt *le petit mort* is more often welcomed than feared, as Shelley welcomed it in 'The Indian Serenade':

> The nightingale's complaint,
> It dies upon her heart,
> As I must on thine,
> O Belovèd as thou art!
> O lift me from the grass!
> I die! I faint! I fail! . . .

His penis

The apparatus that dangles between a man's legs is of immense significance for our species and for him. Freud's belief that the phallus is central to male experience has not been seriously challenged – although its psychological significance for women is a far more contentious matter. As I have described, the penis develops from the same embryological group of cells as the female clitoris – but with very different results; both anatomically and psychologically, the active, large, exterior penis enjoys a psychological and social prestige immensely greater than that of the clitoris.

Everyone is familiar with the image of the penis as a power-tool for attacking and subjugating women, but this is not the whole story. The relation of a man with his cock can be an endearing thing, and for a man in love it can be very congenial. This anonymous fourteenth-century poet was pleased with his 'gentle cock', and was not merely composing a nursery rhyme –

> I have a gentle cock
> Croweth me day;
> He doth me risen early
> My mattins for to say.
>
> I have a gentle cock
> Comen he is of great;
> His comb is of red coral
> His tail is of jet . . .
>
> His eyen are of crystal
> Locken all in amber;
> And every night he percheth him
> In my lady's chamber.[69]

The anarchic cock is the third, irresponsible member of the love relationship which is normally thought of as two. It seems to have a mind of its own, responding vigorously to signals its owner is scarcely aware of, and refusing to respond to those its owner wishes to acknowledge. The bewildered man finds himself sharing his life with a maverick partner, whose objectives are not always as worthy as he would wish. In the first century BC the Roman poet, Ovid, observed this wilful independence:

> Now, when he should not jet, he bolts upright,
> And craves his task, and seeks to be at fight.[70]

And just over three centuries later, St Augustine was ashamed rather than amused by his wilful penis, which is 'moved and restrained not at our will, but by a certain independent autocracy.'[71] Control has not arrived with the passing of the centuries, and the embarrassed male cry is still, 'Down, wanton, down!'

Sexual dominance

In most of the animal kingdom, the male is the more active partner in sex, the one who mounts, penetrates and moves. I shall look later at the more terrible aspects of male mastery and sadism, but meanwhile it is enough to say that throughout Hebraic times, the classical world and the centuries of Christianity up to the present day, the sexual dominance of the male has been justified by the male. Those as sympathetic to women as Chaucer and Spenser and Shakespeare (all unsound on women's inferiority) are very much in the minority, and Milton's views are the more representative; for him, Eve's ringlets waved,

> As the vine curls her tendrils, which implied
> Subjection, but required with gentle sway,
> And by her yielded, by him best received;
> Yielded with coy submission, modest pride,
> And sweet reluctant amorous delay . . .[72]

The pleasure of conquest is inflamed by resistance. As Gerald watches Gudrun, in Lawrence's *Women in Love*, 'Her inchoate look of a violated slave, whose fulfilment lies in her further and further violation, made his nerves quiver with acutely desirable sensation.'[73] The excitement of subduing a resistant citadel is the excitement not so much of sex as of power. The thought of his own dependency is frightening to the male, and by subduing his partner the dominator makes sure that recognition is given to him by the subjugated, and denied to the subjugated by him.[74] As Lionel Tiger proclaims, in *Men in Groups*, there is no lack of voices asserting that male dominance is innate and essential to successful sex, in which the male's very manhood is threatened by women who will not acknowledge his virile and personal superiority.[75]

If aggression is indeed vital to male sex, one root is buried in the physiology of the brain. For both sexes sexual and aggressive arousal emerge from the 'old' limbic area, which originates the production of the sex hormones, and so it is not surprising that Kinsey found thirteen physiological changes common to both sexual arousal and anger, and only four which were different.[76] Freud believed that the drives of *Eros* (love and soul) and *Thanatos* (denial and destruction) are strongly alloyed, and that the best place to observe this merger is in erotic life.[77] At the end of *Between the Acts*, when Giles and Isa are alone at night, Woolf's narrator describes the alliance: 'Alone, enmity was bared; also love. Before they slept, they must fight; after they had fought, they would embrace. From that embrace another life might be born. But first they must fight, as the dog fights with the vixen, in the heart of darkness, in the fields of night.'[78]

There is heated debate between those who believe in the ruling effects of the male hormone, testosterone, and those who fervently do not.[79] This hormone is shared between the sexes, and is vital to the energy of both, but it generally reaches far higher levels in males. Upholders of Nature support research which indicates a strong link between sex and aggression, based on the increase of testosterone in anger and in sexual arousal; the higher the level of testosterone, it is said, the higher the aggressive insistence of the libido.[80] Objecting to the view that we are the victims of our hormones, supporters of Nurture assert that a sex–aggression connection is unproved in humans, that hormonal activity is still a mystery, and that the difference in male and female aggressive behaviour, sexual or otherwise, is not reflected in a similar difference of hormonal levels. What is clear is that the sex hormones are not entirely in charge; their effects can be profoundly altered, and even reversed, by learning, experience and environment.

Men and love

Some researchers insist that the wish for a certain submission is common to both sexes, for in outgrowing their infant dependency both still long for the old safe dominion of the mother.[81] Stoller finds (as any Madam of any bordello knows) that there is masochism as well as sadism in men, and Leroy finds masochism as deeply entrenched in men as in women.[82] But whatever the nature of a man's sexual impulses, love will soften their crudity. Normally, a man in love does not want to offend, does not want to hurt, and however intense his passion he will wait, he will consider his lover's feelings. Longing to make love to his sleeping mistress, the sixteenth-century poet, Ronsard, nevertheless reassures her;

> . . . But, dear, I never try
> To wake you when I see
> Your eyes all sleeping lie
> And beautiful under me.
> Happiest of happy men,
> I never wake you then.[83]

'Bath-house' sex will not have vanished from the lover's being, but love will suppress its more flamboyant displays, and in certain men sex provokes intense spiritual and imaginative sensations, of the kind fervently celebrated by poets and other writers. This gentler view of the sexual male is displayed by innumerable male novelists, whose interest in sex is not confined to casual activity, but to sex in relationships, and in love; in *Women in Love*, Lawrence's Birkin detests the notion of easy sex outside a real relationship, which should be 'a pure union' committed to 'a conjuction with the other'.[84] Pietropinto found that only one in five men considered sex to be the central experience of his life, and other researchers have revealed that many men hope to combine sex with a real relationship of compatibility and companionship.[85] Even taking into account the urge to appear virile in a questionnaire, it seems that most men wish to be loved, as women do; most long for reassurance and warmth, feel the need to be wanted, hope for a degree of dependence, and for a close, confiding bond. In the 'animal-groom' fairy-tales the woman's initial disgust is matched by the animal's terror that she may never be able to love him.[86] The sadness is that so many men still cannot acknowledge their need, even to themselves, for they have been taught that such an admission would be weak. S. B. Barrows, one-time Madam of a bordello, found that men who cannot find these loving qualities will visit prostitutes as much for comfort as for sex – as 'friends, confidantes, companions, even therapists'.[87] Both women and men share a hungry longing for intimacy and love.

In the last half-century, surveys have shown that sexual mores have converged so greatly that polarities are blurring, boundaries between the sexes are wavering, and only a fanatic would dare to state that women are like this and men are like that. We are slowing freeing ourselves, at least in some quarters, of the old sexual imperatives: that women are 'by nature' passive and men are active; that women are subservient and masochistic, and men aggressive and sadistic; that women wait while men pursue; that men have a higher sex drive; that women are faithful and men promiscuous. We need to learn more precisely which differences are truly sex-linked, and which are culture- and gender-linked.

The sexes are not merely replicas of each other, with only simple biological differences, but the divergences between them are tendencies rather than deep immoveable structures. Over thirty years ago Masters and Johnson were struck by the similarity (not the difference) in the anatomy and physiology of men's and women's sexual responses, and no one seems to have challenged this seriously since.[88] Nature provides predispositions, and Nurture, reverberating to and fro with the unconscious, creates that welter of ideas, beliefs and imaginings that simmers in the cortex and exerts such power it can transmute, and even reverse, the guidelines laid down by Nature. No wonder sexual behaviour is hectic, wandering, variable, and reluctant to be grasped by dogma and definition. In sex we are all caught, women and men alike, in ambivalent tangles – to be in control, to be helpless; to be ravisher and ravished; to be hostile yet longing for tenderness. The difference is that while women are usually allowed to admit only their feelings of submission, men are allowed to admit only the urge to mastery; some have suggested that women who demand equality in the world could help by submission in the bedroom.[89] Yet even men's urge to dominate can be infused with feelings of dependency, guilt, fear and the wish for forgiveness.[90]

The unconscious is a chaotic place, containing elements of sado-masochism in both sexes, and those couples who enjoy these practices need not be made to feel guilty. As the prescient Victorian writer of *My Secret Life* observed, 'Nothing can perhaps be justly called unnatural which nature prompts us to do. If others don't like them, they are not natural to *them*, and no one should force them to act them.'[91] What is certain is that successful sex-in-love leaves the imprint of a powerful, embracing experience, as it did for Updike's lovers in *Brazil*: 'Up, down, aggressive, passive, dominant, submissive, hostile, tender — Tristao and Isabel oscillated luxuriously among contrarieties, and gave each other the gifts of physical exhaustion and of a drowsy oneness with the universe.'[92]

Sex has lurked as a dark, beguiling presence through all the days and nights of Western humanity. Because of its ubiquity in our lives, because of its fusion with love, because of its blatant presence in the revelations of analysis, because of its potency in fantasy and dream, because of the ageless pungency of its humour, because of the despair of the old at its loss, because of its alliance with the shadow of death — because of all these matters, one must allow that it lies deeply embedded in our lives. This is not to say we can do nothing about it. Sex is not monolithic, but plastic, diverse, polymorphic, and the severance from reproduction makes it even more so. Ignatieff's proposition, that sex is so changeable there may be no essential sexual self at all, goes too far,[93] yet attitudes, behaviours and fashions can and do change dramatically. We live in times which encourage a new diversity, and the old notion of 'normal' has become only one choice among many; in White's *The Beautiful Room is Empty*, Maria says to Bunny, 'Oh I have a *faiblesse* for men . . . I even prefer making love with men, but I only fall in love with women.'[94]

Mutuality must be the most hopeful aim. In Marilyn French's words, 'Sex is essentially a joyful and harmless activity; by itself it is incapable of harm. When it is mutually shared, it is an act of innocence . . . Sex is an act of simple pleasure when it is unmixed with aggression, power, or the possibility of disease.'[95]

CHAPTER FIVE

Gender

A T FIRST sight it seems that gender has very little to do with falling in love, yet it is always there, in the behaviour and the attitudes and the appearance of each lover. It cannot be side-stepped, for it pervades all personal relations between women and men, and threads itself all through the experience of falling in love. If two lovers are deeply besotted they will not notice gender for a while, but if they are less obsessed it will soon begin to obtrude. Far from blowing apart the gender stereotypes, love often accentuates them, for lovers will remember the gender signals they have learned to think of as attractive, and if one or both of them is playing gender 'wrong' there will be increasing trouble ahead. Because gender trouble, like sexual trouble, worms itself into the very heart of love, some idea of how we acquire our gender stereotypes, and how they come to dominate us, ought to help us trip over them less often. If falling in love is to run sweetly, gender relations should be harmonious enough to be invisible, and if this is so both the first period of love, and its outcome, will have a sunnier chance of success. In this chapter I will look at gender relations which are not too deeply troubled, but later I will turn to their more intractable problems.

I use the word 'gender' to refer not to biology and sex, but to the social and psychological aspects of being seen as female or male, and of thinking of oneself as such. Although sex and gender slip constantly in and out of each other's territory, in rough-and-ready terms sex is a fact of biology, while gender is largely a product of culture, changing with the times. Gender is concerned with how society thinks the different sexes *ought* to look and feel and behave, and so it is confusing to use the word 'feminine' to mean a biological woman, or the word 'masculine' to mean a biological male. It may be one thing to behave in a 'feminine' or a 'masculine' style, and quite another to be biologically a woman or a man. 'I am male' is not the same as 'I am manly'.[1]

Although gender is far from rigid, its tides have swung only between the stereotypes of the dominant man and the subordinate woman. Different periods have different expectations of gender behaviour in love, ranging for instance from the brash initiative of Chaucer's Wife of Bath ('I folwed ay myn inclinacioun') to the blushing reticence of a Victorian heroine ('This is so sudden, Mr—'). The degree of women's freedom or oppression rises and falls; at some periods women have been allowed a limited autonomy, but in others gender polarity is strong, and they are kept firmly in their place. The behaviour expected of men has also shifted, with marked changes to and fro in the notion of the 'masculine'. In fact, through centuries, years, days, moments, we are always 'doing gender', actively constructing, deconstructing and reconstructing it.[2]

In the realm of gender studies tempers fray fast, and opposing dogmas are reluctant to give an inch. Once again, one camp is defended by the supporters of Nature, who hold that traditional gender behaviour is genetically innate and welded to biological sex – that 'women are women and men are men' – while the other camp is defended by the advocates of Nurture, who believe that gender is a social construct, constantly creating and re-creating cultural 'scripts', according to the pressures of the time, with little reference to biological sex. Gender develops as an ideology – or fantasy – about what women and men *should* be like, and then becomes entrenched as a 'natural' mode of living.[3]

The traditional stereotypes

I shall stay with the normal word 'stereotype', rather than with the wider scope of 'model' or 'schema', for my interest is in those rigid hypotheses and assumptions that are unthinkingly accepted, and traditionally assumed to imply what is 'natural'. In certain quarters of society these stereotypes seem to be crumbling at the edges, but they are always lurking, and from time to time their cold grip reasserts itself. In their traditional polarized forms, the stereotypes of feminine and masculine are more or less the reverse of each other, each set providing a mould into which 'woman' and 'man' are expected to fit. There is no need to expand on the old oppositions of dominant/ submissive, strong/yielding, hard/gentle, autonomous/ nurturing – they are all too familiar. (Yet apparently both women and men see themselves as less exaggerated than their stereotypes suggest.)[4]

Engels noted in the last century that the manipulation of these stereotypes varied from class to class; while the male working class made women work and serve, wealthy men turned them into decorative objects of prestige.[5] The situation is not so different today. Although the distinctions between classes have diminished greatly, working-class men are still likely to assert their power more blatantly than other classes, who are often just as demanding but more devious.[6] In a study of schoolchildren in the early eighties, Sarsby found marked class differences in attitudes to gender, but ten years later the Wellings survey revealed that these had become much less defined.[7]

The traditional woman

Before I describe the traditional female stereotype, I have to acknowledge that vast numbers of women are not interested in the struggle against it. Unlike the more fiery feminists, I have little quarrel with them. They have every right to their practice and their views, yet in their anger at the feminist fracturing of old values they might well create a forceful backlash.[8] They could be asked to return tolerance for tolerance, and not to subvert the efforts of those women who would like to find themselves in a wider, airier world.

In whatever guise, and to whatever degree, women have traditionally been taught to be submissive in their relations with men; according to the old gender bargain, if they are pleasing and 'good' they are approved and protected, if 'bad' they are punished.[9] It is still, for instance, not the woman's generally accepted role to pursue and initiate – although she often does, and always has. When she adopts the role of pursuer, male authors often describe the results as disastrous; until the Widow Wadman revealed the heat of her passion, in Sterne's *Tristram Shandy*, Uncle Toby was innocently confident in his courtship, but when he felt the probing of her sexual excitement he became so alarmed he retreated into his safe male world.[10] The women interviewed by Duncombe and Marsden, as recently as the early 1990s, felt that while they were obliged to make the *emotional* running during courtship they had to be wily in concealing their aims.[11] For many women the only brief dominance will be the time of courtship and early love, when they are often the directors, deciding whether the relationship continues. But when the period of courtship is over, a woman is traditionally not supposed to compete. In order to be loved and admired she knows she should aspire to the role of 'Angel in the House', and diminish herself to the point at which, in Tweedie's words, she exhibits only 'small ego, small brain, small voice, small talk'.[12]

With exuberant venom, Greer describes one of the standard female stereotypes, the languorously beautiful doll, clad in enviable clothes, and smouldering with the promise of unattainable sex. The fact that the woman is beautiful, submissive, alluring, with no will and no aptitudes, removes all threat to the men who create and long for her. She is the adman's dream, and the most persuasive seller of goods ever conceived.[13] At the opposite pole to this glamorous vision, the gentle, home-based woman sustains the family, accepts her husband's authority and cares for all his needs. She is warm, nurturing, intuitive, expected to deal with all matters emotional; she is Thomas Hardy's idol, who, whatever he does, 'will not blame me / But suffer it so'.[14]

So the woman is the sex symbol, the subservient partner, the nurturer, the wife, the mother. In order to please, and preserve relationships, she must give up most of her own needs, her anger, her rebellion. Great emotional effort is needed to repress the inner disorderly self – an effort which plays a forceful part in women's depression,[15] and which often escapes in turbulent scenes, in sulks, self-pity and all the ploys of dependency; in fantasies of vampires and madwomen in the attic;[16] in the use of sex and beauty as a tool for the destruction of men. Throughout the centuries innumerable women have felt that their stereotype does not fit them, for like tight clothes it rubs and chafes, and inner experience does not match the required outer shell. Yet even now the stereotype is hard to escape, for it has a power which tugs against the longing to break out. An escaping woman seems to be fighting against herself, yet what she is fighting is not the natural ordained order of her being but a carapace into which she has been fitted so young that it seems to be part of her. Many women grow up filled with self-doubt, believing they are second-best, and somehow not in charge of their lives. Learned behaviour masquerades as biology, so those who approve of gender polarization can easily deceive themselves into believing that these acquired traits are actually innate. All this deeply troubles a woman's relations with men, especially with a man she loves.

Studies of children born with ambiguous genitalia, and assigned to the wrong sex, provide conclusive proof of the influence of learning on biology, for if an infant brought up as a girl or a boy, to the age of three to four years, turns out to be predominantly of the opposite sex, it is easier to alter the sex by surgery than to remodel the established gender behaviour.[17]

Women's protest

In the face of men's physical strength, and their political and economic power, women have always found rebellion an awesome prospect, and because conformity brings the love and approval most humans long for only the wildest spirits have dared it. As Mary Astell bitterly declared, at the beginning of the eighteenth century, women were ' . . . Wise enough to Love their Chains, and to discern how very becomingly they sit . . . She's a Fool who would attempt their Deliverance and Improvement. No, let them enjoy the great Honor and Felicity of their Tame, Submissive and Depending temper!'[18] Women have protested not only with words but with despair, neurosis, mental and physical illness, and anyone who dismisses feminism as a tiresome modern affectation should remember that for millennia women without number have led silent, stunted lives, which even love has not been able to redeem.

Yet very slowly their stifled cries of rebellion have helped to alter our attitudes, and the protests of twentieth-century women are new only in their volume, not in their intensity. A handful of anguished cries from the past might begin with the earliest of all known pro-testers, the Amazons, who (if they existed at all) left no words behind them but only a small, baffling episode. Here, apparently, were women rejecting men almost alto-gether. The Greek historian, Herodotus, described how this society of women warriors arrived in Syria and Phrygia about 1250 BC, and how they eventually settled and spread by conquest over much of the Greek Middle East.[19] They may have captured Troy when Priam was still a boy, and they are mentioned by Priam and Glaukos in the *Iliad*.[20] Many scholars are highly sceptical, insisting that the Amazon story is only an accretion of legend, concocted to reinforce the patriarchal ideal by showing what women might do if given too much freedom.[21] Yet elaborate accretions of legend often conceal some seed of truth; Robert Graves amassed a variety of ancient authori-ties who described Amazon history and customs,[22] and in 1996 tombs of women warriors were discovered on the steppes.[23] Whatever their provenance, the notion of fighting, self-governing Amazons has intrigued the West for three thousand years, providing a fantasy figure for men and a potent symbol for their fear of women's latent aggression.

There are not many recorded protests by women before the seventeenth century, but a few voices pierce the silence. Peter Dronke has collected late-medieval European love-songs in which the woman speaks candidly, chooses the man she desires, and is apparently the active partner in pursuing love.[24] The twelfth-century poems of the twenty known women troubadours,[25] and the contemporary love-*lais* of Marie de France, express the feelings of independent, passionate and often cynical women. For that brief moment, not to recur for centuries, a few privileged women wrote, and were taken seriously.[26]

Into the seventeenth century strode the fantastical Duchess of Newcastle, blissfully married to a man as eccentric as herself, yet protesting vehemently at the deprived lot of women: '. . . men are so unconscionable and cruel against us, as they endeavour to Barr us all Sorts or kinds of Liberty . . . would fain Bury us in their houses or Beds, as in a Grave; the truth is, we live like Bats or owls, Labour like Beasts, and Dye like worms.'[27] In the same century the poems and plays of the prolific, bawdy Aphra Behn demanded both social and emotional justice for women, and meanwhile in Paris a sharp tap of the fan reminded men that women were not merely domestic adornments. In the most celebrated of many mixed salons, a group of sprightly, clever Frenchwomen, known (and much derided) as '*les Précieuses*', gathered to enjoy friendship and learning with talented men, and to assert the presence of women in the domestic sphere.

In the eighteenth century, when women's literacy and the growth of the new print culture both expanded together, women's published protest swelled.[28] Writers came from the working class, the middle class, the aristocracy, from women painfully conscious of their subservient position and the stunting of their emotional lives. In *Evelina*, Fanny Burney covertly challenged the expectations of romance; Laetitia Pilkington described the despair of women who felt themselves denigrated at every turn ('Give me a mind,' she begged, 'to suit my slavish state'),[29] and an anonymous 'Lady' bitterly listed the series of dominating males in her life:

> In youth, a father's stern command
> And jealous eye control her will,
> A lordly brother watchful stands
> To keep her closer captive still.
>
> The tyrant husband next appears,
> With awful and contracted brow;
> No more a lover's form he wears:
> Her slave's become her sovereign now.[30]

In London, in the middle of the same century, there emerged the circle which became known as the 'Bluestockings', a coterie of clever, cultivated women who established a mixed salon, just as the *Précieuses* had done in Paris a century before. The object was to take tea, coffee, or lemonade in the company of sympathetic men, and to exchange wit and learning. They believed the world was not made for men alone, that marriage was not the only possible female career, that women were capable of learning and writing books, and that by extending their traditional roles they could make themselves worthy of respect – which they did. Dr Johnson was their darling, and they were his. He warmly approved their immense learning – though he also approved the fact that 'My old friend, Mrs Carter, could make a pudding, as well as translate Epictetus.'[31] The Bluestockings could never be described as even proto-feminists (Hannah More detested the liberal views of her feminist contemporary, Mary Wollstonecraft); their ambitions were modest, their numbers minuscule. Yet they made an elegant protest against the hapless female stereotype, and left a fingerprint on women's history.

The impassioned, prescient protest of Mary Wollstonecraft, at the end of the eighteenth century, led Virginia Woolf to describe her books as 'so true that they seem now to contain nothing new in them – their originality has become our commonplace'.[32] Fierce and lucid, in her 'A Vindication of the Rights of Women' Wollstonecraft demanded the right of women to stand as full human beings with men, in a common humanity, and complained bitterly that girls were taught from infancy to value only frivolity and pleasure, and to please men, so that 'all their thoughts turn on things calculated to excite emotion and feeling, when they should reason.'

In the nineteenth century the volume of women's protest rose prodigiously. Covertly or overtly, the voices of Jane Austen, the Brontës, Harriet Martineau, George Eliot, E. B. Browning protested at the constricting dominance of men, even in the realms of domestic life and love. As a result of this increasing threat, men began to take serious fright. The advent of the 'New Woman' caused a ferment, and was no doubt one of the causes of the Victorian fascination with male friendship, the founding of new male clubs, the quest for male adventure and a flight from marriage.[33]

'There's no Sex in minds,' wrote John Dunton in 1702.[34] Across the centuries, like fireflies in the dark, certain men have spoken up for women. Few of these men could be described as even primitive feminists, but at least they recognized the plight of their companions in humanity. In the fifth century BC the Greek dramatist, Euripides, gave to the heroine of *Medea* a passionate complaint on the oppressions of a woman's domestic life, and in the surviving fragment of *Tereus* Sophocles provided Procne with a terrible indictment of a woman's fate: 'But now outside my father's house I am nothing; yes, often I have looked on the nature of women thus, that we are nothing . . . Some go to strangers' homes, others to foreigners', some to joyless houses, some to hostile. And all this, once the first night has yoked us to our husband, we are forced to praise and say that all is well.'[35] A long list of medieval sympathizers includes many poets of Courtly Love, and many of the anonymous writers of the Border ballads. Sometimes protest was put into the mouths of fictional women by their male creators; into the fourteenth century, for instance, rode

Chaucer's Wife of Bath, and from her gat-toothed mouth issued a voice which has shrilled down five hundred years, asserting personal views on women's rights which were scarcely heard until the nineteenth century.[36]

The catalogue of sympathy continued, in ever-increasing volume, in voices hesitant or bold, including those of Spenser, Shakespeare, Defoe, Rousseau, Richardson, and on into the chorus of the nineteenth century. J. S. Mill shouldered his way above them all, the first man to have defied public outrage and argued with passion, in *The Subjection of Women*, for women's public rights and for their dignity as human beings as the equal companions of men, in love and in all else; Shelley, Tennyson, Browning, Engels, Meredith, Ibsen, Shaw, Gissing and Hardy followed, all, to a greater or lesser degree, making plain their sympathy, and the rising dawn of the twentieth century was heralded by the mighty figures of Wells and Joyce. Although many of them were rather more than cautious, and could hardly be described as feminists, they were still men women can be thankful for.

However, after all that, it must be said that Camille Paglia (roaring like a lion and writing like an archangel) is not the only woman to argue that the present social construct of femininity gives women everything that is required to be dominant, strong, the arbiters of sexual power, and very far from oppressed.[37]

The traditional man

Innumerable men, today and in the past, have laboured all their lives for their wives and children, and done their best to love and respect them, even when gratitude seemed in short supply. Although sometimes misguided, blundering, bewildered, they will quite justly not recognize themselves in most of the descriptions which follow – but sometimes, in a kind of blind brotherhood, they will also refuse to acknowledge the misogyny of the male world beyond their own orbit, or to admit the fact that innumerable women are still where they always were. There will be many other men who will refuse to recognize themselves because they do not want to. Yet women can assure them that they and their like exist in multitudes, for even if the old male stereotype is cracking it has not disintegrated, and under the threat of feminism it may well begin to reassemble itself again. By delving into the imposition of 'masculinity' – into the man's apparent need for domination, his fear of intimacy and commitment – it might be possible to trace how deep the damage lies.[38]

As everyone knows, male authority is embedded even in our words and grammars. Descriptions of our very beings are based on the word 'man'; mankind, human, humanity, and even 'woman'. The language of the computer, together with socio-critico-psycho-babble, police-speak, management-speak are all the prestige utterance of a dominant male world. As to the everyday language of conversation, in *You Just Don't Understand* Tannen has shown how much difference there is between women and men in the manner and interpretation of speech, and how much the woman is expected to make adjustments to the male style.

As I have said, the standard male stereotype is largely the reverse of the woman's. Until very recently, and often even now, a man is permitted power and dominance, and expected to wield it; sexual power, physical power, economic power, intellectual power, social power. Authority and autonomy are still a man's birthright, and (in spite of girls' recent successes at school) he is generally regarded in all-important worldly matters as a woman's superior, with an innate right to expect all manner of personal and domestic services. Many men eagerly assume this position, gratified to be in charge, satisfied to be the one who knows all the answers. As Ibsen's Nora muses, in the first act of *A Doll's House*, 'How painful and humiliating it would be for Torvald, with his manly self-respect, to know that he owed anything to me!'

It is assumed that sex will loom large in a man's attitude to women, whom he will assess as sexual objects who are attractive (to be pursued) or unattractive (to be ignored), and even today he often expects a sexual freedom greater than his partner's. Innocently but blatantly, romantic fiction exposes the nature of gender under patriarchy; in a romance of 1990, Marlow says to Flame, ' . . . you're my *wife*. You belong to *me*. I want what's mine . . . You're back on my territory now, Flame. And you're going to know it!'[39] He might be Shakespeare's

Petruchio, announcing to the world that Kate is 'my goods, my chattels'.[40]

Many men have always felt women to be nearer the rawness of Nature; a woman menstruates, she gives messy bloody birth, she suckles infants, and she is thus 'lower' than rational, clean, Apollonian man. In the patriarchal world of the Old Testament most women are kept firmly in their place, and (with the half-hearted exception of Plato and certain playwrights) the misogyny of the classical Greeks still corrodes us; even the capacious mind of Aristotle could find no warm corner for women, according them only limited rights as wives, and conceding they were necessary for procreation, yet regarding them as feeble in mind and in general 'a deformity'.[41] For women who love the poetry and plays of the Ancients, and the glittering stones of Greece, the contempt of so many of its greatest is hard to bear. Two later men of prodigious stature, SS Paul and Augustine, followed Aristotle in regarding woman as an inferior creature, and their views were upheld through the Middle Ages and into the Renaissance.[42] Their attitudes cannot be dismissed as remote, old-fashioned stuff, for in our own century, in her *Sexual Politics*, Millett had no trouble revealing the angry contempt for women displayed in the work of Lawrence, Miller, Mailer, Genet.

Like many aspects of gender, fashions in articulacy vary from age to age, and for centuries men have been taught, as part of their stereotype, to believe that it is not a man's role to speak of emotions, or to read and write about them; the inner world of feelings is a place for women, from whose clutches men must escape. Although love will sometimes make a man an ardent communicator, this sudden gift will wither all too soon, and in all matters emotional he will tend to revert to a stereotypical silence; the refusal or inability of many men to express their feelings in spoken words is all too often a problem between a couple in love – one to which I shall return.

As an element of the male stereotype, chivalry is some eight hundred years old, but today it describes little more than a mild consideration to women. Certainly this modest *politesse*, still practised by some modern men, does acknowledge that male physical and social power is being (temporarily) set aside, and this is kindly – but chivalry is not always quite what it seems. The urge to defer and protect is sometimes no more than the smiling face of domination, a device of the would-be male lover looking for a submissive woman – as Wordsworth had hoped of his beloved 'Lucy';

> '. . . This child I to myself will take;
> She shall be mine, and I will make
>   A lady of my own.
>
> Myself will to my darling be
> Both law and impulse: and with me
>   The girl, in rock and plain . . .
> Shall feel an overseeing power
>   To kindle or restrain.' [43]

In Ibsen's *A Doll's House*, Torvald sees himself as the chivalric model for all good husbands: 'Only lean on me,' he says to Nora (his 'little featherbrain'), 'I will counsel you, and guide you.' (All Nora longs to reply is, 'Damn it all.')[44] To such a man women are like children. His protection may seem to him truly affectionate and good, but as with a child the woman's time is interruptible, her efforts are incompetent, her need is for constant indulgence.[45]

Because it is obvious to most women, and many men, that women cannot be truthfully represented by this poor despised creature, we need to know why men have had to create her in this image. It was only in the last hundred years or so that women were able to raise a protest so piercing it had to be listened to. Why did it take so long – at least three thousand years? The answer is that for men so much was at stake: self-esteem, authority, power, wealth, autonomy. And these, it seems, could not be shared. Why? Why have men needed these so desperately and exclusively? The answers must lie deep, and deepest of all lies the 'male wound' – to which I will return.

The sad fact remains that even after a century of exhausting struggle many women are still caught in the gender trap, and often reviled for wanting to escape.[46] But slowly they are breaking out, demanding the freedom to make their own choices, negotiate their own arrangements, decide what to do with their own lives. Protest is all about our ears. Research indicates that success and independence is important to a third of all women, that half are optimistic about their lives, and that this optimism is provoking higher levels of the neurochemicals which work against depression; anger is no longer a wicked emotion which women must suppress, but is being turned to effective uses, and teenage girls (for better or for worse) are becoming attracted by the 'male' excitements of risk, hedonism and even violence.[47]

Many men, too, are waking from a long sleep, and some are beginning to enjoy a new liberation from the old gender constraints. After a sombre century and a half, in the fifties and sixties their clothes again became relaxed and colourful, jewellery was worn, long hair and grooming were expensively attended to, and young men saw none of this as a threat to their virility (though their fathers did). In ever-increasing circles, embracing all classes (though not the older generations), a new respect for feminine values, for intimacy and emotional honesty, is performing a heroic function in restoring his buried feminine aspects to the male.[48] Given opportunity and encouragement, and permission to shake themselves free from their old stereotype, many men would be capable of resigning their assumed superiority, and finding their way into a more equal intimacy and companionship with their lovers.[49]

For and against polarity

Obviously the stereotypes imply polarity between the sexes, and many people still approve of this as 'natural', as they have for millennia. Laurie Lee presses for 'the uniqueness of the sexes, their tongue-and-groove opposites . . . man should still be man, and woman as female as she is able.'[50] It is not only men who approve of polarity; Paglia rides down all who condemn it, for to her woman is the chthonic, Dionysian swamp upon which Apollonian man must impose order and control.[51] Other women find men so impossible that only a fundamental polarity could account for the difference; Formaini, for one, describes men as aggressive, denying, self-destructive and lethal to relationships, while women are warm, relational and whole.[52]

The belief that women are designed for love and the domestic virtues, and men for governance, invites the theory that they complement each other. How happy for everyone if this were the end of the matter, in love as in all else. But not all women wish to be only domestic, and not all men wish only to govern, for gender as a set of immutable traits does not exist. To those who see themselves as human before they are gendered, the stereotypes obstruct the sharing of love and intimacy, for when we are acceptable to others only by not being ourselves we are bound to feel an uneasy mystification.[53] Enclosed within their own models, women remain unaware of the stereotypal pressures bearing down on men and men are blind to the discriminations which act against women. Even if he does not wish it, a man will feel he ought to be in charge, and a woman will be afraid of losing her role if she shows herself to be a person of thought and action.[54] In *Plain Girl*, Miller's Janice is filled with gratitude to the lover who 'had turned her inside out so that she looked out at the world instead of holding her breath for the world to look at her and disapprove'.[55] By throwing off the weight of other people's expectations such a woman will be able to define *herself*.

The psycho-sociologist Craib argues eloquently against the tyranny of the polarized stereotypes, insisting that no one of either sex is a simple entity but inhabits a multitude of contrary roles; we need to hold opposites within ourselves, coping, for instance, with both the need for intimacy *and* for separation.[56] The psychiatrist Phillips agrees, convinced we should live many parallel lives, with our gender categories nomadic, and blurring into each other.[57] Not only does Woolf's Orlando slip over from being a man into a woman, but even within those categories, ' . . . she had a great variety of selves to call upon, far more than we have been able to find room for, since a biography is considered complete if it merely accounts for six or seven selves, whereas a person may well have as many as a thousand'.[58] This is not always easy to accept, for we are usually brought up with a rigidly gendered self-image and we do not like it threatened. But although traditional polarity can be a happy state for some couples in love, others will need to find a difference, an 'otherness', which is not fenced in by the old patterns. Because of our robust variety as human beings, polarity cannot be an accepted norm for all, and the only acceptable gender identity is one that leaves us feeling easy in our skins.

How do we become gendered?

Where do these stereotypes come from, and can they be truly innate and inescapable? In this contentious field one of the few conclusions generally accepted is that gender identity – the sense of being 'girl' or 'boy' – begins at about eighteen months, and will be complete at the latest by three to four years.

The argument from biology

This can range from an insistence that gender is wholly bound to sex (with both sexes enslaved by their hormones), to the less extreme view that there are small, but crucial, gender differences in the developing foetal brains of female and male. I am not concerned here with intellectual difference, but with differences in emotion and emotional behaviour, and here there is (controversial) evidence for pre-natal divergencies. As I have described earlier, in order to turn the embryo into a male the brain is flooded with androgens, and in order to turn the boy into a man at puberty there is a renewed surge.[59] As the argument goes, both testosterone and serotonin appear to be correlated with energetic, risk-taking, dominant behaviour in men (although the same correlations do not seem to be found in women).[60] When present in amounts above normal, the male androgens seem to have a masculinizing effect on girls,[61] while the physiological effects of Turner's syndrome, in which a female infant is born with greatly reduced androgens, enhance her 'feminine' aptitudes and behaviours to an abnormal degree; similarly, too much oestrogen in the male foetus seems to produce less active and aggressive boys.[62] In *The Psychology of Sex Differences*, Maccoby and Jacklin concluded that, after two years, average male infants are more active and aggressive, and their outbursts of anger are more frequent – but there seems no difference between girls and boys in levels of timidity and fear. About this time preferences emerge in activities and toys. These characteristics are linked to genetic factors, hormones and cultural stereotypes – in what proportions no one can yet be certain. Some research indicates that a high level of testosterone produces no aggressive feelings in a majority of men, although in both women and men it is associated with roles which are dominant but not aggressive.[63] Although aggression implies some level of testosterone, the hormone may function as a stimulant to a level of aggression already present. It is not uncommon to find apparently 'normal' women with higher levels of androgens than the average male (although usually the male has about twenty times more), and 'normal' males with higher levels of female hormones than the average woman, suggesting that it could be a high *variability* of testosterone which is responsible for aggression.[64] It is now quite clear that there is a cognitive aspect to the action of hormones, and that their effects are powerfully influenced by needs, by wishes, by beliefs. These interconnections are extremely intricate, but it seems clear that testosterone is usually assigned too dominant a part.[65] As I shall describe later, there is much in a man's life besides hormones to explain his aggression and anger.

As to the expression of aggression in women, it is now found to have increased almost to the level of men's, but their aggression is provoked more by matters of principle, such as unfairness, rather than by offence to the person, and most (particularly older women) still tend to feel it is not right for them be aggressive.[66] It seems likely that the pre-natal sex hormones do not establish rigid predetermined behaviours in female and male, but affect their potential and predisposition, so that a man is moved to aggression by a *lesser* stimulus than moves a woman, and a woman is moved to nurturant behaviour by a *lesser* stimulus than moves a man. [67]

The cultural argument

Determined to prove that anatomy is not destiny, radical supporters of Nurture dismiss biology altogether, and insist that the two sexes are innately alike in almost everything but their sexual anatomy. De Beauvoir was the first of the major post-war feminists to argue that a woman's destiny is positively not determined by her biology; she can be, if she wishes, entirely the mistress of herself and her own fate.[68] Unlike other animals, human babies are born with little truly instinctive behaviour. They will seek the breast, they will cry, and clutch; they seem to possess a fear of falling and a general 'readiness for terror',[69] but there is little other innate behaviour, nor is there any sense of gender. The libido is diffused, not yet directed into socially acceptable forms, and to the advocates of Nurture even attachment to the mother is seen as a matter of learning how necessary she is for survival and comfort. They point to the enormous power of the label 'girl' or 'boy', and to the ways in which from birth girl and boy babies are dressed differently, handled, played with and talked to in varying ways, so no one need be surprised that the infants' sense of difference soon expands to the point where each sex totally accepts dissimilar sets of gender appearance and gender behaviour. The establishment of gender identity is provoked also by a growing awareness of people and by the acquisition of language.[70] In *The Dialogic Imagination*, Mikhail Bakhtin proposes that the chief influence on the infant's development is an endless series of social, linguistic dialogues with others, creating both the reciprocity and the 'difference' necessary for growth, all of it affected by the social attitudes and gender stereotypes of the time. According to these arguments, the determination of gender is, in fact, almost or entirely a post-natal and cultural process.

The idea that gender is taught and learned cannot be dismissed as a tiresome feminist notion, for as far back as the late sixteenth century the French essayist, Montaigne, watched the process of teaching on his own daughter: 'Even from their infancy we frame them [women] to the sport of love. Their instruction, behaviour, attire, grace, learning, and all their words aim only at love, respect only affection. Their nurses and their keepers imprint no other thing in them, than the loveliness of love . . .' [71] Gender is in essence not 'natural' and fixed, but malleable and relative, as in the ambiguities of Shakespeare's comedies, or the novels of Colette, or Woolf's *Orlando*.

However, by whatever process, by the time infants are about five, parents, teachers and peers (often with no conscious intent) will have successfully imposed the traditional stereotypes, and most children will have adopted the gender roles expected of them. Many adults still admire boys for being boisterous and competitive, and girls for being quieter and prettier, and of course adult admiration reinforces these differences. There is a tremendous list prescribed for growing infants to learn – how they shall look, how they shall behave, how they shall feel – yet most of them learn so thoroughly these seem to be natural impulses.

Learning to be a proper man is a harsh task, for the traditional means by which a boy is socialized breed fear of failure, and fear of intimacy; he must learn to be in control, and to disregard whatever is disturbingly emotional. Always sensitive to a child's wounds, Dickens gave Mrs Clennam, in *Little Dorrit*, a glacial description of her son's childhood: 'I have sat with him and his father, seeing the weakness of his father yearning to unbend to him; and forcing it back, that the child might work out his release in bondage and hardship . . . He never loved me, as I once half hoped he might . . . With an empty place in his heart that he has never known the meaning of, he has turned away from me and gone his separate road.'[72] Fortunately such ferocity in child rearing has almost gone – yet there have been many books in the last twenty years describing the lingering existence of the hard male stereotype; in *Manful Assertions*, Lewis recalls the automatic removal and devaluation of almost all womanly influences from his boyhood, leading him to the madonna–whore polarity and to a terror of commitment.[73]

The psychodynamic argument

This has its roots in the complex feelings between infant and parents, and finds the beginnings of gender chiefly in this intense early life. The confident development of gender, and the happiness of the child's relations in adulthood, depend on the quality of these vital early connections. When early bonds are trusted, and surroundings are secure, the growing infant will have the courage to move towards a proper independence, and a happy experience of adult love. In order to grow into adults capable of love and intimacy, boys just as much as girls need an absolute assurance of warmth and approval and love.[74] Home is where we start from.

Gender (it is argued) does not derive chiefly from biology, nor mainly from the imposition of culture, but from an intertwining of both with the psychology of the baby–mother dyad and the baby–mother–father triad. In an area so inaccessible, studied for less than a century, there are bound to be divisions, confusions, angers, rebuttals; but here (so the argument goes), in this knot of tangled influences, gender is somehow made. In crude and simple terms, Freud's founding theory insisted on the immense significance of sexual development in infants, on the supremacy of the phallus, the central importance of the Oedipus–Electra crisis at three-to-four years, and for boys the terror of castration. Girls, lacking the phallus, grew up to feel themselves a failed kind of man, identified with the 'lack' also suffered by their mothers, while boys, identifying with the father's phallus, learned to despise the inferior sex which is without it.

Troubled by Freud's lack of interest in the mother and in the effects of culture, and by his emphasis on the centrality of male sex and the Oedipus phase, Karen Horney, and later neo-Freudians, have shown how his theory can be redirected in order to avoid Freud's dejecting outcome.[75] The significance of the mother, of her womb, of her breasts, of the loss of her, and the attempt to escape her, is now emphasized as much as it was once neglected. Interest has shifted away from the phallus to the pre-Oedipal years and to the 'relational self', a concept centred on the infant's developing ego, its attachments, its social heritage, its growth through language. In *The Interpersonal World of the Infant*, Stern proposes that the infant is primed from the age of three or four months to distinguish itself from others, even from the mother, yet without rejecting her, and while constantly creating a network of new relationships. Whatever their differences, most researchers, of both cultural and psychological persuasion, now seem to agree on the importance of the infant as a social being, with social bonds and interactions, increasingly with the father and others, but first and vitally with the mother.[76] Infants turn their faces to their mothers as plants turn to the sun.[77]

Freud's view of the mother as castrated and powerless is now usually thought to be only half the truth; instead (with all the ambivalence of unconscious life) the infant sees the mother not only as warm and loving, but also as a figure of frightening power, arbitrating love and death.[78] In order to cope with trouble, we have a tendency to deal with a stressful concept by splitting it into parts; in its broadest sense, this 'splitting' describes the division of a whole into polarized pairs, in which one of the pair is idealized and the other devalued; each is projected on to different objects, and these opposites can no longer be integrated. While it can be a destructive process, it can also be creative and promoting of self-awareness. Both girl and boy infants split their intense emotions into love and hate, anger and joy, projecting them on to both mother and father, and furthermore dividing functions between their parents. Because in a patriarchal society the mother is usually the submissive parent, the growing infant begins to see her not only as all-powerful but also as the Object, the one who submits, while the father remains the dominant, outward-bound, exciting Subject.

How a girl is gendered

Freud's theory is devastating for women who look for something more to life than an inevitable passivity and masochism, yet Freud was obviously right in observing that this was the condition of most western women throughout his lifetime. Why should it be so? How is it that infant girls, endowed with the buoyancy and joy and bloody-mindedness of all babies, turn into women who not only co-operate in, but sometimes even desire, submission to men? Why is it that men find in women more complicity than the oppressor normally finds in the oppressed?[79] There is no lack of writing by women compliantly accepting their inferior status; although clever and capable, George Eliot's Dorothea longs, in *Middlemarch*, for a husband who would be 'a sort of father, and could teach you even Hebrew'.[80]

In a dark welter of possibilities, certain recent neo-Freudian theory questions whether the infant girl wishes for her father's phallus. Rather, she regards it as a symbol of freedom with which to withstand and escape from her mother, and for this reason she seeks identification with her father as eagerly as her brother does; but because the father does not normally 'recognize' her as he does his son, his repulse drives her back to identifying herself with her subordinate mother.[81] At this early point in her life she begins to believe in this minimalized creation as if it were her own true self. (But perhaps her situation does not have to be so bleak, and in the last chapter I will look at the means by which she might be rescued.)

Displaced by the age-old excitement over mothers and sons,[82] fathers and daughters have been very much neglected. As women now begin to describe the effects their fathers have had on their adult emotional lives, this neglected relationship is at last emerging from shadow. In Hite's *Report on the Family*, the relations between almost half of fathers and daughters were found to be cold and strained,[83] but other researchers find that many girls have a strong and loving relationship with their fathers, and grow up confident in its warmth, given the proper self-esteem needed for happy adult love, and never made to feel they are 'only' daughters.[84]

For both sexes the mother is the point of departure, but she must not be the destination for either. If the girl remains too identified with her mother she has not escaped, she will live only half a life, she will experience great difficulties in adult love – and she will provide the material for the ideal romantic heroine, seeking romance and a man to justify her.[85] But because a girl keeps a degree of her original identification with her mother, and (unlike her brother) does not have to forge a distinctive separateness, her infant life is in many ways less stressed. For this reason, in Nancy Chodorow's view, the basic feminine sense of self is connected to the world, while the basic masculine sense of self is alienated.[86]

How a boy is gendered

One branch of neo-Freudian theory proposes that the three- to four-year-old boy, beginning to identify himself with his father, will find his way to masculinity only by denying his old oneness with his mother, repudiating her as a love object, and rejecting femininity. His departure from his mother is a painful process, disrupting his identity, creating danger in disentangling himself from the source of all he knows, and burdening him with a longer and more troubled journey than his sister's. Even as he leaves his mother he longs for her, but the terror of being sucked back and losing his hard-won male identity provokes him into becoming superior and aloof. Enduring what Hudson and Jacot call the 'male wound', he finds the journey to masculinity leaves him torn, with an ever-haunting sense of loss.[87] His struggle to escape will tend to constrict his inner psychic life, making emotional demands hard for him, and leave him shakier in his gender identity than a woman, who has had the lesser trauma. But for all its damaging consequences, there will be compensations in the 'wound', which releases intellectual, imaginative and practical energy, encourages the man's objective stance, his involvement with work in a sustaining male world, and provokes creativity in science and art.[88] For Paglia, man is the hero of the West, and her paeons of praise are all for the male, who has sloughed off the engulfing mother, and evaded his anxieties by commandeering the Apollonian world of rationalism, physical achievement and 'thing-making'. Creator of civilization, he finds his armour against chaos in the stillness of work and of art.[89] However much one wonders at Paglia's breathless praise of men, their momentous creativity is not in question.

There is still much argument and uncertainty about the making of homosexuality, in both sexes; in a primitive form it is commonplace in the animal kingdom, so it is surprising that in humanity it is so rare.[90] Possibly, for some reason, the basic bisexuality of all infants resolves itself in identification with the opposite rather than the same-sex parent, perhaps through the combination of one strong parent and one weak or absent. Other explanations might include infant hormonal or environmental or even genetic factors;[91] whatever its origins, fear of it is still strong in the West, and cultural prohibitions are only just beginning to slacken.

As Sam Keen puts it, 'We come to love wounded.'[92] All psychodynamic theories of gender secrete an ineffable sadness, for the mother is lost, leaving a hollow which can never be filled; the world of the nursling at the breast, where all hopes are possible and all sorrows end, vanishes beyond recall. Here, perhaps, lies the land of heart's desire, our hopes of heaven, our desperate trust in romantic love.

A moderate view of gender making

Rational beings will want to take something from all these theories of gender making. Biological theory contributes the various (if controversial) effects of physiology; cultural theories explain the vast acquired structure of the gender stereotypes and their variations; psychodynamic theory points to the intense reverberations between infant and parents, and their shaping significance in adult life. The most hopeful outcome of these pressures should be a state in which each person of each sex can assert the self *and* recognize the other as Subject rather than Object. Women must learn to respect themselves, or men will not. Yet it is possible that the gender revolution may still be less developed in love than in other spheres, because – for whatever reason – women value love too highly, and are fearful of men's reactions.[93]

It seems possible that, in spite of the similarities in their experience of love, each sex usually possesses certain core predispositions, on which culture and individual psychology do their work, either to reinforce or to contradict; most women probably harbour some tendency for nurture and relationship, and most men for autonomy and aggression. While women tend to regard love as personal romance, men may think of it as power, and while women may find mutuality attractive men may see it as a threatening dependence.[94] Another dissimilarity may lie in the different value systems most cherished by women and by men. *In a Different Voice*, Gilligan argues that because of his fear of intimacy the male assumes his need is for autonomy and achievement, and the moral abstractions such as 'justice' and 'equality', while women (although perfectly capable of appreciating such concepts) find equal or greater value in relationships and an 'ethic of care', based on love, friendship, nurturance and peace. Their aims and rules may often be less competitive, and less reliant on status and aggression, for they may preserve something that the boy so easily loses in his struggle to become an autonomous male.

Later I will look at the dire problems of love which arise from differences in gender perception, in upbringing, in intimacy, in articulacy, in the desperate area of dominance and subservience. These are fraught matters, feeding the entanglements between any loving couple, but in a less patriarchal society most of them could probably be eased. Somehow we have to recognize our similarities yet also respect the strangeness of the other sex; find creative tension between familiarity and difference, within mutual respect. We possess our magnificent conceptual cortex, through which we have a degree of free will, and we can go a long distance towards being what we wish.[95]

Is love different for women and men?

If women and men are really as different as their traditional, polarized stereotypes suggest, should they not feel very differently about falling in love? Should not the dominating, autonomous male feel quite differently from the submissive, dependent female? Some find there are indeed divergencies, one of the most marked being women's greater investment in love, and a greater offering of affection – yet not everyone feels these differences are innate. More probably, it is argued, they arise through women's search for value and identity in a patriarchal world.[96] Other differences may arise from a predisposition to nurture in women, and to domination in men. Yet, as work by many researchers indicates, the experience of love is very similar for both sexes; Person found that women were no more preoccupied with love than men, and suffered no more nor less, and that men were just as likely to become enslaved.[97] Men as well as women want love, and women as well as men want sex, and all the symptoms of infatuation, obsession, energy, rapture are shared by both alike. After all, only one pair of our twenty-three pairs of chromosomes distinguishes one sex from the other. We all feel pain, cold, hunger, joy, anger, sex, grief; we seek love, need friends. There is much evidence that these similarities have been recognized over millennia; in arguing his case for women as 'Guardians', for instance, Plato asserted that 'in their original matter' women were the same as men.[98] All this must surely indicate something artificial about the stereotypes, for women and men share a far greater part of their humanity than that which divides them, and human society is such an intricate tangle of culture and nature that we cannot yet be certain which of our traits described as 'feminine' may be innate to the male, and which of those described as 'masculine' may also be innate to the female.[99] What is sex-linked and what is gender-linked is still not clearly known.

As I have said, gender polarization is not so much an expression of difference as a suppression of similarity. Factor-trait analysis, as developed by Cattell and Eysenck, showed that masculine–feminine trait structures exhibit greater similarity than difference, and from his work on

function types Eysenck concluded that it was not biological identity but personality which chiefly governed
sexual and social conduct.[100] Maslow found that lovers
who were in good psychological health made no sharp
differentiation between the roles and personalities of the
two sexes, and did not assume that the female was passive
and the male active, whether in sex or love or anything
else.[101] For the happiness of our relations in love (and all
else), our notions of gender need this fluidity.

CHAPTER SIX

Attractions, Provocations, Inducements

~~~~~~~~~~

THESE ARE even more multifarious than the varieties of love itself, and it is unlikely that any single provocation or attraction will ever precipitate love on its own. But although many factors usually resonate together, one often dominates, producing (for instance) a strong attraction in the first glances; but if this is to result in love there will be a further tangle of provocations in the background. And if some attractions are obvious, others lie in deep shadow.

There is a fundamental biological attraction between the sexes, and within the sexes. But as to further attitudes and attractions, these change constantly, 'learned' according to the fashion of the time, and some researchers insist that attractions and sexual mores are entirely culture-bound.[1] Beauty, for instance, the most celebrated of all provocations, has altered its guise almost from generation to generation for at least three thousand years – but it ranges only within limits. In both women and men, large, wide-set eyes, perfectly symmetrical features, abundant hair and full lips have always been admired – but in different shapes and proportions at different times.

Fashions in what is thought to be charming, glamorous and attractive vary as widely as physical features, and sometimes these requirements are cruelly demanding, excluding great numbers of both sexes, either of which (though especially women) may come to hate and punish their bodies for being the 'wrong' shape. And not only does the importance of different attractions alter over time, it can also vary, as Alexander Pope noted, between people living in the same period –

> But diff'rent Taste in diff'rent Men prevails,
> And one is fired by Heads, and one by Tails . . .[2]

But however fashions in attraction vary, some obstacles are constant and do not change with changing culture. Youth and beauty have always been potent *provocateurs*, but old age, sickness, serious blemish, sexlessness, are usually obstacles to love.

Attractiveness

Alongside the specifically sexual attractions that may lead directly to love, there is a more asexual attractiveness, which appeals to everyone who meets it. Adults notice it in each other, children notice it in each other, and adults notice it so markedly in children that their behaviour towards attractive children is much more attentive than to less appealing ones.[3] Such general attractiveness deeply influences popularity, relationships, careers, and creates a powerful 'halo' effect, whereby a beguiling appearance is taken to reveal a worthy character.[4] As a result, attractive people tend to be over-valued in all kinds of ways, socially, morally, in work, in law. The quality emanates most often from those who are young, verbal, bright if not intelligent, and generally includes a friendly, smiling face (pleasing if not beautiful), a warm, easy confidence, a degree of liveliness, and some tremor of sexual appeal. And laughter, although obviously an *expression* of interest and pleasure, also attracts intimacy. All this amounts to what we call 'charm', a word which comes coloured with all the connotations of magic and spell.

Obviously the physical factors that draw couples to each other are based on the senses, on what is seen, heard, touched, smelled, even tasted. Any single one of these, or more likely a combination of several, may produce a physical attraction which first becomes apparent through the arousal of the genitals, as when Jong's Isadora sits staring at Adrian, in *Fear of Flying*. 'He sucks on his pipe as if he were sucking on me . . . He drags on his pipe. I drag on his phantom prick . . . Little heat-waves seem to connect our pelvises.'[5] Now nearly half a century old, Elaine Walster's studies of physical attractiveness have been expanded but not disproved. She found that among students the unvarying factor deciding whether a couple liked each other, and repeated their meeting, was their physical attractiveness to each other. She also noted the fact, often emphasized since, that a couple is more likely to stay together if each exhibits roughly the same level

of attractiveness.[6] Wryly, in 'Wild Oats', Philip Larkin
described how it is:

> About twenty years ago
> Two girls came in where I worked –
> A bosomy English rose
> And her friend in specs I could talk to.
>
> Faces in those days sparked
> The whole shooting-match off, and I doubt
> if ever one had like hers:
> But it was the friend I took out . . .

To the socio-biologists (supporting Nature), attraction is based on the need for a suitable, healthy mate –
but female and male have diverging priorities. The male
(it is argued) is driven to spread his genes, and therefore
seeks a young, strong, attractive female, who will reproduce only for him and care well for his progeny. Females,
however, are more concerned with the heavy cost of
pregnancy, feeding and nurturing, and want a male who
provides help and protection. Among primates, the
female gorilla is content with the largest, strongest silver-
backed male, and among birds the female bower-bird will
inspect the males' flamboyant nests in order to find the most
brilliant builder. Even though humans are not gorillas or
bower-birds, in his study of thirty-seven human cultures
Buss found that for marrying purposes virtually all males
were attracted by young, pretty women, and almost all
women by dependable, wealthy men.[7] The Michigan
'International Mate Selection Project', studying mate

preferences in thirty-three countries, confirms that women prefer men who show ambition and earning potential, while men value physical attraction and good looks. Time and again, from various quarters and in various forms, the same assertions are confirmed – that women are attracted by achievement, wealth and status in men, while men look for beauty, youth, and social skills in women. In John Braine's *Room at the Top*, Joe and his friend Charles worked out a grading scheme for women, 'having noticed that the more money a man had the better looking was his wife . . . the fact is that Charles and I could eventually work out husbands' incomes to the nearest fifty pounds.'[8]

However, supporters of Nurture argue that, although age and looks have some influence, there is almost no biological basis to human attraction and mate selection; individual differences, together with long social learning, are the bases of our reactions in forming pairs.[9] Yet in spite of an obvious encrusted cultural overlay, the urge to sexual pairing suggests that some part of our evolutionary inheritance still echoes in our heads; the process of falling in love entangles human coupling in a turbulence which must surely tumble out of both an evolutionary past *and* the cultural structures our minds have built.

Youth

'Besides, she's young, she's got all that youth everyone's so mad about and admires. Even if she's not very clever or pretty, she's got good old youth. I'd never use anything else if I could help it . . .'[10] John Osborne's lawyer, Maitland, is describing humanity's age-old devotion to the young, and if one had to select only two stimuli to love, youth and beauty would be the chief contenders. The burst of hormonal activity in puberty creates the sexual body in its morning bloom, when the libido soars, and the heart craves romance.

Most love poetry has been written about the young, and often *by* the young, because falling in love is overwhelmingly the domain of youth and early middle age. In fact, the young regard romantic love as their own territory, and are disinclined to believe that anyone falls in love after their forties. They find love in their elders a rum and ludicrous affair – even though it is likely to disturb them more than they know, with its disquieting reminders of sexual activity between their parents (the 'primal scene'). It is true that mature love inhabits uncertain borderlands, where love and sex and friendship drift and merge, yet Masters and Johnson found that for both women and men sex and sex-in-love can continue into the seventh and eighth decades,[11] and according also to literary evidence those who are no longer young continue to defy youth and to fall in love. In the most heartening of all tracts on love for the middle aged, Antony and Cleopatra fall radiantly into each other's arms, and further heartening words come from John Donne's Elegy, 'The Autumnale';

> No Spring, nor Summer Beauty hath such grace,
> As I have seen in one Autumnall face.

Yong Beauties force our love, and that's a Rape,
This doth but counsaile, yet you cannot scape . . .
Not panting after growing beauties, so,
I shall ebbe out with them, who home-ward goe.

Old men in love have been the butt of young fun
from at least the seventh century BC, when the ageing
Greek, Mimnermus, found himself 'Unloved by youth,
of every maid the scorn'.[12] As everyone knows, an older
man often falls in love with a younger woman – a fact
confirmed in Wellings's survey, which also reveals that
the age gap increases with the years.[13] Many older men
will not achieve the young women they desire, for most
of those women will have partners of their own age – but
all need not be lost. When he wrote his poem 'A Song
of a Young Lady to her Ancient Lover', the seventeenth-
century Earl of Rochester may have been simply
indulging his fantasy – but such relationships certainly
do occur:

Ancient Person, for whom I
All the flattering youth defy,
Long be it ere thou grow old,
Aching, shaking, crazy, cold;
But still continue as thou art,
Ancient Person of my heart . . .

Sometimes the situation is reversed, and a young, uncertain man is attracted to the safety of an older maternal
women, while she is stimulated by his need for care and
compassion.[14] Traditionally, society has found the love

of older men for younger women more tolerable than the love of older women for younger men, for here the shadow of the mother–son relation ignites the most powerful of all the incest taboos. Yet this anxiety is clearly fading; in the novels of Colette, in Vizenczey's *In Praise of Older Women*, in the 'Lonely Hearts' columns of journals, there is much to suggest a newly admitted male need. These younger male lovers may have to bear the description of 'toy-boys', yet more and more of them seem prepared to face contempt in order to acquire a woman older than themselves.

In the realms of love older women fare even less well than older men. Nature is crueller to them, abandoning them as soon as their reproductive life is over by with-drawing the hormones that kept them looking young; as Joyce's Molly Bloom bitterly observes, ' . . . being a woman as soon as you're old they might as well throw you out in the bottom of the ashpit.'[15] All in all, elderly sexual love provides a mine of enduring, edgy jokes – as provided by Peter Porter in 'Sex and the Over Forties':

> It's too good for them,
> they look so unattractive undressed –
> let them read paperbacks! . . .
>
> Back to the dream in the garden,
> back to the pictures in the drawer,
> back to back, tonight and every night.

The face

We are fascinated by faces. The complexity of our facial muscles provides us with the widest range of expression of any living creature[16] and so, as de la Mare described it in his introduction to *Love*, ' . . . the human face is the most pregnant few inches of space in the world.' If the face is also beautiful then it is most pregnant of all. For both women and men, beauty is one of the great gifts of nature. Almost always, it makes for confidence in its possessor – confidence in love, confidence in friendship, confidence in work; for the beautiful, golden prizes line up for the taking. Most people enjoy (as well as envy) the sight of beauty, are happy to bask in its reflected light, and until they learn better they are likely to assume (because of the 'halo' effect) that the beautiful are also the good. In trying to relate to their fellow humans, in love as in all else, both plain women and plain men are cruelly deprived. While they go about devising their own methods of being noticed, appreciated, loved, the beautiful know nothing of their miseries and subterfuges. Only the plain have to decide where their best path lies, whether through wit, animation, eccentricity, subservience, aggression, hypersexuality, or whatever. For three millennia, literature has been riven with male contempt for the plain woman – but the plain man suffers too.

The Greeks, the Hebrews, the Romans, the poets of Courtly Love, the Romantics, the Victorians, the breathless decades of the twentieth century – all have had their own changing notions of what makes a beautiful woman's face, and through the millennia men's admiration of women's beauty has been insatiable, as it was for Byron:

> She walks in beauty, like the night
> Of cloudless climes and starry skies;
> And all that's best of dark and bright
> Meets in her aspect and her eyes: . . .

Until this scouring, searching century, women's beauty had been one of the perennial themes of poetry, provoking sensations of sex and love, stirring the imagination, and inspiring a torrent of unforgettable words. But there is a qualification. Beauty which is too great is overwhelming, and can frighten men away, even in a bordello.[17] Although men are often thought to be more frightened of clever women than of beautiful ones, Pietropinto found that beauty scored even higher than brains as a source of male anxiety.[18] As Thomas Hardy described it in 'The Beauty', women endowed with outrageous beauty are often left loveless and lonely, a prey to adventurers who desire but do not care for them:

> I hate my beauty in the glass:
> My beauty is not I:
> I wear it: none cares whether, alas,
> Its wearer live or die!

Helen of Troy, Mary Queen of Scots, Emma Hamilton, Greta Garbo, Marilyn Monroe and Diana, Princess of

Wales, were not altogether happy women. However, in spite of this, most women would settle for beauty rather than plainness, and if not for beauty then for some kind of an appealing face – the urchin face, the *gamine* face, even the *jolie-laide*.

Because men have produced the vast proportion of western writing and painting, we know far more about their thoughts on women's beauty than we know of women's thoughts on men's; but this does not mean that women are unaffected by men's looks. There has always been a scattering of dashing men pursued by women's sighs and swoons, and sometimes by screams too – from the Greek Adonis through to Lord Byron, Valentino, the film stars and pop stars of the later twentieth century. Some women are also much taken with the 'Bambi-effect', in the twinkling, half-baby faces of men such as Leonardo di Caprio and Paul McCartney – which possibly act as 'releasers' of complex maternal as well as sexual feelings.[19]

The different parts of the face vie for attention, but eyes have probably received more literary homage than any other facial feature. This is partly because all primates are predominantly visual, and western society has glorified the sense of sight.[20] Gazing – what ethologists call the 'copulatory gaze' – conveys a complexity of messages, as the staring pupils dilate and the wetness of the eyes increases, giving them the wide, glistening quality which both reveals and provokes excitement.[21] When Miranda and Ferdinand meet in *The Tempest*, Prospero whispers, 'At the first sight / They have changed eyes.'[22]

Mouths and lips are potent attractions – the roses and cherries of the poets. When attraction is felt, a flush of blood reddens lips and skin, and in bolder writing the lips are paired with the lips of a woman's genitals. Above and around the face, the mobile shape and colour of hair invites touch and provokes all manner of erotic sensations; it is a common centre of fetishism, and has always attracted magic. Just as with clothes, the style of hair reveals attitudes and beliefs, and (as anyone will remember who lived through the furore raised by the long-haired young men of the sixties) it acts as a social attractant or repellent.

The female face (and sometimes the male) has always been adorned to emphasize its attraction, and the cosmetic industry today is multi-billion and multinational, with huge vested interests in our preoccupation with looks.[23] Cosmetics are used most conspicuously for the mouth and the eyes, and sociobiologists have argued that lipstick, kohl and other facial make-ups function as 'releasers', triggering in others an inherent pattern of behaviour, in this case obviously sexual. 'Painting' has produced a stream of vituperation over the centuries, revealing the darker side of sex and the terror it can provoke. The Roman satirist, Juvenal, who loathed women, also loathed their make-up:

> But tell me this; this thing, thus daub'd and oil'd,
> Thus poulitic'd, plaister'd, bak'd by turns and boil'd
> Thus with pomatums, ointments lacquer'd o'er,
> Is it a face, Ursidius, or a sore?[24]

Warner has drawn up a long sequence of denunciations, from the Biblical condemnation of Jezebel through to writers of our own times,[25] yet men's ambivalence about women's make-up has not disposed of it. If a majority of them had detested the practice it would have faded long ago – as it patently has not. In periods of extreme gender polarity the man is expected to reject any kind of make-up, adornment, long hair, jewellery, or coloured clothes, while in periods less stern these embellishments are allowed him. As we move once again into a period when gender stereotypes are loosening, younger men no longer feel threatened by what were once seen as purely womanly adornments.

The body

Either because women did not write a great deal about these things, or rarely had their work published, women's comments on the male's bodily attractions are almost submerged in the torrent of male descriptions of theirs. But (as I have said) most women seem less sexually affected than men by bodily appearance, and even today most women writers do not dwell greatly on the physical parts of men. All the same, women's preferences certainly exist, although men (it seems) have little idea what women like about them; according to one piece of research, thirty-nine per cent of women like small buttocks in men, but only four per cent of men realize this; eleven per cent of women take a deep interest in men's eyes, but only four per cent of men believe this; only two per cent of women are much moved by a man's *exposed* penis, yet fifteen per cent of men believe they admire it and prefer it large.[26] On the other hand, the penis which is concealed but bulging, as in an Elizabethan codpiece or in tight twentieth-century jeans, is an exciting attractant. For both sexes body shape is intimately related to attraction, and bears a statistical relation to the number of partners acquired, for an increase in the body–mass index (thickening or fattening) means a corresponding decrease in the success of the wandering lover.[27] Innumerable women (and more and more men) resort to cosmetic surgery, on face and body, to help them achieve the fashionable shape, and acquire social and sexual success.

Desmond Morris argues that men's highest preference is for women's bodies to be 'girl-shaped', with rounded breasts and buttocks, and a small waist.[28] Women's breasts have received unstinted praise through the ages, and in our own breast-centred culture they hold sway over all other parts of the female body, accentuating the old painful confusion between breasts as erotica and breasts as milk for babies, the place where sex and hunger meet.[29] The disappearance of the Victorian 'bustle' shows how the emphasis moved away from the buttocks, yet, as Morris describes, the breasts and buttocks anatomically mirror each other[30] – an observation made nearly a century ago by the French poet, Verlaine, whose poem 'Foursome' salutes 'Buttocks, big sisters of the breasts . . .':

Here I invoke you four: tyrants, but sweet and just,
The imperial pair, the princely underlings,
That bend the vulgar and admit anointed kings,
Hosannah, Rumpus Rex and Venerable Bust![31]

Obviously the attractive female form changes its shape considerably over time, as a visit to any gallery of classical art will demonstrate: the Greek Venus de Milo, with her wide waist and small breasts, no longer accords with our popular notion of female beauty; Rubens's seventeenth-century women are noticeably plumper, and nineteenth-century Pre-Raphaelite women noticeably droopier than the favoured look today. The present perfect female shape, displayed in contemporary fashion, is becoming that of a waif-like child, with flat breasts and thin buttocks and huge eyes, exuding the allure of sexual immaturity. The fashion in male shape also changes, just as the androgynous, beardless, epicene man, so favoured and painted at the turn of the eighteenth–nineteenth century, has long since given way to the muscled, triangular man of the twentieth-century swimming pool and beach. Men's concern with their own looks – body shape, hair, clothing – has a complicated history, often entangled with the fear of homosexuality, and there is evidence today of a new male anxiety about the look of their bodies, with a creeping increase in anorexia among boys and young men.[32]

The body, moving or still, nude or draped with slivers of clothing, has been the erotic inspiration of countless sculptors, painters, poets and photographers, and at certain periods voluminous robes have also had an effect, provoking the excitement of prohibition and postponement. When used to enhance the attractions of the body, clothes, like cosmetics, have come under the severest strictures; at the turn of the second and third centuries AD the early Christian, Tertullian, demanded that all women dress 'as Eve mourning and repentant'.[33] But outside religious circles few women have ever taken much notice. They understand Burton when he described how clothes, jewels and pigments 'will make the veriest dowdy otherewise a Goddess, when Nature shall be furthered by Art'.[34] Bustles, corsets, long skirts, short skirts – all come and go; the series of shapes and adornments which women adopt is ingenious and endless, including heels so high the wearer can barely progress, yet with the advantage that the legs and ankles are set off, and the breasts thrust provocatively forward.

As we know from drawing and painting, the body in movement and dancing has always been alluring; Salome captivated Herod with her dance, and for Hardy's Eustacia, dancing with Wildeve on Egdon Heath, 'The enchantment of the dance surprised her . . . Wildeve by himself would have been merely an agitation; Wildeve added to the dance, and the moonlight, and the secrecy, began to be a delight.'[35] Once a couple feel an interest in each other, a sequence of unconscious bodily movements tends to develop. Both establish territory, the man stands tall, gestures are exaggerated, both touch their clothes or hair, both smile, wary conversation begins, they move to reduce the space between them, half-accidental touchings begin, and the oddest phenomenon of all occurs when their bodies and actions begin to synchronize, performing the same movements at the same time.[36]

The senses of touch, smell, hearing and even taste are all deeply implicated in attraction. Our skin is our periphery, covering a far greater area than that of any other sensory organ, and it is threaded with an acutely sensitive maze of nerves. Much of an infant's intimacy with the mother is conveyed in contact through the skin, and its sensuality is re-established later in the pubertal explorations of sex and love. The mucous membrane of the mouth and genitals is acutely sensitive, and the pleasures of kissing, so akin to a baby's suckling, are intensely erotic yet keep gratification excitingly at bay.[37] In courtship humans touch each other, and the effects of touch run at electrifying speed through the nervous system, conveying in lightning shorthand the excitement of both the toucher and the touched; as Elizabeth Taylor describes in *Palladian*, 'When one is young the blood bounds forward at a finger's touch, something is – not intolerably – suggested, for the touch is an adventure in itself and may be hoarded, taken to bed as a child takes a present, turned over and contemplated and treasured.'[38]

Compared with many other animals, the human sense of smell is a poor thing, yet smell is deeply bound into our experience of attraction, and unpleasant bodily odours repel as fiercely as pleasant smells attract. As every dog knows, we all have our individual scents, and much work has been done in trying to identify which parts of these are sexually provocative. Highly attractive scents called pheromones have been extracted from a great number of insects, and from musk deer, civet cats and other mammals, and it seems possible that apocrine, the human sweat pheromone, can have an unconscious attracting effect between humans in contact, and also (possibly) at a distance.[39] Without our recognizing it, there could be sexual information in the air.

'Music, moody food / Of us that trade in love . . .'[40] Our response to music is buried deep, in the limbic system of the 'old' brain, and far more primitive than our response to language.[41] Music can be highly emotional, hypnotic, seductive, and since time immemorial has been used to stir the emotions, and arouse sexual excitement; as they echo the pulse of heart and breathing and orgasm, beat and rhythm create deep erotic responses, releasing love's sexual and imaginative yearnings, and melting the boundaries of the self into the sensation of 'merging'. Love-songs are among the most numerous, best remembered, soonest learned and latest forgotten of all songs, and (as Herrick described in 'Upon Julia's Voice') the human voice singing them can be as affecting as the songs themselves:

So smooth, so sweet, so silv'ry is thy voice,
As, could they hear, the damned would make no noise,

But listen to thee (walking in thy chamber)
Melting melodious words, to lutes of amber.

Spoken words take a lesser part in attraction, but they also can have their effect. The entire plot of Rostand's *Cyrano de Bergerac* turns on the glittering eloquence Cyrano employs on behalf of his friend Christian, suitor of Roxanne, who is overcome by the poetry of his words; and in our own less romantic time Jong's Isadora supposed that, 'It was probably Brian's brilliance and his verbal pyrotechnics which made me fall in love with him in the first place . . . My heart (and my cunt) can be had for a pithy phrase, a good one-liner, a neat couplet, or a sensational simile.'[42]

The taste of each human skin and the taste of each human mouth is as different from others as each human smell. Taste is obviously significant in the mattter of food, for in its early stages love is often accompanied by food and drink, first with him dining her, and later on with her feeding him. When eating and drinking are combined with music and dancing, the ambience is recognized by all suitors as a magical stirrer of attraction, and a review of five hundred seduction scenes in literature reveals that ninety-eight per cent are preceded by a meal.[43] Taste and eating are coloured also by confused sexual urges, rooted in the lover's wish to 'eat' the beloved.

Sometimes one particular feature is mysteriously and peculiarly thrilling to the lover, when a lip, an ear, an eyebrow, a turn of the neck, provokes a surge of instant, highly sexual attraction. Thinking of Sarah, in *The French Lieutenant's Woman*, Smithson remembers, 'that generous mouth. Undoubtedly it awoke some memory in him, too tenuous, perhaps too general, to trace to any source in his past; but it unsettled him and haunted him, calling to some hidden self he hardly knew existed.'[44] But the most hopeful physical attraction of all, most likely to lead to successful love, is the all-embracing attraction described by Thomas Carew in 'The Compliment':

> I love not for those eyes, nor haire,
> Nor cheekes, nor lips, nor teeth so rare;
> Nor for thy speech, thy necke, nor breast,
> Nor for thy belly, nor the rest;
> Nor for thy hand, nor foote so small,
> But wouldst thou know (deere sweet) for all.

Social and psychological provocations

It needs little inducement for us to turn our thoughts to love, for most people long for sex, for human warmth, for companionship, and the feeling of being particular. But over and above this, all western women and men are socially conditioned from an early age to expect that one day they must find love, and fall into it; we are inundated with provocations, swarming out of books, journalism, drama, film, pop music, advertising.

The way in which we react to love's provocations is usually governed by the social group to which we belong. The theory of 'cognitive dissonance' proposes that a sense of being at sixes and sevens with our group makes us so uncomfortable that we try to resolve the dissonance by conforming – in this particular case, by seeking, like everyone around us, to fall in love.[45] Those who find themselves socially over-pressed may fall in love not with a person but with the *idea* of love, and will often be left helplessly awash, and ready to transfer their burden of love almost anywhere. Orsino, whose love for Olivia in *Twelfth Night* is 'all as hungry as the sea', was fortunate that someone as peerless as Viola was ready to accept the abrupt transference of his passion.[46]

Another associated theory, that of 'social exchange', argues that we base our love decisions on a system of Reward and Cost. When we fall in love, the social Reward of conforming to society's expectations is the approval and prestige most people enjoy; yet the Cost must be balanced too – the risk of failure and hurt, the loss of freedom. At some level, often unconscious, a proper bargain must be struck.[47] By a process of reciprocity, love sometimes (but only sometimes) provokes love in return; in Austen's *Mansfield Park*, Fanny Price loves Edmund long before he notices her and responds to her love, and in Lawrence's *Women in Love* it is Ursula's love which inspires Birkin's. The interest of an admiring lover can set in train a thrilling rush of amphetamines in the beloved, and even if nothing develops the lover will usually have created at least interest and gratitude.

Studies of a couple's first and later meetings find that they follow the general rules of 'primacy' and 'recency' effects. The primacy effect, combining the impressions made at the first meeting, tends to be disproportionately important, for if the meeting goes well impressions formed at later meetings – the 'recency' effect – are disregarded, the first positive feelings will dominate the negative, and the couple will begin to form a bond. Rightly or wrongly, first impressions do count, and we self-fulfil in trying to make them true.[48]

Another common provocation lies in similarity – physical, social and psychological. Studies dating from well over a century ago have established strong correlations between various physical factors, including height, weight, eye-colour, and in the past ten years further research has uncovered startling resemblances in lovers' ear-lobes, middle fingers, big toes, chin sizes and other small parts of the body.[49] Falling in love tends to homogamy (with the same social class) and to endogamy (within the same social group).[50] Couples who share family, social and character factors will be more likely to feel attraction than those who do not, and will fall in love more readily. Although it is probably not the *number* of similarities which counts, but the proportion of similarity to difference, correspondences in age, race, religion, class, values, intelligence, interests, temperament, background usually provoke greater attraction than dissimilarities.[51] This is no new discovery; speaking in Plato's *Phaedrus*, Socrates declares that 'every man desires to find in his favourite a nature comparable to his own . . .'[52] Added to this, there can be a strong compulsion to repeat the known pattern of past family and parental life. In her book on Dickens and Ellen Ternan (the love of his later life), Tomalin points out a remarkable series of similarities; Ternan bore the same name as

Dickens's own daughter, Ellen, and as 'Nelly' she shared her name with his 'Little Nell'; like Little Nell she had travelled all through her childhood with her actor parents; she had been born in Dickens's beloved Rochester, where he too had been a boy, and she belonged to a profession he loved.[53] Apparently birds of a feather do flock together. But why? Although dissimilarity would seem to be more arresting, sociobiologists point out that it is important not to break up the gene group, and so organisms favour those which are genetically and in other ways like themselves, while psychologists argue that the high element of narcissism in romantic love leads to a similar group and a similar partner.

None the less, for some people difference also has a powerful attraction, and there is now a greater tolerance of mixed pairings, as for inter-racial pairs, and for lovers of different classes. In the grip of a generous youthful ideology, young lovers will sometimes insist that class and colour can make no difference to their love and its future; loving and marrying 'out' can only be good, for anything which helps to dismantle the fears and bewilderments of class and race and sex must be welcome. But there may be problems. While their sensations of love will be the same, each may express them very differently, and the enveloping webs of stereotype and custom into which each of them is born may not be easy to untangle.[54]

Other studies point to the importance of proximity, for apparently women and men who live in the same district are more likely to fall in love and to make lasting relationships.[55] Obviously proximity is often allied with familiarity, and it does occasionally happen that couples who have known each other well during childhood do eventually fall in love; according to their story, written down in the second or third century AD, Daphnis grew up with Chloë, and then in early adolescence, when Chloë briefly kissed him, ' . . . he saw with wonder that her hair was golden as fire, that her eyes were as big as the eyes of an ox, and that her complexion was really even whiter than the milk of the goats. It was as if he had just got eyes for the first time, and had been blind all his life before.'[56] However, it is rare for childhood friendship to end as love, and most studies show that love is more often ignited by a background familiarity but a personal *un*familiarity.[57]

In the purely personal (but non-physical) realm, there are attractions so varied they could never be counted. When a glow of confidence, for instance, arises from a proper self-esteem, it is appealing to most onlookers, and although dominant men are sometimes attracted by shy, submissive women, who flatter their authority, an easy confidence usually provides the assurance that most social encounters flourish on. Confident lovers not only notice confidence in others, they recognize its appeal in themselves, just as Jinny, at a party in Woolf's *The Waves*, begins 'to unfurl, in this scent, in this radiance, as a fern when its curled leaves unfurl . . . I feel a thousand capacities spring up in me . . . All gold, flowing that way, I say to this one, "Come . . ." He approaches.'[58] But while confidence is attractive, perfection is not required

and mistakes can be endearing. Elaborate experiments
have shown that the appeal of attractive and competent
people is often enhanced when they are seen to be
occasionally clumsy, or to make errors.[59] For then, it
seems, they become 'human', more reassuring and
approachable, as Jong's Isadora discovers when, 'I lie in
bed thinking of Adrian (who has just driven off and by
now must be hopelessly lost again). I adore him. The
more he gets lost, the more perfect he appears in my
eyes.'[60]

Although falling in love is provoked by many factors,
sadly worthiness is not often one of them; a sterling
character, who would sustain a long relationship with
loyalty and kindness, is not on its own an instant provoker of love. In 'Did this happen to your Mother', Alice
Walker reveals, how almost anyone can be the recipi-
ent of love, which has a way of remaining blind to
merit:

> I love a man who is not worth
> my love.
> Did this happen to your mother?
> Did your grandmother wake up
> for no good reason
> in the middle of the night?
>
> I thought love could be controlled.
> It cannot.
> Only behaviour can be controlled.
> By biting your tongue purple
> rather than speak. . . .

Given other attractions, a thoughtless and empty character may provoke abject adoration. In his *Liber Amoris*, written in the nineteenth century, William Hazlitt wrote with anguish of his unwished enslavement to Sarah Walker, a simple girl he felt to be unworthy of him: 'I am in some sense proud that I can feel this dreadful passion . . . but I could have wished it had been for an object that at least could have understood its value and pitied its excess.'[61] The comment is not endearing, but one can understand how Hazlitt felt that love had cheated him.

Obstacles in the path of love often heighten its attraction, and double the determination of the lovers. Many theorists of love, including Stendhal, Freud, de Rougemont, Singer, Alberoni, have insisted that if romantic love is to reach its fullest flowering the lovers' journey must include rigorous trials and obstructions, even to the point where life itself is imperilled. Danger is a potent aphrodisiac, and in its presence high levels of the amphetamine PEA provoke the euphoria which increases the fervour of love.[62] If obstructions are not present, argued de Rougemont, the lovers will invent them.[63] Such obstacles may include trials of courage, of separation, class, race, past loves – and family. Research on the effects of parental opposition corroborates everything that was felt by Romeo and Juliet, for it seems parental disapproval positively increases the fervour and determination of lovers.[64]

Preliminary states of mind

States of 'non-specific arousal' are fruitful grounds for the burgeoning of love. Exultation, anxiety, isolation, exhaustion, even menstruation can all leave the mind in what Alberoni calls a 'nascent state', highly receptive and suggestible, ready to coalesce emotion on whatever lodestone presents itself. Some argue that such a state of mind comes about when there is a mismatch between goals and the means of achieving them, resulting in the discontent necessary before the sufferer finds the love which will (it is believed) dispel all sorrows.[65] This is Maslow's 'Need' love, which may strike those who feel rootless, and who long for some experience which will lead to self-fulfilment.[66] Such 'free' suspended emotion may tumble equally into hate or patriotism or religious conversion or devotion to a charismatic leader – or into love; the individual is swamped and 'taken over' or 'reborn'.[67] Especially likely to occur in youth, it is a state of expectant readiness, such as Guillardun feels when she gazes on Sir Eliduc, in the medieval *lai* by Marie de France; 'Her eyes might find no blemish in his person, and Love knocked upon her heart, requiring her to love, since her time had come.'

In the fourth century BC the Greek philosopher, Theophrastus, noted that love was 'an affection of an idle mind . . . youth begets it, riot maintains it, idleness nourisheth it', all of which makes it 'the proper passion of Nobility'.[68] Millennia later, Engels asserted that romantic love did not exist for the poor, whose minds were distracted by hunger and work, and therefore ill-suited for the reception of love;[69] modifying Engels, Stone argues that until the eighteenth century love was an emotion experienced by only a minority of the poor, and cultivated only by the idle rich.[70] This view is still vigorously propagated (in Tweedie's words, for instance, 'Love is a club for the well-to-do, and peasants are not elected'),[71] yet there is much evidence to show that the age-old pangs and joys of love were indeed experienced by the poor. The Border ballads, which were probably first written down in the fourteenth century (although much older), are filled with the hectic loves of lords and ladies, but they are also riven with the loves of the poor – of those who, in Burton's words, 'fare coarsely, work hard, go wool-ward and bare'.[72] Fair Annet had no dowry, the Great Silkie's love was a nurse, Childe Maurice's love lived in the greenwood; Hynd Horn was a woodman, Hynd Etin a forester, Brown Adam a smith.[73] There seems no reason why those who wrote these ballads needed to falsify or romanticize the under-classes. And although marriage was no doubt an unusual outcome between the well-to-do and their underlings at the time, in the fifteenth century the Pastons' bailiff fell in love with Margery, daughter of his wealthy employers, and she with him; to the fury of the family, they doggedly persisted with their *mésalliance* and married.[74]

Sarsby has excavated impressive testimony of love, just as obsessed and devoted as love in the aristocracy, among the working and lower middle classes of the sixteenth and seventeenth centuries. She cites several tales, including that of a shoemaker who described how he 'fell desperately in love with the farmer's handsome dairymaid', and of two servants who 'fell in love and were married'. Intrigued as to why love should have been thought impossible for the working classes, Sarsby suggests that the new prestige accorded to love in the twelfth century meant that for several centuries a sentiment so refined could not be imagined in beings so far down the social scale.[75] Of course, wealth and leisure give time for the rich elaborations of love – for the poems, the games, the dancing, the intrigues – and obviously these activities are less ornamentally developed among those with little time or energy to spare; but there seems no doubt that the poor have always experienced love as real and raw as any of their betters.

Other spurs to love can be created by deliberate manipulation. Many of those falling in love play the risky trick of blowing hot and cold with their lovers, for even without scientific knowledge they know that a steady state cools down faster than one constantly cooled and re-excited; this 'habituation effect' slows down the firing of neurones and lowers excitement – but with fresh stimulus the effect is counteracted and excitement is fired again. Literature is full of women who use this trick to fire a lover's fervour; Shakespeare's Cleopatra plays it on Antony, Austen's Mary Crawford on Edmund, Hardy's Arabella on Jude.[76] Ethologists are interested in the 'leading-on' flight behaviour of female animals, which probably occurs in order to raise the temperature of the encounter,[77] and it is tempting to see this shadowed in the advance–retreat behaviour of Shakespeare's Beatrice, and in her glittering descendent, Congreve's Millamant.[78] Another spur created by the canny lover is a pretended dislike, the game of playing seriously hard-to-get; as Shakespeare's wily Cressida muses, 'Men prize the thing ungained.'[79]

There are more brutal manipulations than these. Although in the usual course of events love cannot be summoned up, nor ordered away, if a certain state of mind can be engendered it is possible to plant a kind of love. Such a state of 'non-specific arousal' can be encouraged by the distasteful process of 'brain-washing' – exactly what Petruchio practised on Kate in *The Taming of the Shrew*. To put it briefly, the brain is so confused by alternations of terror and hunger and sleeplessness, interspersed with kindness, that it becomes highly receptive to whatever is offered, at which point almost any belief or attitude or feeling can be induced, and the victim will enter a state of dependence and even gratitude.[80] Kate even finds she 'loves' Petruchio.[81] There are other situations which give love a high chance, including all moments of intense emotional arousal, or unexpected encounters in unaccustomed settings. For Hardy's Bathsheba, in *Far from the Madding Crowd*, the sun, the surprise, the loneliness, the brilliant danger of Troy's flashing sword create an erotic intensity she cannot resist.[82]

There are also many means (it is said) by which love can be cured. Burton gathered up an array of remedies, including those of the eleventh-century Arab philosopher,

Avicenna, who provided seven methods, and the monk Savonarola, who in the late fifteenth century offered nine. Summing them up ('for I light my Candle from their Torches'), Burton listed the remedies of fierce exercise, spare diet, constant occupation, blood-letting and various repellent medicines – the very methods employed to extremes by the desperate desert hermits of the fourth century AD. But in Burton's own view, the only real cure for love is 'to withstand the beginnings; he that will be resist at first, may easily be a conquerer at the last.'[83] As so often, he was right. There is no sure way to cure love, but before provocations and inducements have done their work there is one way to escape it, and that is to run.

The mystery

Chaucer's Wife of Bath perceived but could not explain the mysteries of attraction:

> Thou seyst som folk desiren us for richesse,
> Som for oure shap, and somme for oure fairnesse,
> And som for she kan outher synge or daunce.
> And som for gentilnesse and daliaunce;
> Som for hir handes and hir armes smal . . .[84]

Nearly six hundred years later, we can say little more than the Wife of Bath. Still no one knows exactly what it is that passes between two strangers across a crowded room, arrests two people in their tracks, fills them with an iron determination to meet again. Some provocations are obviously more powerful than others, with beauty and youth the most powerful of all, and those who possess these, woman or man, will provoke attraction far more widely than those who do not. Yet these may take a couple no further than sex, and stop well short of love. As I shall describe in the next chapter, the only trigger powerful enough to ignite the full blaze is buried, unconscious experience — perhaps of parent, perhaps of sibling, perhaps of some other intensely valued person, once precious in infant life, who stands at the heart of each individual's 'lovemap'.[85] As D. G. Rossetti described in 'Sudden Light', 'I have been here before / But when or how I cannot tell . . .'

As I have said, certain core attractions (such as the female interest in the male's status, or his in her sexual allure) are probably built deeply into us. Possibly there are chemical attractants still beyond our knowledge, and electrical fields still uncharted. Interpenetrating all these possibilities loom the huge pressures of culture, and the processes of learning. All these provocations to love will operate most fully only when several of certain conditions come together, most often from an infinitely complex web of sight, sound, scent, suggestion, memory, and then only when there is readiness, when appearance and personality appeal, when culture, geography, psychology are propitious, when the mood is right, when the ambience is provocative, when chance decrees. When all these come together, love will strike, and the nuts and bolts of reason will fall into rattling disarray.

CHAPTER SEVEN

What Happens, and Why?

❦

ONCE LOVE has possessed its victim, and the diagnosis is positive, what is it that has happened? All we know is that some shift has turned indifference or affection into the state we call love; sometimes the shift is so slight the lovers are uncertain if they are in love at all, but sometimes it is cataclysmic, as it was for Forster's Maurice when he fell in love with Alec: ' . . . he had swallowed an unknown drug: he had disturbed his life to its foundations . . .'[1] But what if love does not exist at all? As Lodge's Zapp reflects on his friend, in *Small World*, 'Hasn't he learned by now that this whole business of being "in love" is not an existential reality, but a form of cultural production, an illusion . . .?'[2] I have already described the belief that love is in fact only an idea, altering over time, felt to be love only because we call it love, and that most of us would never fall into it if we had never heard of it. But whatever the truth of the matter, the event of falling is usually felt as utterly 'real', and through the millennia its processes have taken up vast amounts of energy and ink and time.

Falling in love, even abruptly, is not a discrete, static

experience but an evolving process, and many attempts have been made to devise 'stage' theories or 'narratives', which roughly accord with the experience of most lovers. In his eloquent essay 'De L'Amour', written in the early nineteenth century, Stendhal detailed a sequence of admiration, anticipation, hope, euphoric love and 'crystallization' (in modern parlance, 'projection'); then doubt and fear, then in a second 'crystallization' the confirmation of ecstatic reciprocal love.[3] In this century Barthes described falling in love as an 'adventure', beginning with instantaneous capture, followed by encounters and exploration of the beloved's perfection, and finally doubt and distress.[4] In this experience of the narrative of love lies the theme and sequence of the age-old love-story. However, the traditional sequence is under challenge; Stacey and Pearce, for instance, argue that the 'narrative' of romance (which they describe as Encounters, Transformations, Negotiations, Refusals) has been radically dislocated by new attitudes to gender, race, class, sexuality,[5] and is therefore open to many new influences, including that of the charismatic movement, which draws multitudes into abject devotion to a leader.[6]

There is no monolithic explanation for love, and little agreement on what actually happens. The vast majority of people, who believe that falling in love is a genuine, palpable event, know that its essentials include sexual excitement, obsession, intimacy, idealization, fantasy, an urge to commitment – and (in an elementary form of 'merging') the creation of the new entity, 'we'.[7] Attempts to explain the arrival of these feelings fall roughly into the familiar groups, one based on biology and the urge to propagate, another calling on the ethological process of 'imprinting', another emphasizing the force of social factors, another pointing to cognitive elements, another arguing for the inner dynamics of the unconscious. All these explanations, in varying degrees, have something to offer.

Biological theories

Falling in love disturbs the body's normal physiology, for when the amphetamine PEA is stimulated it induces the soaring, euphoric urgings of sexual love.[8] The sex organs engorge, the skin tingles (as in the prickly sprouting of wings described in Plato's *Phaedrus*);[9] the eyes dilate, the heart beats faster, the rate of breathing rises, and it is possible that the excited body also puts out aphrodisiac chemical odours.[10] Another neurochemical, oxytocin, although primarily involved in birth and mother–infant attachment, seems to have a role in encouraging sexual touching and orgasmic pleasure in love-making.[11] To the biologist, love is a state of intense physiological arousal, directed to sex, reproduction and bonding, founded on evolutionary urges, and for convenience given the dubious label of 'love'. For those whose theorizing stops here, 'love' is sex in fancy dress, a straightforward biological impulse hazed about with the false colours of romance.[12]

What Happens, and Why?

The ethological view

First studied in birds, 'imprinting' is confined to an early, brief, critical period during which the nestling's brain is imprinted with the image of the mother; before or after this critical period imprinting does not occur. So emphatic is the effect that during this particular time the nestling becomes bonded to whatever it first sees, mother or otherwise; the devoted (and celebrated) ducklings which waddled after Konrad Lorenz, as if he were their mother, proved the dominance of the bond, in birds at least, and proved that 'mal-imprinting' was as potent as the real thing.[13] During this critical period, the nursling can receive no other imprint, and requires no reward for maintaining the bond, which survives any punishment. The bond is vital to survival, for it ensures that the infant attaches to the protecting parent and teacher, learns to recognize its own species, and acquires a first pattern for bonding in adult sexual life. Although the situation is less defined in infant mammals, most of these are susceptible to imprinting and to mal-imprinting, and in fact the theory has its very own nursery rhyme:

Mary had a little lamb, its fleece was white as snow,
And everywhere that Mary went the lamb was sure to go.
It followed her to school one day, which was against the rule;
How the children laugh and play to see a lamb at school.

Mary was obviously present when her troublesome mal-imprinted lamb was at its critical period.

Soon after the middle of this century, John Bowlby

established that in human infants a similar crucial process occurs, which he described as 'attachment', or a bonding of infant to mother (or prime carer) which is likely to affect all emotional ties in the infant's future life, and certainly the process of falling in love. When the thunderous and poetic patriarch, Isaiah, wanted a human parallel to illustrate God's great love for Zion, he turned to a woman with her suckling baby.[14] According to this theory, falling in love erupts in adult life as an elaborate variant on the first imprinting with the mother. Although in humans it has no absolute critical period, it is normally first triggered by puberty, when it is described as the 'secondary imprinting'. When all goes well, attachment is shifted from mother to the adult beloved, and for a woman it may lead to yet a third imprinting, between her and her baby.[15] (Mal-imprinting occurs in humans as well as in animals, and is one of the chief sources of fetishism.) There are impressive comparisons between imprinting, attachment, and adult human love. The dependence, the obsessiveness, the exclusivity are all there; often love persists without reward; there is a sensitive period – youth – when it is most likely to occur; and it often occurs rapidly.[16] Perhaps neatest of all, the (approximate) three-year period Bowlby gives to the infant's attachment phase is the fullest likely period of the incandescence of adult romantic love.

Many writers have described the lifelong influence of first adult love,[17] and if love is indeed an adult reworking of imprinting and attachment, the first fall could well

leave just those haunting traces described in William
Motherwell's nineteenth-century poem 'To Jeannie':

> I've wandered east, I've wandered west,
> Through mony a weary way;
> But never, never can forget
> The luve o' life's young day!
>
> . . . O mornin' life, O morning luve!
> O lichtsome days so lang,
> When hinnied hopes around our hearts
> Like simmer blossoms sprang! . . .

But however great the significance of imprinting and
attachment, they cannot account for the colourful turbulence of human romantic love; imprinting may be the
primitive blueprint, but in itself it is no more than a
series of basic, instinctive responses.

The psychodynamic view

The various theories grouped under the heading 'psychodynamic' – for instance, Freudian, neo-Freudian, Jungian,
attachment theory – bring different emphases to bear,
and give different values to the dyad of mother and
child, and the triad of mother, father, child. They find
varying significance in the pre-Oedipal and Oedipal
phases of infancy, and in the pre- and post-linguistic
periods, and they plot somewhat different maps of the
unconscious. But whatever their differences, all agree

that we carry into our adult lives the shadow of our infancy, where the real fuel of adult love lies ready to ignite.[18]

Freud wrote little about falling in love, for to him it seemed obvious that it was simply a repetition of infant experience with the mother. He saw the state of love as akin to a hypnosis, involving the same subjection, compliance and absence of criticism towards the hypnotist as towards the loved one.[19] Puberty reactivates the passionate Oedipus–Electra family drama of long ago, and in an attempt to repair the ancient separation from the parents the couple fall in love, repeating in their love the old jealousies, rivalries and angers, but also the old comfort and adoration.[20] Adult kissing, caressing, oral sex and the breast all offer recapturings of infant pleasure. In an impossible longing to restage the old primal unity, and to find freedom at the same time, lovers project on to each other great tracts of the self, and the ego of each seems to melt into the ego of the other, creating the sensations of 'merging' and the 'oceanic'. This transference of ego leaves the lover deeply dependent on the beloved, highly vulnerable to suffering, and the greater the transference the greater the commitment; as Jean says to Crimond, in Murdoch's *The Book and the Brotherhood*, 'It's a meeting with an absolute. When you see what is perfect, what is imperfect falls away, it withers. Now it's face to face, not in a glass darkly. One cannot dispute, one cannot resist.'[21] The more self-aware and 'self-actualized' the lovers, the less they will be confounded and deluded – but they will still be subject, to a greater or lesser degree, to the disorientations which beset every lover.

Some believe there is an almost total transference of love of the mother to the object of adult love, but according to Freud's melancholy conviction the mother is irreplaceable, and the most that romantic adult love can do is to 'stand in' for her. If this is so, romantic sexual love is always haunted, beset by a greed for unconditional devotion,[22] and as this yearning can never be satisfied it stands forever at the sad heart of romantic love. But none of this is apparent to new lovers, for to them the possession of the beloved seems to restore all lost unity and joy, and the clouds of disillusion hover well below the horizon.

Psychodynamic explanations of love include the unconscious processes of projection, idealization, narcissism and bisexuality; reacting with sexuality, and with imperious social influences, these psychic forces control the choice and experience of adult love.

Projection

This redoubtable process involves the outpouring of a part of one's own unconscious on to another person or object or group, and attributing to them the troublesome feelings and thoughts which come from oneself, and which one would often rather be without. The receiver of the projection is the 'scapegoat', and was in fact once an actual goat, which was charged by a Hebrew high priest with all the sins of the tribe, then sent off into the wilderness;[23] the crucified Christ, bearing away the sins of the world, is a spiritualized descendant of that same act. As an aspect of love, however, projection can turn out to be benign, offering the remaking of previous beliefs and behaviours, which then become the agents of welcome transformation. Some propose that there is a 'gap' in the would-be lover's sense of self, and the lover hopes that the beloved will fill that gap with qualities unfulfilled or even forbidden, and so allow the living of a life which had seemed impossible before.[24]

Among its other effects projection creates the idealization of the beloved, the process of Shakespeare's 'shaping fantasies', which cause such havoc to the lovers in *A Midsummer Night's Dream*, and provoke the grotesque infatuation of Titania for Bottom the donkey.[25] As an ingredient of idealization, fantasy plays a vital part, responsible for the enchanted perfection each lover sees in the other. In Pasternak's *Dr Zhivago*, Zhivago returns again and again to the wonder of Lara: ' . . . what was it that made her so lovely? Was it something that could be named and singled out in a list of qualities? A thousand times no! She was as lovely by virtue of the matchlessly simple and swift line which the Creator in a single stroke had drawn round her, and in this divine outline she had been handed over, like a child tightly wound up in a sheet after the bath, into the keeping of his soul.'[26] Seeing the idealization of the beloved as a repetition of the infant's idealization of parents, Freud believed that because of the past relation with the mother men idealize women more than women idealize men.[27]

Idealization may be modest in its effects or it may be gross. Either way, what lovers see in each other is a common cause of bewilderment to the outside world, where everyone else notices how the beloved is praised far beyond any obvious merit. When, in Morrison's *Jazz*, Joe gazes at the photo of Dorcas, whom he loves, he sees something quite distinct from the vision presented to his jealous wife, Violet. For him, 'No finger points. Her lips don't turn down in judgement. Her face is calm, generous and sweet.' But to the unhappy Violet the girl's face looks greedy, haughty and lazy. In the wretchedness of her jealousy, Violet tries to recapture her long-ago idealization of Joe: 'I picked him out from all the others wasn't nobody like Joe he make anybody stand in cane in the middle of the night . . . Any woman, not just me. Maybe that is what she [Dorcas] saw. Not the fifty-year-old man toting a sample case, but my Joe Trace, my Virginia Joe Trace who carried a light inside him, whose shoulders were razor sharp and who looked at me with two-colour eyes and never saw anybody else.'[28] Because of its distortion of reality, idealization offers powerful ammunition to those enemies of romantic love who believe, with de Rougemont, that it is nothing but a misfortune.[29] But idealization is also stoutly defended, as it is by Singer, who sees it as a function of the imagination and as part of the act of 'bestowal', enhancing and re-creating the beloved as a unique being, with a value which exceeds any objective assessment, and often provokes a creative response.[30]

Idealization implies some internal model in the lover,

which needs to be matched, and is then projected on to the one who becomes the beloved. One theory is that of the 'lovemap', which enshrines the template of a longed-for ideal being, and at puberty takes on the semblance of a future love, often with very specific traits and looks. When such a person appears in real life, this new beloved provides the screen for the projection of the lover's internal psychic need, the 'map' is projected and love is born.[31] Psychodynamic theory proposes the more elaborate 'ego-ideal'. Founded on the parents, and on an amalgam of all loved and admired figures, this ideal shapes itself in the unconscious throughout childhood, providing a model both of what its creator wishes to be, and of the hoped-for beloved. When love strikes, the beloved has replaced the ego-ideal, taking much of the lover's ego with it.[32] As it was for John Donne in 'Aire and Angels', there is often an overwhelming sense of recognition: 'Twice or thrice had I loved thee / Before I knew thy face or name.' This ideal image may remain in the unconscious, secretly directing the lover from within, but it can also appear in conscious life and become the spur to an endless deliberate quest. Those who have resolved their infant Oedipal problems, and who have warm, secure childhoods behind them, will eventually adapt this ideal figure to reality, but those with a less happy past may create ideals which no future lover could meet, and the result could be much suffering.

Jung's cartography is not drawn with lovemaps or ego-ideals, but with 'archetypes', numinous structural elements buried deep in the unconscious, which (he believed) hugely influence the behaviour and experience of humanity.[33] Inherited, amoral, they act as nucleii, interfusing with our experience and taking a dynamic part in creating the myth, symbol and fantasy with which the Western world has been familiar for at least three thousand years.[34] As so often in psychology, some prescient person has been there before; in the nineteenth century, the essayist Charles Lamb saw gorgons, hydras and chimeras as 'transcripts, types' and supposed that 'the archetypes are in us, and eternal'. If we could understand the power of these images, Lamb believed, they might afford 'a peep at least into the shadow-land of preexistence'.[35]

Jung supposed that every woman has in her unconscious a blurred but powerful impression of maleness, and every man has the equivalent impression of what is female; these are the archetypes of the *animus* in the women and the *anima* in the man, and it is these which mediate love. *Anima* and *animus* shift slightly in shape, according to the needs of those possessed by them, but basically the woman's *animus* is rationalizing and authoritarian, while the man's *anima* is erotic and emotional. Like all archetypes, they can be both malign or good, ugly or beautiful; the form of the woman's *animus* can range from god to demon, sometimes Hero, sometimes Law-giver, or Teacher, or Father – but may also appear as Wild Man, Demon, Beast. Shakespeare's Cleopatra found the Hero aspect in Antony, while in Eliot's

Middlemarch it was the Father–Teacher whom Dorothea found in Casaubon.

Ranging from the devouring Medusa through the Wanton, the Witch, the Mother, the Goddess, to the all-wise Sophia, the man's *anima* may appear all goodness, a Beatrice or a Virgin Mary, or all spirit, as in Shelley's 'Epipsychidion':

> . . . a being whom my spirit oft
> Met on its visioned wanderings . . .
> In many mortal forms I rashly sought
> The shadow of that idol of my thought.

Or it may be sphinx-like and paradoxical, as it was for Martin, musing on Honor in Murdoch's *A Severed Head*: ' . . . I knew that I was looking at her as I had never looked at any human being but as one might look at a demon'; and at the same time, paradoxically, 'Her solemn face of a Hebrew angel regarded me . . .'[36] In its positive aspect, the *anima* eases the man from mother love to happy adult love, but in its merciless aspect it brings only desolation, as 'La Belle Dame sans Merci' brought to the narrator of Keats's poem.[37] Sometimes love is drawn first by one aspect of the archetype and then by its opposite, just as Tristram first loves the erotic Iseult (Iseult the Fair), then transfers his love to the homely Iseult of the White Hands, and is then re-captivated by the first Iseult. It is not by accident that both women share a name, for both are opposing aspects of his *anima*.

When a woman loves and is loved, she has met a man who seems to be the living embodiment of her *animus*, and the man has apparently met his *anima*; as she searches for her buried masculine aspect, and the man for his feminine, she unconsciously projects her *animus* on to him, and he projects his *anima* on to her, and each becomes the custodian of these aspects of the other's self. If the archetype has been deeply repressed it may be projected with extreme violence, and the lover is overwhelmed; Kundera's Tereza 'knew what happens during the moment love is born: the woman cannot resist the voice calling forth her terrified soul; the man cannot resist the woman whose soul thus responds to his voice.'[38]

Although both the *anima* and *animus* can be destructive, they are also inspirational, and the bond between love and creativity has been acknowledged since the time of the ancient Greeks, with their nine goddess-muses. The male writer's muse is not always the beloved, and not always a woman (Blake's muse was the spirit of his dead brother, Lewis Carroll's was the child, Alice) but these instances are rare, and far more often the man's muse is a woman he loves, as Dante loved Beatrice, Shakespeare loved the Dark Lady, Keats loved Fanny Brawne, Yeats loved Maude Gonne, Graves loved Laura Riding. For Graves, 'A Muse-poet falls in love, absolutely, and his true love is for him the embodiment of the Muse.'[39] Jung recognized a particular type of sphinx-like *femme inspiratrice*, equivocal and elusive, who attracts a man seeking a muse, and who will draw his *anima*, and who works in him beyond the frontiers of consciousness, mediating between the tiny conscious ego and the deeps below.[40] In her human form, such a woman will almost certainly supplant whoever holds the role of wife and mother in the poet's life, for in Graves's words the Muse is 'anti-domestic', the perpetual 'other woman'.[41] Some, contemptuous of the whole notion of a 'muse', find such theorizing the very opposite of the truth[42] – yet it is common experience that the psychic energy released in love can provoke a driving creativity.

Whether lovemap, ego-ideal, or archetype, in psycho-dynamic theory these plangent unconscious images are deeply implicated in the processes of falling in love, and the pursuit of their shadows make marvellous tales of quest, endlessly repeated through the centuries. In his novel *The Well-Beloved*, Hardy ingeniously divides the search through three generations of men, and in an eighteenth-century novel of captivating lunacy the rambles of Amory's John Buncle lead him to union with a succession of seven exquisitely beautiful and learned women, in each of whom he hopes to find perfection. Usually the quest fails, as Buncle's failed, for reality rarely matches up to the dream of the ego-ideal, or the power emanating from the archetypes. As Christina Rossetti described in 'In an Artist's Studio', these unconscious images cloud the lover's perception of the real human person on whom they are cast, and the beloved woman is 'Not as she is, but as she fills his dreams'. However, some lovers are more aware than others of love's transformations and deceptions; although admiration and awe still hold sway, the truly sophisticated (like the poet Ronsard) understand they are deluded yet they do not care:

> Everyone says: 'Your mistress doesn't bear
> Much likeness to your words.' I wouldn't know:
> For I'm a fool, I'm not myself, and so
> I cannot tell the ugly from the fair . . .
> I'm blind and foolish: day to me is night,
> To me a thistle's just a bonny rose.[43]

Another element that rides on projection is the lover's narcissism. Just as the Greek Narcissus saw himself in a pool, and fell in love with his own image, so an infant first meets itself in its mother's eyes, and loves what it sees there; the love object is the self, which is also the mother. The literature of love is filled with pools and mirrors; Plato observed that the lover 'does not realise that he is seeing himself in his lover as in a glass',[44] and two and a half millennia later Proust's narrator returns often to his conviction that both Gilberte and Albertine were created by himself, and his love for Gilberte was, ' . . . an internal state in which I drew from myself alone the particular qualities, the special character of the person whom I loved . . .'[45] Narcissism is a necessary condition of helpless infancy, for only through concentration on the self – on the needs of food, warmth and safety – can a human infant survive. When we fall in love we relive something of this primal narcissism, and find in the lover our own long-buried self, our old feelings of omnipotence, of oneness with another being, the bliss of gratification, the suspension of guilt, the loss of reality, all reactivated from the unremembered past. If the lover seems also to have encountered a buried self in the other, then love is mutual, explosive, propitious, filling both with the conviction that they are actors in some destined cosmic drama. Repeating their infant narcissism, lovers alone together indulge in baby talk, and turn themselves into *alter egos*, such as cuddly nursery animals, creating an escape from the harsh adult world to a fantasy of the narcissistic nursery.[46]

Remarkably for his time, in 'Epipyschidion' Shelley sensed in his love 'echoes of an antenatal dream'. Such experience is highly contentious, but apparent fleeting memories of infancy and the mother are not uncommon in lovers: when Updike's Tristao is with Isabella, he realizes that, 'A smell from her skin – sun lotion or a secretion sprung by her surprise and fear – brought back to him an odour from the swamp of his mother . . .'[47] Like Aeschylus, like Shakespeare, Dante sensed the buried relationships of the mother and the beloved long before they were excavated and named, but the blurring of the figure of Beatrice the Beloved with Beatrice the Mother was not fully examined until this century.[48]

Narcissism has a bad name, and its amoral dream world is often sternly contrasted with the next stage of the infant's development, the responsible realm of Oedipus in which conscience is made. De Rougemont argued that romantic love was at root no more than a contemptible narcissism, the self-magnification of the lover,[49] and certainly narcissism lies at the root of much self-regard and social disruption. Yet it is imbued with all the ambivalent qualities of the unconscious, sometimes regressive, sometimes magical and creative.[50] For all its follies and treacheries, it acts throughout life as a well-spring of self-esteem, creativity, rebellion and dream. To a greater or lesser degree, we live with this narcissism all our lives, and never more so than when we fall in love.

Bisexuality

Freud thought it probable that there is no such thing as pure masculinity or femininity, either in the biological or psychological sense.[51] The difference is precarious, and the uncertain sexual identity of the unconscious will haunt both sexes all their lives, through love and out of it. The pre-Oedipal infant (up to three or four years) is psychologically bisexual, with no concept of gender, or of 'female' or 'male', and some have located at least one of the origins of romantic love in this pre-Oedipal bisexuality.[52] In spite of its high sexual content (it is argued), falling in love provokes a re-eruption of infant bisexuality, bypassing the constrictions of the later Oedipal phase, and urging the lovers towards a regressive 'merging' into the psychological sexlessness of their infancy.

Love at first sight

In this, the *coup de foudre*, the lover rides a tidal wave straight into bemused, lunatic love. Some doubt this can happen, and insist that such a sensation can be based only on intense sexual attraction, while love needs knowledge and time.[53] Perhaps it appears to be instant love only because that is the interpretation put on it. But in both life and literature the conviction remains that the experience of love at first sight is of love full-blown. The event has been described again and again over centuries, and the only problem is to choose illustrations from a multitude; when in the early fifteenth century the narrator of James I's 'The Kingis Quair' first sees his future love, ' . . . sudaynly my hert became hir thrall / For ever, of free wyll.' In Shakespeare's plays there are several couples, including Romeo and Juliet, Ferdinand and Miranda, Oliver and Celia, who ' . . . no sooner met, but they looked; no sooner looked, but they loved . . .'[54] When, in nineteenth-century France, the young Alain-Fournier saw Yvonne de Quievrecourt he was captured for life, and transformed his experience into the sumptuous romance of *Le Grand Meaulnes*; in the first moment Tristao meets Isabella, in Updike's *Brazil*, ' "This dolly, I think she was made for me," said Tristao, impulsively, out of those inner depths where his fate was being fashioned in sudden clumsy strokes that carried away, all at once, whole pieces of his life.'[55]

What is rare about the *coup de foudre* is the coincidence of all those factors which are needed for the precipitation of love; not only the particular image of the beloved, but a nascent state of readiness in the lover; the uncanny sense of familiarity arising from re-imprinting; a correspondence with the lovemap/ego-ideal/archetype; probably barriers; possibly a provocative ambience. If love at first sight ignites at all, it will be on the very rare occasions when all these come together.

Cultural theories

Some supporters of Nurture accept that a shadowy repetition of the infant–mother imprinting may lie hidden under the formidable structures of culture. Imprinted in infancy with the image of a vital adult being, or even with the narcissistic self, the adult is ignited into love by cultural forces and by the urge for sex. Shaped by learning, the environment and the historical situation, love emerges from the social life of the group, which is seen as far more influential than infant experience or the hidden psyche. Even if the unconscious exists (it is argued), almost nothing we do is innate or instinctive, and falling in love is in no sense inevitable or 'natural'. The 'dialogic' theory proposes that we are modelled by our unending socio-linguistic encounters, and that the search for another in love is based on this varying historical–cultural experience, with no determining infant phases.[56] The starkest cultural theories, stemming from 'Behaviourism', have nothing but contempt for the so-called unconscious, and assert that only external reality rules us; through a process of 'social engineering' our behaviour is controlled by the denying or offering of reward, or 'reinforcement', and sexual bonding operates in the same way.[57]

Love takes its direction through our knowledge and use of 'love-scripts', the series of expectations and actions we have absorbed from the society in which we live. When we want to know what love expects of us — how to feel, how to act — it is these we turn to. The fact that the script is 'learned' does not mean it can be easily discarded, for like most social learning it is so deeply encoded it can appear to be innate.[58] Although their behaviour is now converging, young women and young men still grow up with different scripts; even now, girls are less likely to be the pursuers, less likely to instigate sex, and still expected to show a higher interest in romance than boys. And they now have a whole new script to learn, which tells them that sex, love, career, children, home can be managed all at once.[59]

Cognitive theories

I have already mentioned the theory of social exchange (which describes our unconscious or semi-conscious balancing of reward and cost), and the theory of cognitive dissonance (which explains our tendency to conform to our 'reference groups'). Spurred by sex, and by the expectations of our group, we try to control our looming love by balancing these rewards and costs, based (as it were) on the value of the merchandise to the buyer. After the bedazzled phase of love is over, the cost may well turn out to have been too high, both in material terms and in terms of emotion, energy, time. Yet rewards can also be great, including social approval, sex, companionship. High reward with low cost is the sunniest outcome, as with many famously happy lovers – Rosalind and Orlando, Beatrice and Benedick, Ferdinand and Miranda. But the most enduring love-stories involve both high costs and high rewards; although love does not *have* to embrace suffering, for its most impassioned apotheosis it demands suffering as well as joy, as it did for Penelope and Odysseus, Tristan and Isolde, Antony and Cleopatra.

The notion of love as a blind messenger of destiny has always had its supporters; Cupid shoots his arrow, love strikes, nothing is done by the self. But for over two thousand years others have believed that, through a complex reverberation between the mind and the senses, our cognitive, appraising faculties play a vital part. In Plato's *Phaedrus*, the would-be lover is described by Socrates as one who seeks in the beloved the qualities he admires – an obvious act of cognition.[60] If the lover's mind is in a nascent state, love may sometimes emerge from just such a cool, deliberate selection – a directing of loving and sexual emotion, already awash, on to a carefully chosen subject; when he feels it is time his drifting intimations of love should settle on a particular girl, Proust's narrator selects Giselle: 'And yet, what would she have thought of me had she known that I had hesitated for a long time between her and her friends, and quite as much as with her I had contemplated falling in love with Albertine, with the bright-eyed girl, with Rosemonde.'[61] More than we often realize, our love is thought-directed.

Although related to cost—reward theory, the cognitive view embraces a greater variety of desires, impulses and needs, and incorporates another vital element of cognition, the imagination. In Singer's view, the process of a would-be lover's appraisal is less a judgement than an imaginative evaluation, a twofold act which assesses how the beloved might be valued by others, and how much this individual is personally worth to the prospective lover. Appraisal is one of two complementary events, the other being the act of 'bestowal', which offers 'gift-love' in all its wild confusion of crazed admiration, adoration, commitment. In the early phase of love, the surge of emotion involved in bestowal is likely to overwhelm appraisal, just as the urges of lust may temporarily swamp the thought-directed 'interpersonal intent' of love. Although the effect of both processes will depend on the lover's personality and understanding, the relation of appraisal to bestowal will become clearer as emotion subsides.[62]

The faculties of cognition also assist lovers to settle realistically for the best they can get. Everyone wants the most perfect possible mate, but (as I have described) each must usually settle for one of about the same level of attractiveness — in bald terms, the most cost-effective available. Those lovers who are secure enough to be flexible will have discovered their range and realized their own limitations, as Edward finds in Austen's *Mansfield Park*, when he fails to achieve the worldly and attractive Mary, and so sensibly (and with a higher chance of happiness) turns his affections to the less glamorous Fanny.

Choosing

Whom one meets, and when, and where, lies largely in the juggling hands of chance. But given those boundaries, do we in any sense choose the person with whom we fall in love? Obviously there are wide breaches between those who feel that sexual attraction chooses for us, those who believe we make a cognitive, appraising decision, and those who hold that the unconscious decides the matter more or less on its own. For most people the degree of choice will emerge from a confused experience of all these factors; if, for instance, the lovers do not even greatly *like* each other, the cognitive appraising process will have been overwhelmed by unconscious forces, and to outsiders their choice will often seem baffling. In arguing for 'confluent' uncommitted love and free-wheeling 'plastic' sex, in a relationship which is intimate but without the obsession of projection, Giddens approves the cognitive approach, and may seem to offer an attractive solution; but anyone waylaid by love could find such a target very hard to hit.

A forceful projection may deliver the most glittering two to three years of our lives, an endless drift of tall blue days which no later misery can obliterate; but love glimmers with illusion, it provides no accurate map of reality, no authentic guide to the future at all. Sometimes it can happen that a relationship based on illusion will succeed indefinitely, when both partners remain blissfully unaware of the real nature of the other and live in a childlike oneness, but for most lovers the day the first

wraiths of disillusion drift around them love will have
run its shining morning course, and as in Thomas Stanley's 'The Deposition' that day will mark the first
withdrawal of projection:

> Beauties, like stars, in borrow'd lustre shine,
> And 'twas my Love that gave thee thine.

But, as I have said, not all love stories *have* to end in
tragedy. When the lovers' projections are reintegrated
back into themselves, each will begin to see what the
beloved is really like, and will have to decide if the projection has been a disaster, or if a realistic and loving
relation can now develop. If luck is with them, the
withdrawal of projection will reveal two people chipped,
cracked and slightly foxed, but still pleased to be
together. In Lessing's 'A Habit of Loving', it suddenly
seemed to George 'that he was seing Bobby quite newly.
He had not really known her before. The delightful little
girl had vanished, and he saw a young woman toughened
and wary because of defeats and failures he had never
stopped to think of . . . He was appalled at his egotism.
Now, he thought, he would really know her, and she
would begin to love him in response to it.'[63] This is the
time when lovers cease to gaze only at each other, and
turn their eyes to the future instead. They can now begin
to build a structure of mutuality and sex and trust and
affection and loyalty and humour, bone to bone, which
will be the envy of all who have never succeeded in
building it. But if luck is absent, only one lover may

withdraw, leaving desolation in the other, or there may be a mutual legacy of indifference, contempt, or even hatred.[64] Love which grows from affection, with a less violent projection and a cool, cognitive appraisal is the safer course, for although there will be a loss of impetus, through a landscape of drabber colours, a balance of appraisal and bestowal will be more likely to survive disillusion. The great hope is always that love will alloy both the real and the ideal. Love is not only an emotion, nor cognition, nor learned behaviour, but something which includes aspects of them all. It is, in fact, labyrinthine, integrating at least the three behaviour systems of attachment, care and sex,[65] and knotted up in strands of biology, culture, cognition, chance, expectation, learning, looks, personality, readiness, infant experience and the unconscious. Some people are so daunted they will not face it at all, fearful of being picked apart, but for prospective lovers, willing to fall into it, most triggers must be at least half-cocked. Or, in Nin's more poetic words, 'The fascination exerted by one human being over another is not what he emits of his personality at the present instant of encounter but a summation of his entire being . . .'[66]

In spite of millennia of hope, falling in love is absolutely no way of getting to know someone. With good fortune, that will come later, but in its early iridescent days love is a blind bewitchment, which may or may not turn out for the best. Musing on Antony after his death, Cleopatra asks the abiding question, and softly Dolabella answers her:

CLEOPATRA: Think you there was, or might be, such a
              man
              As this I dreamed of?
· DOLABELLA: Gentle madam, no.[67]

Why do we Fall in Love?

Why should humans, alone of all creatures, be subject to these fits of insane exultation, heartache, dependence, trust, obsession; why did such a unique behaviour ever evolve, and how can such an experience be of any benefit to us? Apes sometimes show distinct preferences for each other, and a few mammals are monogamous,[68] but none of these exhibit anything like the bedazzled loving activity of their supposed superiors, *Homo sapiens*.

Biology and ethology

In evolutionary terms, if a species lives and flourishes it has succeeded, and if it dies out it has failed. The successful propagation of the species is all that counts, and the only sexual strategies which persist are those that pay off. Far from failing and dying out, the human species continues to increase its flagrant dominance over all other creatures, and it seems likely that bonding and falling in love must have made its contribution to this doubled-edged evolutionary triumph.

Convinced that the bonds created by love could come only from our evolutionary ancestry, some biologists propose that the brain chemistry governing imprinting and bonding was already evolving some three and a half million years ago.[69] Before about three million years ago, hominids had probably not advanced to a stage of consciousness in which individual couple-bonding was possible; as Gunther Grass's narrator describes in *The Flounder*, ' . . . in the beginning, when Awa ruled, when all women were called Awa and all men Edek, we didn't have love . . . And undoubtedly our Superawa would have sternly tabooed love between two individuals – if such madness had ever cropped up among us – and banished the offending pair . . . To us the individual meant nothing.'[70] By about two million years ago a primitive sense of individuality had probably emerged, and the bonding of couples was slowly selected for various reasons, first because of its benefit to the infant, which increasingly required many years of physical and mental and emotional growth before it could look after itself. By about a million years ago the foetal brain had grown so large that the mother's cervix was only just able to give it birth, and to get out at all the baby had to be born, as it were, prematurely, in 'atricial' or semi-embryological form, as it is today. For a species which concentrates on quality rather than quantity, and gives birth to so few infants, each of which takes many years to grow, obviously pair-bonding has enormous survival value. If the parents were bonded into a reasonably long-lasting pair, this extended infancy was protected by two rather than one, and the various tasks of baby-caring, food-gathering, hunting and defence could be shared.

In order to hold the bond through the long infancy of the offspring, adaptations had to include the enhancement of sex. The female hominid became, uniquely, receptive all the year, and the couple constantly strengthened the pair-bond by unrestricted sexual activity. Morris argues that the evolution of naked skin, elaborate facial expression, full sensitive lips, rounded female breasts, the intensity of orgasm, the size of the man's penis, face-to-face sex, and the high sexual energy of both human female and male would all have encouraged a pair to stay together at least long enough to rear an infant successfully.[71] If the male confines himself to one female, and so limits his freedom, he is compensated by being able to make sure his partner's offsping are his own, and by frequent available sex. Evolutionary psychologists propose that as consciousness advanced, and social life developed, primitive pair-bonding evolved into the passion and commitment we now call 'love', and eventually gave rise to all the painful entanglements of jealousy, incest taboo, promiscuity, monogamy and fidelity. If these speculations have any truth in them, then love's primitive blueprint is old indeed.

Cultural explanations

As I have described, radical sociologists argue that the emotions of love are socially constructed, created by the dominant ideology of each society, and specific to each historical period. Love is a component of social relations which has evolved its own 'love-script' to meet certain social needs, and to dictate the emotions and behaviour considered appropriate to its time. Those supporters of Nurture who accept that 'falling in love' is a discrete and recognizable experience provide various explanations which have little to do with ethology or sex, and are based on the premise that reproduction and rearing are not the main functions of love. As individual consciousness emerged slowly over the aeons (it is argued), so did an awareness of loneliness, of shifting moorings, alienation from the unity of the tribe – a condition first described in the nineteenth century as 'anomie'.[72] Theorists from all camps seem to share at least one common belief – that we humans need one other. We have developed as intensely social creatures, seeking comfort and warmth with our own kind, and banding together against fear, cold, hunger, loneliness; we cannot develop fully without social contact.[73] And so perhaps the complexities of love evolved, at least in part, as a defence mechanism helping us to control our primal terrors, and a consolation for the lonely individual in a detribalized world. Love offers a safe space, soothes the troubled human brain and its lonely consciousness, assuages the fear of death, and offers a luminous purpose for living. If loneliness and fear and anxiety are not escapable, love can make them bearable, and even for a while forgettable.

Some argue that when the animal nature of lust became a moral problem, the social structures of love were encouraged in order to provide a cloak of respectability for sex[74] (and Freud was therefore right in supposing that love is 'aim-inhibited sex'). Love is thus no more than self-interest, cloaking sexual desire, and the determination to keep the beloved for oneself, at the same time respectably ensuring the orderly descent of wealth. The bearers of children were taken into the power of the non-bearers so the latter could recognize their children.[75] Love was nurtured, in fact, as a means of social control, protecting and masking patriarchal institutions, and exploiting the dependency of women for the perpetuation of patriarchy, while at the same time providing consolation for conforming to the demands of dynasty, of marriage, of the nuclear family. It developed, in short, as a patriarchal scarcity mechanism, apparently enhancing what is in truth the repression of sex, which is then tamed through marriage, family, dynasty, and bound to the service of patriarchal society.[76] Or could it be just the opposite? Perhaps love did not evolve as a repressive mechanism at all, but as an act of defiance and rebellion, an anarchic wish to be free in an impersonal world, liberated from the harsh conventions of adult life?[77] In this view, love is anti-social, a force not *for* but *against* wealth and power and institutions. Might it also have been encouraged by women themselves, as a path to a little brief power?[78] These possibilities – repression or rebellion – are not as contrary as they first seem, for once the edifices of love were put together in order to control they could also become the provocation to revolt.

Psychological explanations

In Fromm's view, the helplessness of the human young at birth ensures that desertion is the deepest human terror, and our profoundest need is to overcome separateness and leave the prison of our loneliness.[79] As adults we need the body intimacy we once found in our parents' arms, we need wordless communication, a sense of oneness and union with another. If love is linked to the search for completion we are back with Aristophanes, describing the search by each half of the original double-being for the other.[80] As so often with the Greeks, he touched a nerve which still quivers, and has inspired through the millennia images of something lost, some longed-for wholeness just out of sight. As I have described, some see this sense of absence arising from the alien and forbidden spaces in the self; others see it as the warm place once inhabited by the mother, and argue that we are forever in pursuit of the old dyadic relation of infancy, a oneness with this lost being. According to this argument, the deepest of all sources of love lies in the desperate need to re-establish this relation, and in adult romantic love, when the infant's fusion with the mother becomes the adult fusion with the beloved, we have created its nearest conceivable equivalent.

As a part of this re-establishment of past security, the evolution of love brought with it confidence, self-esteem and a sense of personal significance; in Lacan's words, 'the first object of desire is to be recognized by the other.'[81] Everyone needs to feel unique, craves a sense of worth, and nothing fulfils this need more exultantly than being loved. Love helps to establish the wavering self in an impersonal world, to find a way through the uneasiness of 'anomie', and through Alberoni's 'nascent' state, when mind and heart are on a threshold, tremulously waiting. Falling in love presents an escape, sweeping the lover away from the old life and creating a new configuration, filled with fresh experience, offering new self-realization, a new route to growth. Even some of those who find romantic love merely egotistical admit that it may transform the ego and open new paths of consciousness.[82] But there is nothing neat about human beings. With all the contrariness which besets us, we look to love for both safety and danger, commitment and freedom, and as the Christian myth fades we watch love stealthily usurping the realms of religion, absorbing transcendence and offering new salvation, in this world rather than the next.

As Bellow's Uncle Ben asks his nephew, Kenneth, ' "If love cuts them up so much, and you see the ravages everywhere, why not be sensible and sign off early?" "Because of immortal longings," I said, "Or just hoping for a lucky break." '[83] Our answers, like Kenneth's, need to cover all possible sources. It seems reasonable to accept that the seeds of romantic love lie in a primitive imprinting, in which they germinated through perhaps three or four millennia, and that the processes of evolution selected them because they proved helpful to the survival of the species, and brought us a sense of significant self. The success of the helpless human baby was ensured by the various strategies evolved for its care, and when it grew to adulthood it would repeat the pattern of its parents' bonding and bring its own offspring the same advantages. But eventually, through the long growth of consciousness, an elementary reproductive bonding seemed no longer enough, and the human adult felt the need for more. Only a few millennia ago – very recently in our human time-scale – a confused and compelling welter of emotions evolved, in its floundering way, to meet these needs, and what had happened was romantic love.

CHAPTER EIGHT

Trouble

LOVE IS bedevilled by trouble. However ecstatic it may seem at first, it is not always going to be proof against the confusions of sex and gender, conflicts of personality, different attitudes to the world. There are all manner of stresses which can prize lovers further and further apart, until a tangle of mystification and guilt has corroded all their early confidence. They may find, for instance, that their stereotypes do not 'fit' either for them or for each other; or one of them may find that the other does not correspond to a stubborn 'ideal' whose image will not fade; they may suffer from incompatibilities in which there can be no compromise; hidden needs may struggle against conscious hopes; attitudes to love, sex, gender, politics, religion, money may veer apart rather than together. In spite of its glittering scenes of transformation, love carries the old hidden baggage, and cannot dispose of it all. Infantile rages and resentments lurk in the shadows, and sooner or later they will re-emerge. The lovers' state of dependence leaves them acutely vulnerable to the anger or malice of the other — yet sometimes an effort at harmony can be positively destructive, for when both lovers try to eradicate their differences both may find they have lost in themselves what each of them most valued.[1] Jung described the possible dangers for a couple in which one is the 'container' and the other the 'contained'; the first, being the more developed personality, 'contains' the less complex partner, who will begin to feel inadequate and trapped,[2] as Crimond felt when he had parted with Jean, in Murdoch's *The Book and the Brotherhood*, ' . . . we were bound to destroy each other. We both realised it. I was devouring her being and making her less. And after a time, she would have hated me.'[3]

Sex, sin, anxiety

Of all the problems besetting love, these loom as ominously as any. Guilty sex is poison to love in all its phases. It has a long history behind it, but for the last hundred years it has been struggling free of the ancient, destructive shibboleths, and Freud was only the greatest of the many midwives who helped the birth of a new understanding, and a new conviction that sex was neutral, neither good nor bad unless we made it so. Many of those born in or after the fifties have cheerfully burst the chains which bound sex to sin for so long, and find themselves no longer badgered by guilt. Yet research indicates that perhaps 'the sexual revolution' trumpeted a greater change than has actually taken place,[4] and many lovers are still half-haunted by the old ghosts.

Lust has always been the most enthralling of all transgressions, and although in theory Pride is the most terrible of the deadly sins it has never enjoyed anything like the celebrity of Lust. For well over two thousand years sin has been seen in the guise of lust more often than in any other; the Old Testament story of Eve teaches (as one of its lessons) that sexual knowledge was central to the Fall, and even now sex still tows that shadow behind it. Most western people have been taught to regard sex as dirty. Why? The answers are buried deep, but the word 'dirty' provides an obvious clue to one of them. The organs of sex and of excretion are physically so close together that urine, faeces, menstrual blood, sperm and the effluvia of sexual diseases are crowded in such a way they almost seem to interpenetrate. As W. B. Yeats described in 'Crazy Jane Talks with the Bishop':

> A woman can be proud and stiff
> When on love intent;
> But Love has pitched his mansion in
> The place of excrement . . .

Add to this the ancient earthy tradition of nature–body–woman, against the clean clarity of god–mind–man – Dionysias against Apollo. Because she is earth and body and blood, woman is dirty, and man is contaminated in his contact with her.

But sex was not only dirty, it was sinful, and woman who provoked temptation must be evil.[5] Sexual sin is often thought to be the invention of Christianity, but the pre-Christian world was thoroughly familiar with it; the virginity of Artemis was sacred to the Greeks, and if a Hebrew bride was found to have faked her virginity she was stoned to death.[6] The same attitudes were confirmed in the new sprig of Judaism which came to be known as Christianity. As far as can be understood from the New Testament, the founder of Christianity almost entirely ignored the place of sex in his own and others' lives[7] – but this may be the fault of the men who wrote the Gospels, and of the early Christian Fathers, who wished to exclude all stigma of sex from the Son of God.[8] St Paul's was probably the first of the thundering Christian voices to denounce the evil of sex, grudgingly conceding that for those who could not achieve the holy state of chastity, 'it is better to marry than to burn.'[9] Whatever else he may have done for the Church, his elevation of chastity, and his insistence on the split between 'the flesh' and 'the spirit', left a disturbing legacy.

By the fourth century AD, monks and hermits were fleeing to the deserts of North Africa and the Middle East, either alone or joining various sects already settled there, in the hope of avoiding the sins of the flesh, and especially of sex. St Augustine's cry to God in his *Confessions*, 'Give me chastity and continency, only not yet',[10] has remained (at least until recently) one of the great cries of the Western dilemma, and it is dispiriting to watch his progress from kindly lover and father to the celibate ascetic who found mankind in danger of perdition because of the pleasure of sex.[11] Following Paul, the Saints Jerome, Ambrose and Augustine, bestriding Christian thought in the fourth and fifth centuries, led a Church which believed that only the celibate life could be truly pure, and the only pure bride was a consecrated virgin, a bride of Christ.[12] (Nearly a thousand years later, a long fourteenth-century poem, 'The Pearl', endearingly mingling tenderness and doctrine, described the writer's dead infant daughter as one of Christ's brides – a company, she tells her father, of 140,000 wives.)[13] For the early Church female flesh was abhorrent, women were evil – except for the one who was wholly exempt. By the third century (some two hundred years after her life and death), the mother of Christ had been transformed into a figure of angelic purity, uncontaminated by the crudity of sex, and the split between Madonna and Whore, which was to haunt the West for centuries, became blatantly visible.[14]

The Church's prolonged and grudging acceptance of sexual love as a promoter of the love of God, and of loving-kindness towards one's fellow beings, hindered the approval of sexual love even in marriage; but the great writers of the Renaissance, including Dante, Petrarch, Chaucer, Spenser, Shakespeare and many of their fellows, began to feel their way towards a reconciliation with the body. After the repression of the puritans' Commonwealth in the mid-seventeeenth century, sexual exuberance burst out vehemently at the Restoration of 1660, when Dr Samuel Collins described the female sexual parts filling with a 'choyce Juyce' in coition, and reported enthusiastically on women's sexual pleasure.[15] In the eighteenth century came a surge of bawdy literature, from street ballads to the erotic elegance of Pope's 'Rape of the Lock', and the novels of Fielding and Smollett.[16] By the early nineteenth century the Romantics were flaunting their contempt for the old notions of sexual sin, and William Blake was only one among many who struggled to establish sex as sinless and joyful:

> Abstinence sows sand all over
> The ruddy limbs and flaming hair,
> But Desire Gratified
> Plants fruits of life and beauty there.[17]

But as I have described, in the succeeding Victorian era, in spite of the efforts of the Romantic poets, sex was once again transformed into a forbidden subject for polite society and polite literature. In that strange time (more alien to us than many further away) the iron corselette snapped shut on the middle classes, for whom sex became as shrouded as the bodies of women. Serious middle-class writers, such as Thomas Hardy, chafed at having to bow the knee to Mrs Grundy, and detested the 'false colouring' with which a novelist was obliged to tint his story, instead of presenting life as 'a physiological fact'.[18] But alongside the drive to social purity there also ran an explosion of sexual excitement, producing wide research into sexual diseases, prostitution and sexual problems (many of which became labelled as 'perversions'); it created new classifications, new Acts of Parliament, and burst out in the riotous sub-culture of unexpurgated writing, brothel and music-hall.[19] Soon Ibsen, Hardy, Reade, Browning, Shaw, the Fabians, the New Women were on their way to rescue the middle classes, and under their restless pressure the adamantine tablets began to crack. Sexual guilt was again in retreat, and permission to talk out loud came with a new shift of attitudes, in which Freud's was the most momentous voice. From about that time our twentieth-century devotion to sex began to burgeon. The explosion of interest provoked by depth-psychology, and by research on physiology and the brain, was enormously encouraged by the arrival of the Pill. Sexual pleasure was finally severed from unwanted conception, and publicly, powerfully, for the world and Philip Larkin, sex had re-arrived;

> Sexual intercourse began
> In nineteen-sixty-three
> (Which was rather late for me) –
> Between the end of the *Chatterley* ban
> And the Beatles' first LP.[20]

Guilt provokes anxiety, and until very recently sex has acted as the most compelling of all the magnets (like money, or food, or body shape) to which our wandering apprehensions fly like iron filings. In spite of our liberation, shifting public panics still latch arbitrarily on to various categories of sex, such as homosexuality, prostitution, masturbation, or any other kind of sexual 'deviance'.[21] For couples in love the sexual bond is vital, but there is much evidence of extreme unease in sexual relations, both in and out of love.[22] The belief that sex, and sex-in-love, should be natural, joyful and unencumbered is highly attractive – but it is not always like that for everyone. Desiring a man other than her husband, in Jong's *Fear of Flying*, Isadora broods on this intransigence; 'Why was it all so complicated? Why couldn't we just be friendly and open about it? "Excuse me, darling, while I go off and fuck this beautiful stranger." Why couldn't it be simple and honest and unserious?'[23] Why indeed? The reason is that for both women and men sex is affected by an intricate tangle of beliefs and attitudes and emotions, making many sexual partnerships stiff with tension. For some, as Amis's Jake describes, new knowledge and information is not helpful: 'I was doing fine when things really were repressive, if they ever were, it's only since they've become, oh, permissive that I've had trouble. In the old days a lot of people, men as well as women, didn't know quite what to expect of sex so they didn't worry when it didn't work too well. Now everybody knows exactly what's required of them and exactly how much they've fallen short . . .'[24]

Some researchers find greater insecurity in women's sexual feelings than in men's, with the fear of inadequacy, fear of rejection, and levels of guilt all higher; but others find that men are even more anxious than women.[25] Orgasm in women is less predictable than in men, and *The Hite Report* produced the sad statistic that out of a sample of over three thousand women nearly two-thirds never, or very rarely, experienced orgasm in intercourse, and eleven per cent never experienced it at all.[26] All researchers have found the faking of orgasm is a frequent female device[27] – one not unknown to Chaucer's Wife of Bath:

> For wynnyng wolde I al his lust endure,
> And make me a feyned appetit.[28]

Although one reason for the failure of orgasm is that the clitoris is not precisely placed where it can respond to the male's thrusting, the cause of failure is not always the clitoris, or the clumsiness of the lover; it may be rooted in psychological damage inflicted by early experience, such as a girl's inability to resolve her feelings towards her mother or father.[29] Masters and Johnson found that women were more affected than men by harmful psycho-social influences in childhood and youth, and in their latest work they emphasize the dire effects of fear, early trauma, and above all of a puritanical religious upbringing.[30] However, the editors of *Sex in America* found that conservative, Protestant women enjoyed more orgasms than any other female group[31] and one can only assume that it is the *degree* of repressive religious upbringing that is significant. As Sylvia Plath describes in 'Spinster', a traumatic background can produce sexual inhibition so deep-frozen it will never be thawed:

> ... And round her house she set
> Such a barricade of barb and check
> Against mutinous weather
> As no mere insurgent man could hope to break
> With curse, fist, threat
> Or love, either.

Men may also suffer from the effects of childhood trauma, which can destroy their capacity for sex and love as cruelly as for the frozen male figures in L. P. Hartley's *The Go-Between* and *The Brickfield*, who grow up unable to make committed loving relations with adult women. Sometimes it is possible to love only after the death of the beloved, when there is no more terror of giving or rejection; Hardy's piercing love poems to his first wife were written long after she had died,[32] and with his *Birthday Letters* to Sylvia Plath Ted Hughes has followed in the same track.

Men live in a culture today which encourages them to compete as sexual athletes, although not all wish, or are able, to join in the hurly-burly of rampant male sex; some are anxious about their sexual prowess, others are frightened by the strength of their sexuality, others cannot manage the relation between sex and power. Even those who try, like the boy in Dworkin's *Mercy*, may find themselves bewilderingly out of control: 'The pain wasn't supposed to rip through him; from wanting me; every second; now. He was supposed to come and go, where he wanted, when he wanted, get laid when he wanted. . . . He's burning towards death and a man's not supposed to.'[33]

Except in old age, impotence is more often caused by anxiety than by physical problems. Fear of it is profound, and as far back as we can reach in history men have felt that an inability to perform was one of life's cruellest humiliations; when the nineteenth-century author of *My Secret Life* found himself inadequate ('. . . it was a sucked gooseberry, a mere bit of dwindling, flexible, skinny gristle') a wise doctor told him his condition was due to 'nervousness', and to the fact that he had tender feelings towards the woman.[34] Long before it came to be known as 'splitting', this doctor had stumbled on the male process of dividing women into Madonnas and Whores; for some men, Madonnas are so sacrosanct the penis refuses to defile them, and only prostitutes can stimulate it to rise. As Roth's young Jew, Portnoy, discovers when he is with a Gentile girl, 'I am so awed I am in a state of desperation *beyond a hard-on*. My circumcised little dong is simply shrivelled up with veneration.'[35] Sometimes, as in Amis's *Jake's Thing*, it is the combination of powerful women and psychiatry which terrifies the penis into collapse, and although in many surveys men assert they like women to be clever, in fact this is often not so, for clever women may make them feel threatened and inadequate.[36] And yet, although male anti-feminists often cite over-confident women as the culprits, Pietropinto found that it was not liberated but passive women who were the greater cause of impotence.[37] Obviously there are many causes, including long abstinence, but age is probably the most glaring, and sadly for the male his longing does not wane with his waning powers. The despair of old men surfaces in an acute sense of deprivation, a mourning for the wilting of a life-driving system, and sometimes in a desperate recourse to monkey-glands, powdered horn, injections, surgical dildoes, young women and a frantic search for love.

The anxieties of infidelity will not trouble a besotted pair of lovers, for they will want only each other. But those who are less committed could easily be haunted by the old uncertainties; an insecure woman will dread the roving tendencies of men, and an apprehensive man will remember endless stories of the fickleness of women. The only body of evidence as large as that describing men's infidelity is that describing women's. In all hearts but that of Chaucer (who was acutely sensitive to women's pain), Cressida has become a lasting symbol of woman's inconstancy, immortalized by Homer, Boccaccio, Henryson and Shakespeare as the lovely, faithless woman whose treachery breaks the heart.[38] But she is only one among many, for as Captain Harville insists to Anne Elliot, in Austen's *Persuasion*, ' " . . . I do not think I ever opened a book in my life which had not something to say upon women's inconstancy. Songs and proverbs all talk of women's fickleness." '[39] (In an intriguing new slant on adultery, a piece of research has found that women are more likely to be unfaithful during the few days after ovulation, when they are most fertile, and most under pressure to seek the fittest sperm[40] – you may take it or leave it.)

Yet because the variety of human conduct is so great there is as much literary evidence for woman's constancy as for her infidelity. In 'Wulf and Eadwacer', one of the small handful of Anglo-Saxon lyrics to survive, the woman laments:

> Grieved have I for my Wulf with distant longings.
> Then it was rainy weather, and I sad,
> When the bold warrior laid his arms about me . . .

O Wulf, my Wulf, my longing for your coming
Has made me ill. . . .[41]

She, and Chaucer's Patient Griselda, who endures her
husband's savagery yet remains 'constant as a wal,'[42]
provide two of a thousand noble prototypes of fidelity
to counterbalance the treachery of Cressida. In these
annals of male literature, women suffer and wait as
often as they betray, and in the writing of women themselves the case is not much different. Replying to
Captain Harville, Anne Elliot says, 'All the privilege
I claim for my own sex (it is not a very enviable one;
you need not covet it) is that of loving longest, when
existence or when hope is gone!'[43] Often women are
as bewildered as men as to why they ought to be
faithful, as Jong's Isadora discovers when she and her
husband are driving with Adrian, in *Fear of Flying*,
and she complains how, 'We drove to the hotel and
said goodbye. How hypocritical to go upstairs with a
man you don't want to fuck, leave the one you do
sitting there alone, and then, in a state of great
excitement, fuck the one you don't want to fuck while
pretending he's the one you do. That's called fidelity.
That's called monogamy. That's called civilization and
its discontents.'[44] Socio-biologists generally argue that
women want long-term relationships in order to stabilize
a family, but Fisher advances the theory that women are
as sexually restless as men and, like them, tend to have
close relationships in periods of roughly four-year cycles.
As men are driven to spread their genes, so women are

driven to accumulate new alternatives, opportunities and resources.[45]

Literature written by men (who ought to know) offers an unending history of male deceit. Following in the footsteps of Zeus, the great progenitor, wandering human males have littered the West with the broken hearts of women. Lothario, Casanova, Don Juan, Tom Jones, James Bond — they and their brothers sparkle through their literary lives, always attractive and alluring, whatever damage they may do to women on the way. Their victims have been the perennial butt of jokes and songs, but so great is the young blade's sexual glamour that everyone except the deserted (and possibly pregnant) woman smiles and urges him on.

By dividing the concept of 'woman' into separate physical parts, and further dividing them off into different sexual personae, a man can enjoy sex with almost any woman, even if she is unattractive, hostile or indifferent. Under present conditions of child-rearing, she is the silent bearer of his ideology — Virgin, Mother, Wife.[46] And as the Object, the 'lack', the 'not-me', distanced and emptied, she becomes a gulf into which he pours his polarized fantasies of Whore and Madonna, Eve and Mary, Witch and Angel. In 'Siren Song' Atwood complains of the life of the woman who can please the man she wants only by accepting the split-off role of Siren:

> . . . Shall I tell you the secret
> and if I do, will you get me
> out of this bird suit?

> I don't enjoy it here
> squatting on this island
> looking picturesque and mythical . . .

Many men find it easy to blind themselves to women as real people, and readily see them as a commodity for using, selling, packaging, in sexual and commercial exchange.

Yet men may not be as 'naturally' promiscuous as the reputation they enjoy – and often cultivate. Innumerable true and steadfast men are there for the finding: the faithful Orpheus descends into Hades to try and win back Euridyce, Launcelot gives up a lifetime's honour and friendship for Guinevere, and even today, when interest in such matters is limited, Murdoch's Arrowby waits half a lifetime to be reunited with Hartley in *The Sea, the Sea*. In *Tropic of Cancer*, Henry Miller was amused to note the kind of crooked faithfulness he felt 'not to Germaine but to that bushy thing she carried between her legs. Whenever I looked at another woman I thought inadvertently of Germaine, of that flaming bush which she had left in my mind and which seemed imperishable.'[47]

The inclination of some women to see their bodies symbolically seems to be less often shared by the man, and those who take a sacramental view of sex – the body as outward and visible sign – will not be happy to pair for long with those who see it as a source of casual pleasure. Those who regard it as casual will despair of a partner who gives it a symbolic value – as Bellow's Herzog despairs of his Ramona: 'She wants me to believe the body is a spiritual fact, the instrument of the soul. Ramona is a dear woman, and very touching, but this theorising is a dangerous temptation. It can only lead to more high-minded mistakes.'[48]

The classic socio-biological view may partly account for society's greater tolerance of the male's sexual restlessness; the notorious double standard, by which it is thought natural to allow men a sexual freedom denied to women, is directly reflected in sexual vocabulary – a promiscuous man is 'a bit of a lad', a 'stud', whose pride is to 'score', while a similar woman is still, to some, 'meat', a 'slag', a 'cunt'. However, times are changing, and women's protest has become vociferous. Even in popular romance (the most conservative of literary forms) it is possible to read: ' "I expect the fidelity he expected of me," replied Flame tartly. "I don't accept double standards. Why should I?" '[49] The double standard is part of the tangle of power and *eros*, seen by Marxists and their successors as a patriarchal device for ensuring male freedom and the control of women, in order to sustain capitalist society. A man needs to be sure his offspring is his own, or the descent of property falls into chaos, so whatever a man may do, his wife must be faithful. The Marquis of Halifax, who in 1688 published his *Advice to a Daughter*, seems to have been a tender father, but he knew his priorities. In delicately referring to men's 'Frailties', he explains: 'The World in this is somewhat unequal, and our Sex seemeth to play the *Tyrant* in distinguishing *partially* for ourselves, by making that in the utmost degree *Criminal* in the *Woman*, which in a

Man passeth under a much *gentler Censure*.'[50] As an excuse for male promiscuity, the acceptance of the 'double standard' drives feminists to fury – but they have a reply in the argument that we ought to have superseded such primitive influences. The human cortex ensures that men have access to will-power, and to a sense of justice, so whatever their animal ancestry there is no just reason to allow promiscuity to them if it is not allowed equally to women.

In general agreement with previous work, Wellings's survey finds that over a lifetime men have more sexual partners than women, and over twenty per cent more men than women have more than ten partners. But the survey also points out that this difference may simply reflect society's tolerance of male sexual behaviour as compared with women's.[51] Added to this, it is very difficult to know how much these differences in sexual behaviour are innate, and how much conditioned by society. Contrary to common belief, there is no general homosexual appetite for a large number of partners; half of homosexual men, and two-thirds of women, have only one partner in a lifetime, but it is true that nearly four per cent of such men have over one hundred partners, which is a much higher number than for heterosexuals.[52]

Gender problems

Gender is all problems. Because of our acceptance of the ideology, traditional stereotypes still encourage man's domination over woman, and woman's contempt for herself, and until these iniquities are righted love will be beset by them. The assumption that the male is dominant and the woman subservient leads to a desperate misrecognition, by which the man knows he must *appear* strong and the woman must *assume* she is vulnerable.[53] Even in love certain men will feel it is their right to dominate and degrade, and women in love are notoriously compliant, especially if the relationship is threatened. In a desperate moment she later recognizes as madness, Jong's Isadora wants to run to Bennett and 'promise to serve him like a good slave in exchange for *any* bargain as long as it included security. I would become servile, cloying, saccharinely sweet: the whole package of lies that passes in the world as femininity.'[54] The potency of love distorts behaviour and, if they are not watched, stereotypical gender patterns can become even more exaggerated and destructive than in more normal times.

It is often believed that love interests women more than it interests men, that they place a greater value on romantic emotion and on the 'staging' of romance and ritual,[55] and certainly (although their interest seems to be decreasing) girls and women are far more devoted to popular romantic writing than are boys and men. Why? Is this innate? De Beauvoir argued that women's over-emphasis on these matters was caused not by any 'natural' disposition but by society's denial of her need to do and to dare; the lack of self-esteem derived from traditional nurturing leads her to look for her justification not in her own self but in love.[56] As long as women are brought up to exhibit the characteristics men are brought up to suppress, men will suppose that emotion and need and words and commitment are what women want, and therefore cannot be properly masculine.

Yet from the earliest written works we know, it is obvious that men have profound feelings of love, and have never had inhibitions about expressing them in writing. For over three thousand years, male poets and story-tellers and dramatists have described the loves of both women and men with dazzling, heart-breaking perception. It is only when men find themselves in intimate situations in real life that they often resort to their silent stereotype, and are happy to let language fail them; in an Old English poem, written down some time between the seventh and eleventh centuries, the melancholy 'Wanderer' muses:

> . . . I know it for a truth
> That in a man it is a noble virtue
> To hide his thoughts, lock up his private feelings,
> However he may feel.[57]

Even though a lack of verbal intimacy may arise from a fear of giving, and appearing weak, anyone deliberately withholding what is wanted by the other establishes a position of power, and male inarticulacy provides a method of asserting it.[58] Men's refusal or inability to express their feelings in spoken words is a frequent complaint of women, and often gives trouble between a couple in love. While men feel threatened by verbal intimacy, women feel comforted – as men feel *in*vaded, women feel *e*vaded.[59] New brain-imaging techniques reveal that women speaking make some use of the right side of their brains as well as the left, while men use only the left, and so it may be possible that the spoken word is indeed more difficult for men.[60] In *Women and Love*, Hite found that only 17 per cent of the 4,500 women in her sample felt that men were able to communicate their feelings, and 47 per cent believed the only way to have any real verbal contact was to quarrel.[61] Work, doing, things; these dispassionate activities form a large part of the stereotyped male world, yet women who find men refusing the intimacy of words feel rebuffed and lonely, and in retaliation may refuse to give proper importance to this male 'doing'.[62] Men's 'work' is often seen as an obstacle to the kind of committed relationship a woman wants, and she cannot understand that many men seem to define themselves through what they do, rather than what they think or speak.[63] Women are often thought to be in touch with their feelings, while men are split and closed off from theirs. In Nin's *The Four-Chambered Heart*, Djuna no doubt speaks for many women when she grieves over 'man's great need to build cities when it was so much harder to build relationships, his need to conquer countries when it was so much harder to conquer one heart . . . Man's need to invent, to circumnavigate space when it is so much harder to overcome space between human beings . . .'[64] Yet there is a great deal of evidence (to which I shall come) that men need warmth and intimacy as much as any woman, and that even if they appear cold they are often engaged in intense inner emotional work.[65]

But women should not be too complacent, for even in the sphere of love they have no right to present themselves as sole occupiers of the high moral ground. There is no overwhelming evidence that they are innately better at loving than men, and plenty of evidence of their dependency, treachery, cruelty, selfishness. Quite apart from their well-documented aggression against their lovers,[66] women are notoriously jealous, not only of men's infidelities, but of their work and outside interests. They are capable of imposing love like a suffocating tyranny, and of playing with men's affections like a cat with a mouse, sensing that in our present society their only brief power lies in their ability to arouse men in sex or love, and then to submit or withhold. They can be venomous as nettles to their own sex, and in the pursuit of love no quarter is given to rivals. They are full of wiles, not only sexual, and by all manner of devices, overt or covert, they find ways to get what they want from men, and from love. As Chaucer's Wife of Bath observed, women are thought to be excellent liars:

> For half so boldely kan ther no man
> Swere and lyen as a womman kan.[67]

Skilful flattery is another favoured device, shamelessly employed by Ibsen's Nora in *A Doll's House*, as she praises her husband's taste, his goodness, his cleverness – and thereby captivates and uses him. The artful use of tears is also notorious; tears, wrote Burton, 'they have at command: for they can so weep, that one would think their very hearts were dissolved within them . . . they wipe away their tears like sweat, weep with one eye, laugh with the other . . .'[68]

But do women have to be like this? Could such behaviour be a result of the dominance embedded in the traditional male stereotype, and the conditions of women's lives and upbringing? The imperatives of traditional masculinity are listed by Miles as, 'the fantasy of heroic endeavour, the competitive urge to dominate and excel . . . the need to blunt all tender feelings, the search for significance through the transcendence of fear and weakness, the centralizing of the penis and its demands . . .'[69] Faced with even the shadow of such a being, women are aware from childhood of the power employed against them, and if they want to be survivors they have to learn means of coping. Their tearful insecurities, wiles and strategies are the undignified devices of the weak, who long sometimes to be allowed to speak out, to be right, to have things their own way, and are compelled to find manipulative routes to a little personal autonomy. With the power of decision in their hands, many men find it delightful to be wheedled, but the woman doing the wheedling may wearily wish for less devious means. Eysenck finds the conflict between feelings and behaviour is far greater in women, implying a discord in self-image, for in order to please, and secure advantage, women behave in ways they themselves dislike about four times as often as men.[70] When Nora finally rebels, she says to her husband, 'I lived by performing tricks for you, Torvald.'[71]

In growing into women girls do not suffer the painful journey away from the mother and into another gender, but from very early on they suffer from dissimilarity with their fathers, and from a sense of being the inferior, subservient sex, as their mothers so often are. Given their chance in a less patriarchal structure of child rearing, girls could grow into, women able to see themselves as Subjects rather than Objects, and confident enough to reduce their dependence on whines, tears, strategies and jealousies.

Power and domination

Power may be a man's reward for dealing with both the problem of women and the demands of wordly success, yet it is an investment which does not always bring the expected reward, and it can be a heavy burden, achieved at the cost of expressive emotion. When Henchard casts off the world of women, in Hardy's *The Mayor of Caster-bridge*, he must live by the harsh male codes of power – through paternity, money, law – and when he fails to retrieve the love he has lost he is finally destroyed by them.[72] Split and closed, dominating, inarticulate, angry, this male ogre remains in essence the traditional model of the man, and something like him is still never far to seek.[73] But it is an arid, sterile model, and pushed to extremes, as Grass describes, it works fiercely against a loving heart:

> men for whom not possibly possible goals
> but the ultimate goal — a society free from care —
> has pitched its tent beyond mass graves;
> men who from the sum of dated defeat
> draw only one conclusion: smoke-veiled ultimate victory
> over radically scorched earth . . .[74]

Domination swells easily into aggression, and the alliance of male sex and aggression is as old as mythology. Zeus seizes his pleasure where he chooses, Pluto abducts Proserpine, the Sabine women are seized by the followers of Romulus. Some men are unable to see themselves as sexual beings unless they feel dominant, and when carried to extremes, rape is not always a sexual demand but a means of dominating and degrading the woman. As Angela Carter described it, 'Always the object of punishment, she has committed only one crime and that was an involuntary one; she was born a woman, and, for that, she is ceaselessly punished.'[75] Always we come back to the question, *why* do so many men, in love or out of it, feel compelled to maintain a punishing superiority and dominance over women?[76] Some propose (controversially) that this male need for rank and attainment and conquest is a by-product of testosterone, 'wired' into the neuro-endocrinology of the brain, and therefore 'natural' and justified.[77] Others emphasize the fact that men enjoy and want to sustain a patriarchal society, which depends

on the subordination of women in the social and family
structure, and on the inheritance of wealth down the
family line. Yet men's urgent need to dominate,
throughout the millennia, might point to sources deeper
in the psyche, into the various symptoms of the male
'wound'. Perhaps women are punished for the sexual
thraldom they impose on men, and because they are a
fearsome threat to proper masculinity. Fear breeds anger,
which may all too easily lead (as King Lear revealed) to
a disgusted terror of women; the womb is a deep, dark
hole and the dread of re-engulfment is the stuff of
nightmare:

> Down from the waist they are Centaurs,
> Though women all above:
> But to the girdle do the gods inherit,
> Beneath is all the fiends':
> There's hell, there's darkness, there's the sulphurous pit,
> Burning, scalding, stench, consumption.[78]

It is no secret that boys do not always succeed in
disentangling themselves from their mothers. Oedipus
did not complete it, nor did Hamlet. There is a plethora
of literary problems between sons and mothers: 'Edward',
a medieval ballad of anguished hate, ends in Edward
crying, 'The curse of hell frae me sall ye beare, / Mither,
mither . . .'; in Goethe's *Faust*, the hero's path to adult
love with Helen can be achieved only by passing through
and beyond the threatening 'Mothers'.[79] Sometimes it is
the man who cannot make the break, sometimes it is the

mother who will not let go: ' "Her *lover* she calls me . . .!" ' cries the young Portnoy, despairing of the suffocating parent who has emotionally seduced him.[80] The 'wound' such a boy suffers in leaving his mother will not heal over, and although he is longing to escape, and become a full, autonomous man, he cannot do so. No doubt Hite's interviewee spoke for many when she complained that men seem afraid to fall in love.[81] (It is not only sons who have trouble with their mothers; in works such as Greer's *Daddy, I Hardly Knew You* daughters are revealing painful, lifelong entanglements with their fathers, which are no doubt just as blighting to their adult loves.)[82]

There is probably no more chilling example of men's angry fear of women than the hunting of witches. While the Virgin slowly emerged, through the first millennium AD, as a figure of female perfection – lovely, gentle, sexless – her split-off shadow represented women as the evil daughters of Eve. For two terrible centuries the male's wandering guilts and fears and furies coalesced on the so-called witch. Persecutions for witchcraft are known in Europe from the seventh to the nineteenth centuries, but the most violent eruptions were from about 1560 to 1760, during which time between seventy-four and one hundred thousand souls were tortured, burned, hung, and drowned, about eighty-five per cent of them women.[83] Once again, as in the Middle East in the fourth century, women were singled out as the source of sin, the instigators of man's Fall. Innumerable reasons have been advanced to explain this horrible episode, but only an explanation which points to the repressed power of the unconscious could account for something so baleful and omnipotent. Whatever the overt cause, the tap-root grew from guilt and fear – sexual guilt provoked by religious and social repression, and fear of the latent power of women, of the threat to rational male rule and to male potency.[84] It seems, in the end, to have been a sterile outflow of energy, for women did not depart, sex did not depart, nothing was solved, and Western society was left with an even greater burden of sexual guilt. And above it all floated that counter-image, the serenely lovely (and sexless) Virgin.

Together with his fear of woman, the man has a grim humiliation to contend with in the woman's ability to conceive, bear and nurture babies. Even when, millennia ago, men had discovered their part in procreation, and considered themselves the chief begetters, certain fathers must have felt the humiliation of not carrying the baby, not giving birth to the baby, not suckling the baby; among her male patients, in the first half of this century, Karen Horney found this envy still intense.[85] Such humiliation translates directly into the kind of rage felt by Birkin, in *Women in Love*: 'It filled him with almost insane fury, this calm assumption of the Magna Mater, that all was hers, because she had borne it. Man was hers because she had borne him.'[86] It was surely such envy that incited the male creation myths of the Greek Zeus, the Slav Svarog, the Teuton Amir and all other male world-makers.[87] To these we could add the case of Eve who was (as it were) born of Adam, having been fashioned from his rib. To turn the male into the sole creator is a bizarre inversion of the obvious biological facts, and must have its reasons.

Torn from womb and breast, threatened by re-engulfment, tormented by sex, unable to conceive or give birth, man rages until someone pays. This is no modern, post-Freudian perception. In 1696, Mary Astell wrote, ' . . . Men being sensible as well of the Abilities of Mind in our Sex, as of the strength of Body in their own, began to grow Jealous . . . therefore began in good time to make use of Force (the Origine of Power) to compel us to a Subjection, Nature never meant . . .'[88] The lurid evidence of misogyny is gruesomely documented throughout history and literature, and is too commonplace to dwell on. Myth is not short of tales of matricide by men, while patricide by women is very rare: Marduk cut up his mother Tiamet to form the universe; Horus decapitated his mother, Isis; Orestes slew Clytemnestra. The savagery of Bluebeard is endlessly paralleled in real life by such figures as Jack the Ripper, the Yorkshire Ripper, Frederick West, and constantly represented in violent pornography, and in the words men use of women – bitch, slag, cunt, scrubber, meat, slit. In a story by Martin Amis, Vernon deliberately ejaculates all over his loved wife's face, yet 'It distressed him greatly to reflect that his rare acts of abandonment should expose a desire to humble and degrade the loved one. And she was the loved one.'[89]

As a protection against fear and anger and humiliation, 'Men must speak to one another.' Male bonding was a passionate interest of D. H. Lawrence, and at the end of *Women in Love* Birkin declares that male friendship is as vital as the love of women.[90] The tribal male brotherhood of the street gang, with its rituals of dress, behaviour, language, is not such a far cry from the exclusive brotherhood of Freemasonry or gentlemen's clubs.

New Men

Not all men are happy with the stereotype delivered to them. Although the male role is highly privileged in various ways, many men find it hard to inhabit;[91] their lives seem to them alienated, riven with role-conflict, and many are finding it no easier than women to devise a new mode for living.[92] Masculinity is, in fact, fragile stuff, and the male psyche cannot always cope with the dominating image demanded of it. After the stately curate of Haworth, Mr Nichols, had proposed to Charlotte Brontë, she wrote to a friend, 'Shaking from head to foot, looking deadly pale, speaking low, vehemently yet with difficulty – he made me for the first time feel what it costs a man to declare affection where he doubts response. The spectacle of one so ordinarily statue-like, thus trembling, stirred and overcome, gave me a kind of strange shock.'[93]

Many men of a gentle nature cannot bring themselves to assert authority, and prefer an unconventional subservience; Macbeth is clearly dominated by his wife, yet theirs is one of the few obviously close marriages in Shakespeare. Pride, and the possibility of ridicule, stop many men from asking for help when they need it, yet their state of trauma may be no less than a woman's; while women tend to consult and warn before killing themselves, men often do not, for the fear of exposing weakness and pain is even more terrible than the fear of death.[94] They are more often ill than women, more vulnerable to certain stress-related diseases; eating disorders recently doubled, anxiety is high, suicide is increasing, sperm counts diminishing.[95] With the disintegration of their familiar stereotype, they begin to feel threatened, marginalized, with their importance as wage earners in decline, the status of 'head of household' gone – and they do not even have to be personally present for the conception of their children.[96] Menaced by the demands of feminism, diminished by mothers and lovers and wives, suffering from absent or dominant fathers, troubled by indefinable griefs, men are facing their own revolution, and they will need to come to terms with their 'new' selves, and with 'new' women too.[97] In *Fire in the Belly* Sam Keen acknowledges the historical humiliation of women, but makes plain that men's suffering is also a fact, and no reasonable woman could disagree with him. Although men have had the best of the world so far, there is no doubt that their road through it is also a troubled one. Gently Amis touches the sore: 'Cities at night, I feel, contain men who cry in their sleep and then say Nothing. It's nothing. Just sad dreams.'[98] If it were possible for men to recognize their hidden disquiets they might be able to free themselves of their anger, of their drive to dominance, of their swaggering fragility.

Some men are trying to find a proper pride without resorting to the old stereotype. In the face of much derision, trailing unwanted 'Wild Men' and various lunatic followers, Robert Bly and his New Male Consciousness Movement, the Wild Dance workshops and various other Men's Movements are struggling towards a new pattern for a new man – a man who, even in love, does not need to dominate or to deny words and feelings. Masculinity, they argue, does not have to be equated with patriarchy, but neither does the New Man have to be softly passive, eviscerated of his maleness;[99] there must be something between the stereotyped patriarch and the hen-pecked emotional cripple.[100]

How are men to reject their destructive traditional stereotype, to learn to see women as Subjects rather than Objects – and at the same time retain their spirit and virility? Not all women like the idea of the New Man (just as many men detest the New Woman) and, for those who see our best hope in him, his coming may still be far away.[101] And how are women to change, to claim their rights as Subject, and escape from all the demeaning wiles and deceptions and strategies of their subordinate stereotype? There is still a huge majority of both women and men who, for psychological or social or political reasons, resolutely maintain that men are men and women are women. Yet millennia of this polarizing gender, which denies so much of our common humanity, has not done much for our wavering human happiness. It seems that women may be more willing to help heal the divisions, for many would like their voice to be shared with the world of men; the failure of so many women's separatist ventures – *The Women's Review, Spare Rib*, Radio Viva! – suggests that women want a way to join rather than a separate camp. The enormous overlap of their nature and experience should enable women and men to exist as true equals, in love as in all else – but it can happen only when both become Subject and neither is cast as the alien Object. There is no simple answer; while some, such as Giddens, see a way in the 'democritization' of intimate personal relations, and a conscious emancipation from traditional gender, others regard this as a destructive and unattainable goal.[102] Nothing here is easy, yet it is just possible that with greater understanding more and more women might be able to raise their confidence and self-esteem, and more and more men might feel able to loosen their desperate grasp on authority. In the last chapter I will turn to our best hopes of reaching this happy state.

Sex and gender and love are troublesome matters, and not everyone rejoices in them. Sometimes, as for Forster's Mrs Moore, the whole commotion becomes utterly wearisome; in *A Passage to India*, the unsolved crisis in the Marabar caves 'presented itself to her as love: in a cave, in a church – Boum, it amounts to the same'. People are important, she feels, but their relations in love are not: '. . . centuries of carnal embracement, yet man is no nearer to understanding man.'[103]

CHAPTER NINE

Agonies

V ERY FEW griefs match the raking grief of love gone awry. As Sarah reads through Stephen's diary, in Lessing's *Love Again*, 'The cries from the country of grief are impersonal. I am lonely. I am unhappy. I love you. I want you. I am sick with love. I am dying of a broken heart. *I can't endure this non-life. I can't endure this desert.*'[1] As often as not, love drags pain in its wake, and its miseries are as tormenting as its happiness is ecstatic. Agony instead of rapture, rejection instead of welcome, degradation instead of salvation. As I have described, there are those who argue that what we call 'love' does not exist, and 'love' is no more than a linguistic construct, which for millennia has provided an excuse for a stream of social, literary and political con tricks. Or 'love' is only a state of physical and psychological arousal on which we confer the resounding name of *Eros*, deluding ourselves with illusory grandeurs. But in this chapter I shall not concern myself with what may or may not be illusory, but with those lovers to whom love feels as real as rock.

Many writers have insisted that suffering is endemic to

love, that love cannot be love without it – and for love's highest romantic apotheosis this is probably true.[2] For every love-story which ends in joy (Penelope and Odysseus, Beatrice and Benedick, Fiorentino and Fermina)[3] there are two shaken with pain and ending in despair (Tristram and Iseult, Antony and Cleopatra, Karenina and Vronsky, Gerald and Gudrun.)[4] Although suffering is not *necessary* to love, it adds a poignant grandeur, and if their love survives the lovers will grow in depth and range, and their agonies will intensify the force of their feelings.

Transience

The time of wine and roses is not long. As everyone has always known – but hoped in their case would be different – love in its first enchantment will never last till the rocks melt i' the sun. It is true it can be prolonged by obstacles, and by a deliberate effort to keep it romantic, but the relevant neurones in the brain are affected by 'satiation', an inability to respond indefinitely to the same stimuli, and as the stimulus fades the past parental incest taboos may begin to emerge, forbidding the woman's love of the (replacement) father, and the man's of his (replacement) mother;[5] added to which, the two-to-three-year duration of intense infant attachment to the mother, which prefigures the intense first period of adult love, is not programmed to endure, and as the bond between the lovers is now forged their hectic relationship can now calm down, with benefit to the rearing of their child.[6] The buried parts of the psyche are always on the move, shifting, transforming and leaving little at rest.

During the time of being 'in love', the lover's vision of the beloved will seem unshakeably authentic, for the messages of Eros come like those of a god, with the apparent authority of the eternal world.[7] But to a greater or lesser degree projection will cloak reality, leading the lover to pursue an idealized image rather than a flesh-and-blood human being. During this time, and some-times beyond, the beloved is an actor in the internal drama of the lover: 'I thought I loved her for her sake,' says Nora of Robin in *Nightwood*, 'and I found it was for my own.'[8]

When the projection fades and is withdrawn, the lovers' egos are no longer disrupted by loaning themselves out, and the couple at last begin to look real to each other.[9] The dispersing of these veils can be acutely disil-lusioning, and life and literature abound with tragedies of lovers who (as in Shakespeare's sonnet), 'had thought thee bright / Who art as black as hell, as dark as night'.[10] If lovers find they can make nothing of each other, some must watch a vacant heart fill with frost, or with the bitter remorse endured by Helen of Troy, who cries out to Paris's father, Priam, 'Oh if only vile death had been my choice when I came here with your son, leaving behind the house of my marriage, and my family and my darling child and the sweet company of friends!'[11] For others more fortunate, love may slip off quietly, as

Barthes described, 'into another world like a ship into space, lights no longer winking...'[12] For the time being, the disenchanted lover will find no comfort in the fact that love can be exactly the same another time round, or even again and again. When, in Forster's *Maurice*, Durham loves for the second time, 'Besotted with love, he gave her his body and soul, he poured out at her feet all that an earlier passion had taught him, and could only remember with an effort when that passion had been.'[13]

Loss

When love is still new, the loss of the beloved by death can be so terrible the human frame can hardly bear it. A large part of the lover's psyche is still invested in the lost love, and the greater the transference of ego the greater the anguish and mourning; little seems left but a searing wound. And, as the Greek hero Achilles discovered, after the death of his beloved friend, Patroklos, even at a maturer stage of loving the pain can still be almost insupportable; he 'took up the sooty dust in both his hands and poured it over his head, soiling his handsome face: and the black ashes settled all over his sweet-smelling tunic. And he lay there with his whole body sprawling in the dust, huge and fallen, tearing at his hair and defiling it with his own hands.'[14] Some three millennia later, after Cathy's death in *Wuthering Heights*, Heathcliff howls, ' . . . *do* not leave me in this abyss, where I cannot find you! Oh, god, it is unutterable! I *cannot* live without my life! I *cannot* live without my soul!'[15]

Death is not the only ending. As Ariadne watches Theseus restlessly turning away in Graves's 'Theseus and Ariadne', 'Dread of his hate was thunder in the air . . .' Dread of an unwanted ending reanimates in the lover all the infant's terror of separation and abandonment, and may corrode a relationship to the point where loss becomes ever more likely. Love that has been first enjoyed, and then rejected, creates pain less final than death, but often just as cruel, sometimes leaving as a residue the brilliant nightmare defined by Graves in 'Lost Love': 'His eyes are quickened so with grief / He can watch a grass or leaf / Every instant grow . . .' Or, as Emily Dickinson described, rejection may create a wholly opposite pain which deadens a once warm and open heart:

> There is a pain – so utter –
> It swallows substance up –
> Then covers the Abyss with Trauma –
> So Memory can step
> Around – across – upon it –
> As one within a Swoon –
> Goes safely – where an open eye –
> Would drop him – Bone by Bone.

The lover who is rejected after enjoying a time of love has known what mutual love is like, but the unrequited lover has had no taste of it at all. There is probably little difference in the suffering each experiences; those eventually rejected know the misery of the child expelled from paradise, the unrequited know the desolation of the child not allowed into it. The need for returned love is so urgent the lover often finds it impossible to believe that love does not automatically evoke love, as Murdoch's Martin describes in *A Severed Head*: 'I was perhaps moreover a little the dupe of that illusion of lovers that the beloved object must, somehow, respond, that an extremity of love not only merits but compels some return.'[16] Unrequited love is a poor maladaptive failure of nature, an eruption of suffering leading to no increase of the gene pool and (except in exceptional characters) to nothing but wilderness and waste. If there is evolutionary advantage in the feelings and behaviours we call love, it should surely have evolved as a dual relationship, or not at all. Just as mothers and their babies flourish in each other's light, so (one would have hoped) lovers should mutually flourish in love. The reason that they do not must stem, throughout the aeons, from our ever-increasing psychological and social complexity, which has defeated any simple system of mutual attraction.

Grieving has an approximate sequence, whatever the loss. First the bereft person will not believe or accept; then comes anger, then overwhelming tears, depression and despair; then usually some manner of recovery. But when the sequence does not follow through to recovery, disaster may follow. Rosalind, in *As You Like It*, briskly pronounces that, 'Men have died from time to time, and worms have eaten them, but not for love.'[17] She was wrong. As many rejected lovers know, rejection can provoke utter despair, hate, rage and terrible vengeance; as Euripides related in his play, the abandoned Medea killed Jason's new love, Glauce, and slew the two children she and Jason had had together; in the ballad of 'Barbara Allen', the rejected Jemmy Grove turns his face to the wall and dies; Ophelia, the once-beloved of Hamlet, loses her mind and drowns herself, Goethe's Werther shoots himself, Lawrence's Gerald walks out into the snow to die.[18] As when Anna Karenina throws herself under a train, her suicide, like many, is as much for revenge as because of pain: 'I will punish him and be freed from it all and from myself.'[19]

To be forced to become one person again, after an intense experience of being two, is among the bleakest tasks of life, and sometimes it cannot be completed. When any of our attachments are threatened we feel emotional turmoil, and when love is lost this turmoil can become deeply disrupting. Any of love's endings can be a potent provoker of acute depression, which is one of the mind's mechanisms for blanking out pain, and seems to the sufferer less terrible than the suffering it replaces.[20] Or the overwhelming feelings of despair may be converted into physical symptoms, proliferating in headaches, ulcers, fatigue and all manner of debilitating general ailments. Those who feel guilt in withdrawing their love may also suffer, for guilt can be haunting, and the guilty often feel a strong need to preserve it as self-punishment;[21] in a twelfth-century *lay* by Marie de France, the knight Eliduc falls in love, but 'He had neither peace nor delight, for he could not get her from his mind. He reproached himself bitterly. He called to remembrance the covenant he made with his wife . . . But his heart was captive now, in a very strong prison.' (But not all lovers feel guilt, for love is an unscrupulous solvent of conscience, and while it holds sway the normal kindnesses of social behaviour can be under direst threat. Lovers will invent all manner of excuses why they should let down those who trust them, and easily persuade themselves that those whose trust they betray will soon recover and not mind too much.)

Jealousy

> Love like heat and cold
> Pierces and then is gone;
> Jealousy when it strikes
> Sticks in the marrowbone.[22]

As this medieval Irish poet knew, jealousy is one of the most obsessive, most degrading and most persistent agonies of love. The destruction of Shakespeare's noble, adoring Othello is brought about by jealousy fuelled by the flimsiest evidence, and his journey through love, hate and back to remorseful love again reveals the closeness of love and hate. All jealous love is partly sexual, creating tormenting fantasies of the beloved in the arms of another, but its tentacles spread further, embracing humiliation and bitterness, rage with the thieving interloper, anguish at the loss of centrality in the beloved's heart. And, again, the old terror of loss and abandonment. As Sappho sat at a banquet on Lesbos, watching her love courted by a handsome man in the sixth century BC:

> . . . My tongue is shivered and at once
> Soft flame infiltrates my skin
> In my eyes no sight remains
> And roaring fills my ears.
>
> Sweat cascades off me and
> Tremor completely savages me
> I am paler than dry grass
> And in my craziness I seem
> To have reached the threshold of death . . .[23]

The most devouring jealousy is born from insecurity and low self-esteem, and a lover who feels guilty or worthless will all too easily become caught in its coils, as Anna Karenina found when she was losing Vronsky: 'As she had no subject for her jealousy, she tried to find one, and at the smallest provocation transferred her jealousy from one subject to another.'[24] If jealousy cannot be brought to an end, it will gnaw at a relationship that once seemed blooming, and eventually destroy it. Studies have shown that neither sex is more susceptible to jealousy than the other, but women are more often prepared to heal the rift, while men are more likely to feel themselves demeaned, and abandon the relationship; but sometimes jealousy provokes murder, and it is a leading cause of murder in the United States today.[25] To the revenger, revenge seems to help in restoring order and justice, and in reducing intolerable humiliation.[26]

Only socio-biologists have anything good to say of jealousy. Because jealous males will guard their partners possessively, in order that they may father more offspring and pass on their own genes, jealousy (it is argued) has been selected as a life-enhancing strategy, good for the species.[27] But however that may be for birds or monkeys, for humanity the cost is dire.

Raging love

Love has always been seen as akin to madness, and its intensity can drive a lover clinically mad. Plato described it as a frenzy, in which reason is overthrown;[28] nearly two thousand years later Malory's Lancelot leaped from Queen Guinevere's window and 'ranne furth he knew nat whothir, and was as wylde [mad] as ever was man. And so he ran two yere . . .'[29] In her work on love in the Middle Ages, Wack has shown how medieval doctors regarded 'lovesickness' with great gravity, knowing that it could result in madness and death.[30] The lunacy of some lovers can be likened to the manic phase of manic-depressive illness, when creativity, speed of thought, scintillating perceptions and linkages combine to make anything seem possible. A magnificent euphoria, but a desperate distortion of reality.

Addiction is another problem of excess, and love can

so beset a lover that the whole being is enslaved in idolatry. Many people dream of just such a great consuming passion, but although it can make an enthralling story it is not a healthy episode for the psyche. Obsessive attachment is a negative experience, for too much of the lover's ego is handed over, and too great a dependency creates too great an instability. In its full-blown extravagance, the condition is recognized as a psychotic disorder, known as Clerambault's syndrome, and recovery can be long and painful, if it occurs at all.

In the grip of such an addiction the lover seems to be experiencing a primitive imprinting, and like an infant bird or mammal, however ignored, however attacked, however humiliated, is unable to give up and go:

> . . . Over my left eyebrow is a greenish bruise.
> There is you and there is me. I cannot choose
> But love you, though you wrong me,
> And make angry love to me, a smack
> Like a caress, a careless move, and a crack
> Appears in your loving, widening, widening . . .[31]

For the woman in Bartlett's poem, escape is not even desired.[32] Such a compulsive dependence seems to occur more often with women, and again it happens to women with a low sense of worth, who grew up expecting rebuff yet desperately needing approval, and became the kind of adults who feel confident only when they are nurturing or redeeming.[33] Women who grow up with this corrosive self-doubt are secretly convinced that any close relation with an adult lover is certain to fail, and in order to avoid the pain of rejection they will sustain any abuse, or make the relation fail by doing the rejecting first. Others (either women or men), who have never been able to resolve their relations with their mothers, may find themselves caught up in a doomed attempt to mend the past, and choose lovers who will abandon them exactly (as it seems) as their mothers did.[34] This is the 'repetition compulsion', the treacherous 'flight forward' from reality to the apparent safety of a situation which may be hideous but at least feels familiar.[35]

In extreme cases this sense of worthlessness compels the would-be lover to seek out the direst possible humiliation, creating a kind of contract between the participators to become 'things', in order to be free of pain.[36] Such a woman (for it is usually a woman) will choose an autonomous, cold and controlling man, as in Selby's *Last Exit to Brooklyn*, in which Tr-la-la offers herself eagerly to contemptuous male brutality; likewise in Reage's *Story of 'O'*, 'O' withstands her terror of dissolution only by becoming the eager object of savage sexual attention. Linked in this way with the supremacy of their oppressors, such women find a vicarious power which compensates for their inadequacy, and gives them some sense of value in being sexually wanted and used. Such desperate women have often endured family trauma in childhood, such as sexual abuse, beatings, or alcoholism, whose terrible legacy is an adult addiction to 'love'.[37] And they may also suffer from a malfunction of brain chemistry, requiring constant new charges of calming endorphins to make life feel secure and endurable.[38]

Another kind of addictive love is expressed in a compelling impulse to burn up one love then hurl off to another, and another, pursing endless love affairs; although the addicts may also be women, the problem is usually epitomized in the legends of Casanova and Don Juan. Such addictive pursuers barely qualify as lovers, for their lives are usually dominated by loveless sexual pursuit, yet they sometimes experience brief bursts of personal affection. Part of their problem may be an addiction to the euphoria induced by the amphetamine PEA, which, when it wears off, leaves a depression that can only be lifted by seeking out yet more 'love', and so sexual relief from stress becomes more and more compulsive, and the problem grows in stages until it can barely be handled.[39] Like the women who need to humiliate themselves, such sexual addicts are often looking not only for sex but for total control, in an attempt to deaden the pain of childhood trauma, and its legacy of self-contempt.[40] Sex (disguised as 'love') becomes a drug, a defence against anger and, in men, against the feared power of woman; perhaps also a hopeless quest for the perfect lost love of infancy, and at the same time a revenge for the mother's abandonment.[41] For other addicts, their malady leaves them devoted to love yet quite unable to commit themselves. Having striven feverishly to achieve the beloved, the successful lover promptly loses all interest, as happened to Proust's narrator when after his long pursuit of Albertine he realizes that, 'My brain assessed this pleasure at a very low value now that it was assured me . . . My nerves and brain then started a discussion as to the real value of the pleasure that there would be in knowing Albertine.'[42]

As I have said before, secure feelings of self-worth are vital for happy relations in love. And self-esteem is made in infancy, when confident assumptions about the safety and pleasure of love become embedded. Matters which have gone wrong can be positively remedied, in childhood or in adult life, but for children who have thought themselves unloved, and grown to adulthood without help, happy love will be outside, in a foreign land.

No one should belittle the agony love can thrust on lovers. Its ferocity provides a justified cause of anger in those who wish to be rid of love and all its works, for no one but a sadist would want to inflict such pain on any human being. But there it is. Love will not go away for the asking, and our best hope is to understand something of what it is doing to us, and why.

CHAPTER TEN

Love Tomorrow

EVEN THOSE who believe romantic love is worthless will sometimes admit that it seems indestructible, shows no signs of departure, and remains the hope and expectation of almost everyone. Falling in love is still the grand and memorable story, thriving on elevated fantasy, mystery, sex, agony, adoration and joy, as it always did. In life, in story, in popular music, in advertising, love is still a king, and even our twentieth-century cynicism has done little to dethrone it. Second only to our preoccupation with sex, the ancient emotions of love still drive couples through all obstacles to a romantic dream in each other's arms.

How love should be

Many writers reflecting on love concentrate on the maturer stage which emerges (if all goes well) after the tumult of 'falling in love' has subsided. But the early hectic state is not contemptible. When still 'in love' lovers are, to each other, and often to others, more

unselfish, more considerate, more benevolent, more spir-
ited, more confident than they will ever be again. Sex
will be blissfully integrated into their lives, and they will
exchange the 'gift-love', which is not a traded commodity
but a free donation outreaching the selfish 'I'.[1] Happiness
is good for us. Nor are lovers in this early stage always
totally out of control: while the violent projection of the
self may blind each to the character of the other, it need
not blind the wish for equilibrium in Lawrence's 'free
proud singleness',[2] or for the equality-in-difference by
which each recognizes the other as Subject. Ideally, they
will be capable of the 'co-feeling' which shares in mutuality without domination, for they will understand the
difference between submission as an unhealthy response
to power, and the self-surrender which comes willingly
from within.[3] And they will know that neither must be
the justification for the other's existence: 'People don't
complete us,' broods Jong's Isadora. 'We complete ourselves. If we haven't the power to complete ourselves, the
search for love becomes a search for self-annihilation.'[4]
Lovers will happily appreciate Laurie Lee's conviction
that love should be an act 'of passionate patience, flexible,
cunning, constant; proof against roasting and freezing,
drought and flood . . .'[5]

From Aristotle onwards, no one has ever had anything
but good to say about friendship.[6] Its qualities of affection, trust, support, generosity are praised beyond
measure, sometimes beyond family, and often to the detri-
ment of love. Some believe that these qualities of
friendship can also be those of romantic love, but others

insist that this is impossible, arguing that romance and friendship are contradictory and that the egotistic drama of love is deflated by the calmer realities of friendship.[7] It is true that affectionate friendship is nearer the condition of mature love than of love's first eruption, yet the borderlands between new and maturer loves are not rigid, and it should be possible to create, with conscious awareness, a distillation of both states. This is exactly what Shakespeare gives us in Beatrice and Benedick, for when love erupts for them we can have no doubt they are 'in love', yet we also know they are friends of long standing, matched in background and character and exuberance and sparring wit. (However critically incorrect, we cannot help having high hopes for them.)

In advocating a new 'true' love, sexual but not monogamous, Tweedie argues that it can emerge, not from hectic emotions, projections and idealizations, but from 'a rational apprehension of another being and a logical assessment of his or her particular needs, virtues and failings, in the light of reality'.[8] This is a description of affectionate sexual friendship, the *amitié amoreuse*, and it is true that a relationship coolly and rationally taken on, clean of emotional turbulence, might seem a wholesome alternative to the commotion of love. Perhaps it need not even be sexual, but more like the 'passionate friendship' explored by White's Edward, in *The Beautiful Room is Empty*, in which 'Maria recognized the ways in which I feared sexual intimacy and firmly ended that possibility between us. But she didn't cut the thread of courtship, of gallantry, even of romance that lent vitality to our love. We coined the notion of "passionate friendship" and we suspected that ours would last a lifetime.'[9] This sexless relation cannot precisely be defined as being 'in love', yet it seems there may be a shift by women today into exactly this kind of celibate intimacy, in which all the problems of genital sex are laid aside as inessential to affection and love.[10] But we have no word for this kind of chaste commitment – even 'friend' is now suspect.

Some have argued that our inclination to love should not be concentrated on one beloved only, but that love's benevolence could be spread among many, when (as Bacon believed) it 'maketh men become humane and charitable'.[11] His belief is forcefully echoed by various modern writers, who argue that it is possible to diffuse sexual excitement and joy over the spectrum of our lives, instead of confining it in one narrow, difficult experience.[12] Certainly we can try – yet love, as we know it, will not easily accept diffusion by reason; it is forever lurking round corners and, unless it is dodged resolutely and soon, it may explode ferociously, disrupting the most confident and affectionate partnership.

The attack on love

' "In love!" – said the corporal – "your honour was very well the day before yesterday . . . !" '[13] Trim's cry to Sterne's afflicted Uncle Toby is not unique. Those innumerable writers and institutions that have had no high opinion of love include many of Plato's debaters in the *Symposium* and *Phaedrus*; the Church, which has never found it possible to bless love out of wedlock, and not always in it; and countless writers who have felt, with Burton, that 'for the most part love is a plague, a torture, a hell, a bitter sweet passion . . .'[14] Certain twentieth-century feminists have fiercely dissected what they see as the illusory and degrading aspects of love; in Greer's words, 'Love, love, love – all the wretched cant of it, masking egotism, lust, masochism, fantasy under a mythology of sentimental postures, a welter of self-induced miseries and joys, blinding and masking the essential personalities . . .'[15]

For millennia the West has been living out its masculine aspects at the expense of the feminine, and traditional love, under the sway of the dominant man, no longer suits women who wish to feel free, and who will no longer accept a conventional subservient relationship. Radical feminists go further, arguing that real love between men and women is impossible in a patriarchal society, for as long as the phallus is allowed to be the great signifier of power and difference only the male will have access to freedom. Women may rage at men, but men's contempt for women also grinds on: for more than half a page in *Jake's Thing*, Amis's Jake indicts the faults of women, their concern with surfaces, their way of getting everything wrong, their air of injury, their assumption of rectitude, their directionless discussion, their appropriation of the major share of feeling.[16]

In spite of love's public glamour, Pietropinto's research sample revealed that a quarter of those questioned felt that although love was good they could very well live a full life without it,[17] and Lawrence Stone is only one of many men who despair of the romantic love complex – 'the notion that there is only one person in the world with whom one can unite at all levels; the personality of that person is so idealized that the normal faults and follies of human nature disappear from view; love is often like a thunderbolt and strikes at first sight; love is the most important thing in the world, to which all other considerations, particularly material ones, should be sacrificed; and lastly, the giving of full rein to personal emotions is admirable . . .'[18]

Psychological attacks include the argument that love is in essence egotistical, based on our own projections, our own expectations, our private fantasies. It is, in fact, love not of another person but of ourselves. Falling in love is, therefore, and should remain, a path to our own inner world, and it should not attempt to encompass a new outside relationship. Furthermore, romantic love has become disastrously confused with our worship of the divine, by trying to appropriate what we have lost of numinous myth and dream.[19] Other enemies of love object that it is no more than a hypocritical dressing-up of sex. In *Othello*, Iago tells the lovelorn Rodrigo that love is 'merely a lust of the blood and a permission of the will'[20] and nearly four centuries later Henry Miller, in his 'Tropic' books, spits venom on 'this love-crap'.[21]

As I have described, love has constantly been attacked as no better than a kind of madness. In *As You Like It* (that awesome debate on love) Rosalind declares love to be 'merely a madness'; Freud saw it as the pattern of the psychoses, and in Murdoch's *The Black Prince* Bradley muses: 'Is it not insane to concentrate one's attention exclusively on one person, to drain the rest of the world of meaning, to have no thoughts, no feelings, no being except in relation to the beloved?'[22] When the usual connections with the everyday world are severed, love may develop into severe psychosis, possibly ending in death. Its euphoria is magnificently airborne but, as Bellow's Uncle Ben discovers, 'I am a phoenix who runs after arsonists.'[23] Auden's Prospero was glad to be done with it, and –

> . . . very glad I shall never
> Be twenty and have to go through that business again,
> The hours of fuss and fury, the conceit, the expense.[24]

Is love changing?

Some say it is in crisis, undergoing violent change and fractured as never before. Sex has become the locus of serious trouble, for the relentless sexualization of society, embracing sex as pornography, sex as obsession, sex as a commodity, sex as a driving force of commerce, undermines the values of love, and withers its growth.[25] Further, the traditional single 'narrative' of love is now disrupted by new attitudes to gender, race, class, sexual-orientation, reproduction, and by a new distrust of traditional expectations. In a story by Self, the girl broods on her predicament at the end of a relationship: 'Perhaps all this awful mismatching, this emotional grating, these Mexican stand-offs of trust and commitment, were something in the air. It wasn't down to individuals: me and him, Grace and John, those two over there . . . It was a contagion that was getting to all of us; a germ of insecurity that had lodged in all our breasts and was now fissioning frantically, creating a domino effect as relationship after relationship collapsed in a rubble of mistrust and acrimony.'[26]

More hopefully, the Poststructural dissolving of gender boundaries, and the determination of many women (and some men) to rethink gender relations, will re-create our attitudes to romantic love, both homo- and heterosexual. Giddens is certain that we are experiencing a radical transformation of intimacy, shifting away from romantic love, into a 'confluent' experience in which the lovers are equal and free, in a 'pure relationship', of autonomy, respect, trust, within which sex is contingent and pleasurable, stripped of the complexities of marriage, reproduction and 'one-love-for ever'. Yet he admits that it is not easy to reorder the emotions of love[27] – and others think it is impossible, for our hidden psychodynamics will not be tamely suppressed.

As I have emphasized, the complex of emotions which are the heart of love do not alter, but our attitudes to them shift profoundly, and just such a radical change is now stirring in women's new perception of their needs, in their search for autonomy in the intimacy of love, in a new balancing and fluidity of gender. But, although we have explored and emphasized gender more than any period before us, gender equality is not our own twentieth-century invention: two millennia ago, the Roman Ovid described the relations of Baucis and Philemon, in which,

> Command was none, where equal love was paid,
> Or rather both commanded, both obeyed.[28]

If there are to be new women, so there must be new men. There have always been men willing to admit the age-old injustice of gender relations, and now there are increasing numbers who believe they might themselves enjoy some freedom from their old stereotype, and who are trying (in the face of much mockery) to remodel it, to admit into daylight the feminine aspect of their beings, while still retaining their maleness.[29] There are now fresh sparks of interest in the old Goddess, not as a Mother-in-the-sky but as a representation of the suppressed feminine aspects of the psyche. In Greek myth the goddess Gaia emerged from Chaos as the first progenitor, and for the Hebrews the first creator was the androgynous Elohim, with lesser goddesses around her.[30] Unlike later Judaism or Islam, Christianity accepted the intrusion of a minor goddess, in the form of the Blessed Virgin, who has provided boundless comfort, but in pointing to a subservient, sexless and maternal role she has been of little use in helping women to shape their lives. For at least three millennia the balance has been tipped in favour of the masculine, *logos* over *eros*, patriarch over matriarch. 'In the beginning was the Word' – *logos*. Yet it seems more likely that in the beginning was the earth, fertility, the moon, the Goddess or the Mother,[31] and that patriarchy is a comparatively recent arrival, fostered by its practitioners until it seemed innate and everlasting. While there is no evidence for the existence of truly matriarchal societies,[32] there is a huge body of evidence, based on painting, artefacts, legends, myths, remnants of customs, scraps of the Old Testament, suggesting the pre-eminence of a great Goddess until about 1900 BC,[33] when the archaic Greeks began their move from earth-cult to sky-cult.[34] What is certain is that by the first millennium BC the supreme Goddess was dethroned, and a monolithic male god, presiding over a patriarchal society, was firmly established in Mesopotamia.[35] The modern monotheistic religions – Judaism, Christianity, Islam – took charge in the Middle East and the West. Freud felt that understanding male domination as a reaction to early maternal omnipotence was like discovering the Minoan–Mycenean civilization behind that of classical Greece.[36] No one (except on the outer fringes) would suggest we return to the worship of the old Goddess, or that we try to replace male with female, reason with emotion, *logos* with *eros*. But if men could permit a resurfacing of the female principle, they might find it possible to achieve a better balance, and in this way to modify the more oppressive demands of patriarchy. Jung believed such a readmittance was essential for our psychic health, and Ted Hughes writes passionately of our need to rescue the Female and salvage the Goddess.[37] Of course not everyone wants this to happen; obviously devoted patriarchs do not want it, and to Paglia, for instance, such a shift would be a regression to narcissism, undoing the great achievement of the Western male.[38] But even some western males are beginning to wonder if they have their achievement exactly right.

Androgyny has fascinated the West since at least the days of the classical Greeks and Romans; legend has it, for instance, that Venus and Mars (polar examples of feminine and masculine), together had a child, Harmony, in whom the fusion of opposites made for completeness. For some, the word 'androgyny' has lurid connotations, and is often confused with 'bisexuality', but I use it to describe the non-biological attributes of both sexes; 'bisexuality' refers – quite separately – to sexual relations with both sexes. Our natures are not neatly defined according to our sexes, but fragmentary, even unstable, and to a high degree we all share attributes of both female and male. Androgyny encourages the move away from polarization and the domination of the masculine, offers a humanizing freedom from the stereotypes, the chance to choose whatever qualities make for a comfortable sense of self, a move towards a reconciliation between the sexes,[39] and the experience of feeling 'both/and' rather than 'either/or'.[40] It does not dispose of gender differences, for androgynous women do not feel compelled to conform to the complete masculine stereotype, any more than androgynous men conform to all that is regarded as 'feminine'. Androgynous women can still be attractive, elegant and beautiful, and androgynous men strapping and handsome. Even in an androgynous world it will still be acceptable to wish to *please*.[41] Androgyny does not mean the obliteration of 'difference' for, if there is mutual recognition of each other as Subject, each will yet remain for the other as an *other*.[42] The need is to dislocate the stereotypical connections between exterior appearance and interior qualities. Contrasexual tension does not vanish, for women and men remain biologically (and to a degree psychologically) different beings, and will still retain their propensities, their difference-with-equality, in their own directions.

Cancian reports that in the United States more and more couples are living an androgynous life,[43] yet initiations into gender, in childhood and through the traditional attitudes and customs of puberty, do all they can to destroy androgyny. No doubt some lovers are happy with a high polarization of gender, but for others love could be happier and more prolonged if there were a deeper and more conscious sense of balance, not only between but *within* each partner. The projection of the unconscious struggle between 'female' and 'male' elements in each can only result in trouble.

For many couples in love stereotypes are accentuated, but other lovers will be at their most androgynous, feeling release from the traditional demands. In times when the feminine element has been more acceptable – the periods of Courtly Love, the Renaissance, the cult of Sensibility, the Romantic movement – men who still retain their energy and bravado have not feared to cultivate sensitivity, colour, the arts. Being in love can lead a man who is not afraid into an understanding of his new androgynous nature, show him the ease of his relations with his beloved, and offer him a better chance of preserving what is good when the hurricane of love subsides. Woolf brilliantly created the split androgyne, Orlando, but the great twentieth-century androgynous novel is Joyce's *Ulysses*, throughout which Bloom attempts to harmonize female and male within himself; many-faceted, unboundaried, tenuous, provisional, he struggles to put the traditional male heroics of domination and violence behind him.[44]

A woman in the traditional style (retiring, dependent, submissive) is unlikely to alter much when she loves, for love does not usually promote the masculine element in women, and indeed, often the reverse. However, from the Greek Artemis, through Spenser's Britomart, Shakespeare's Rosalind, Austen's Emma, Brontë's Shirley, Hardy's Sue and on to the twentieth-century novel, literature brims with glorious young women who could only be described as androgens, escapees from the strait-jacket of gender, taking what they will from the male role and making themselves free and active spirits. But they must beware of insidious social pressures; as Atwood's Marian finds when she becomes engaged to Peter in *The Edible Woman*, even an independent, androgynous woman, used to running her own life, can allow her independence to be undermined by love, until she is reduced to the kind of inert icon she would have once despised: ' . . . I heard a soft flannelly voice I barely recognized, saying, "I'd rather have you decide that. I'd rather leave the big decisions up to you." '45 Until women learn to value *themselves* men will never value *them* in the ways that they would wish. However, if a woman has some understanding of the danger, she will have a better chance of creating and sustaining an androgynous self, and come through the magical, threatening realm of love without too much harm.

As might be imagined, there are many objections to androgyny. Some have felt that the chasm between woman and man is too deep to be bridged, for even though gender can 'wander', and both sexes are androgynous to a high degree, the 'male wound' is so cataclysmic it creates a true gender difference.[46] Post-structural objection is based on the argument that because gender is plastic and fluid there is nothing to be androgynous *about*; in Winterson's *Written on the Body* the narrator is genderless, and so sex and behaviour cannot be bound to either female or male expectations. Others argue that androgyny can mean an escape from true sexual identity, that it defeats the male power which created the achievements of the West, that the contra-sexual tension essential to love will be destroyed. Yet when a sample of male students were asked which kind of women they found most attractive they did not choose the most 'feminine' but those who were psychologically androgynous – emotional, gentle, understanding but also independent, active, competitive, confident.[47]

There is no doubt that we live in a time when our thoughts and feelings about love are in flux. If the traditional forms of romantic love are on the way out, the charismatic movement may be on the way in. Lindholm argues that its unnerving growth is beginning to siphon off at least a part of those needs which have always found their home in romantic love, much of whose character it shares. He points to the devotion, to the single-minded 'conversion', to the sense of 'merging' and the loss of self, to the unquestioning subjection to the leader, whose status is semi-divine, and to the high sexual activity of the group. The parallels with falling in love can hardly be missed.[48]

Many women, as well as many men, would passionately like to see a change in our attitudes to love; but they also fear the uncertainties, the freedom from old gender roles, from conventional sexuality, from traditional concepts of love, and the vastness of unknown liberty.[49] The polarizing of gender is still an entrenched and powerful force, and to many the traditional sex roles remain immovable. Yet, if we are not to remain love's stupefied victims, we must somehow learn to adapt them.

How can we make love 'good enough'?

For some lovers, falling in love as it is today and has been (it seems) for ever, is already 'good enough'. Not everyone's expectations are high, and there are many women and men who do not worry about stereotypes and gender and sex and what love really *is*. But, for those who concern themselves, there are changes afoot, and for some of these feminism must be thanked. However noisy, however riven, feminism is bringing a new and proper dignity to women, and if all goes well it will alter not only the experience of love but society itself for the better – but it must steer between the extremes of the destructive militant and the whining victim.

> Ah, what a dusty answer gets the soul
> When hot for certainties in this our life.[50]

Meredith's piercing nineteenth-century sonnets on 'Modern Love' recognize that certainties in love are impossible. Yet we are not helpless, and love is not hopeless. We might start by trying to make the shift into a situation in which behaviour was judged by its nature, and not by the sex doing it. A reinforcing mutuality should be able to survive those awkward paradoxes whereby each lover needs both freedom and security, independence and protection. These contradictions need to be held, for if they are avoided the mechanisms of polarization and splitting will intrude; lovers need to acknowledge and respect the other's strangeness, not to fight it, for the outside Other has to be recognized as different *and* alike, commonality must be found in difference, and the tension held between contradictory forces.[51] This holding of contrary pulls together in tension is far more difficult than collapsing into stereotyped roles – but then no sane person ever thought that living was easy. Both lovers need to forgo power and control, and find ways in which the militant symbol of the phallus is humanized into a penis. While he assures her of her autonomous, intrinsic worth, she can acknowledge and calm his buried fear of the female, and help him to repair the broken line between his penis and his heart.[52] Men as well as women want companionship, compatibility, an understanding of their vulnerability. When this begins to be accepted, patriarchy will be closing its iron reign; new insights from psychology and sociology, the stumbling progress of feminism, the power handed to women by modern contraception, a modifying of the old divisions of labour are all undermining it.[53]

In exploring a way through the interactions of psychology and culture, Benjamin does not discount or try to alter love but to describe more hopeful and happier means in which it might be lived. One way into the reshaping of attitudes is through the rearing of children.[54] The creation of gender polarity in adult life arises from various related sources, including the inferior sterotypical status of the woman–mother, the virtual absence of the father in parenting and the related problems invested in the father's phallus. While her brother's waves proudly, the young girl finds she has no obtrusive sex organ, and this emphasizes her lack, affects her self-esteem, and symbolizes the superiority of her father. Benjamin argues that the girl desires the phallus for the same reason as her brother – as a route of separation from the matrix of the mother to the thrilling, unavailable outside world. If the father shares his autonomy and status equally with the mother, this will offset the influence of the phallus, both girl and boy will have a chance of growing up assuming gender equality, and making happier relations in adult love. To help her achieve this, the father must learn to recognize, approve and love her as he does his son.[55] If he can show affectionate paternal qualities, and appear to both daughter and son as equal in attachment – stimulating, cuddling, kissing, rocking, playing, without encouraging aggression – his gender will be less important than his role.[56] As to the mother, if she is seen not only as incomplete but as submissive and inferior, she will appear as a 'lack', Object not Subject, and girl or boy will grow up with a traditional polarized sense of gender. But if she confidently enjoys her autonomy and self-esteem, and joins the father in fostering independence, the child will grow up in an androgynous world without assuming that gender must be polarized. Both parents will then be figures of attachment *and* separation for their child, who will learn to live with both sameness and difference, accepting and expressing both female and male aspects of its self; if a girl, she could experience alternately, 'I, a woman; I, a genderless subject; I, like-a-man.'[57] Gender would become flexible, easygoing, tolerant of difference, and the core sense of being one sex or the other need not be compromised. None of this will cancel the male's inevitable 'wound' in separating himself from his mother, but his identificatory love with an affectionate father will provide him with an escape route, and a conviction of his father's love and approval will profoundly help him through his trauma, and heal him in such a way that he renounces but does not reject his mother, or, through her, all adult women.

There is a new confidence in the cognitive aspects of love, particularly in the intimate meeting of minds and the deliberate expansion of self-knowledge.[58] All through this book I have emphasized the hopeful nature of knowledge and self-knowledge about love; but this is a two-way system, for love itself is a route to self-knowledge, to the awareness which can help us out of servitude to the unconscious, and to a new understanding of ourselves and our relationships.[59] Those who are so inclined may think of love as a spiritual journey, undertaken by Orpheus, formalized by Plato, explored by Dante and Shakespeare, dug out of the dark by Freud and Jung and their fellow explorers. Self-awareness can help lovers to stand a little outside and, if they can accept love with some degree of consciousness, they will realize that they do not see the beloved plain but blurred through a projection of themselves, which will not clear until the phase of 'falling in love' has run its course. What they will then find may be acceptable, or not. Although it is impossible for a lover fallen in love to 'know' the beloved, some knowledge of what is happening, some increase in understanding, may help towards a happier experience, and towards a warier and less reverential view of romance. Our expectations of love are already high, but new concepts of partnership could carry their own danger in driving expectation higher still.[60] We need to find a new critical irony, which consciously sets aside love's deficiencies, and plays on our fantasies of all-conquering, all-perfect love.[61] Although some people might fear that the change to a more conscious awareness could leave love withering in a new glare of day, that is a risk we have to take.

Lovers still living on mountain air cannot force time to stand still, but they are not helpless. Even in their euphoric state, it is wise not to assume that love is their due, nor take it for granted when it comes; love has a need to be expressed, physically, affectionately, with praise, self-disclosure, emotional support, gifts.[62] To which could be added the virtue of tolerance, an acceptance of shortcomings, an acknowledgement of needed space – and the nostrum of humour. An easy verbal intimacy is also above price; most lovers laugh and talk unstoppably, but they might sometimes find it possible to direct their babble on to the arrival and growth of their love, their cost–reward balance, their attitudes to gender, the nature of their projections and fantasies, the roots of personal pain, what they want of each other, the influence of parents and siblings. Both might then realize that we all (not only the other) harbour secret demons of aggression, rage, revenge.[63]

Love struggles against the daily sameness which fogs over so much we hold dear, yet love is also subject to dulling, and needs to be deliberately polished by what Alberoni describes as 'adventures', departures from routine, the distancing of everyday.[64] Excitement may be intermittently rekindled by Person's 'love-attacks', renewals sometimes triggered unpredictably, but also provoked by rituals, anniversaries, holidays, play, the unexpected, the unconventional – and even by outside threat.[65]

Danger besets us whatever we do. Women need to reject their passive role, yet if radical feminists succeed in dismembering the male he might rebel with unparalleled violence. Although men often state that they look for women who are their intellectual and economic equals, most seek no such thing.[66] Under the pressure of competition, a man may be provoked into a total withdrawal of his feelings, into angry assertions of dominance, into hectic promiscuity, into violence and rape. Or he might virtually vanish. Losing power is a difficult thing for a man, and somehow women will have to find ways to avoid demonizing the men who for millennia have demonized *them*. In 1988, ten years after *In the Name of Love*, Tweedie saw emerging signs of true equality, Cancian detected hope in the United States, and a recent survey of feminism finds the outlook more optimistic.[67] But Faludi sees the opposition now swelling again, goaded by women's threatening approach to equality, and the achievement of personal, economic and intellectual success.[68] Laddish magazines, such as *Loaded* and *Esquire*, vibrating with aggression and misogyny, flex their muscles and become more and more successful. And out on the crazed fringe, spitting out the old venom of fear and hate, lurk the New Right and the fanatical Fundamentalists.[69]

Is love worth it?

Hector, the Trojan leader, does not think so. Facing his brother, Troilus, to talk to him of Cressida –

HECTOR: Brother, she is not worth what she doth cost
          The holding.
TROILUS: What is aught but as 'tis valued?
HECTOR: But value dwells not in particular will . . .[70]

Hector was right, but then he was not the lover. In their brief space of being 'in love' lovers find profound value in the other, and intense happiness in companionship as they share mirrors of the self, find themselves as sexual beings, search out their capacities for loving and being loved, enjoy emotional support and esteem, growing all the while in self-discovery; their intensity of emotion and imagination creates the sense of another world and provides the energy to work at it. Love changes the boundaries of the self, explores, liberates, challenges.[71] As Gerald realizes when Gudrun rejects him, in *Women in Love*, even after disaster love can still be seen as a creative event: ' . . . this unfolding of his own covering, leaving him incomplete, limited, unfinished, like an open flower under the sky, this was his cruellest joy . . . Why should he close up and become impervious . . . when he had broken forth like a seed that has germinated.'[72]

No doubt there are lovers whose experience has been so black they wish they had never loved, but their testimony is hard to find, and Tennyson's celebrated proposal that "'Tis better to have loved and lost / Than never to have loved at all' is generally shared.[73] As Barthes concludes, 'Despite the difficulties of my story, despite discomforts, doubts, despairs, despite impulses to be done with it, I unceasingly affirm love, within myself, as a value.'[74] Nostalgia for past love is full of resonance. Even when pain and failure lie at the end of it, for most people love is an event of high significance, helping to heal the disjunction between emotion and intellect, between the unconscious and conscious mind. Even if it is frightening, sometimes we should take the risk and jump, rather than remain trapped in aridity.[75] Chaucer's Wife of Bath jumped five times, and had no regrets:

> But, Lord Christ, whan that it remembreth me
> Upon my yowthe, and on my jolitee,
> It tikkleth me aboute myn herte roote.
> Unto this day it doth myn herte boote [good]
> That I have had my world as in my tyme.[76]

Love will not vanish because we strip it of reverence, refuse the unequal gender relations it appears to demand, ignore its ego-comforts, co-rear our children with our partners, raise our self-esteem. Into the far distance its mechanisms are here to stay, and our best course is not to attempt to transform or abolish it, but to find ways of soothing the worst of its effects.

There is much rethinking to be done, on gender, on sexual relations, on the rearing of children, on experiments and alternatives, on more sceptical attitudes. But we have consciousness, conscience and compassion, and we can learn to be more understanding of the worlds within and without us.[77] Given these caveats, we should not disdain the awesome, entrancing, iridescent, galvanizing, resurgent experience falling in love can bring.

Notes

(After the first use in full, subsequent citations will be given as chapter and note number of first use in square brackets.)

Prologue

1 Phillips, *On Flirtation*, ch. 3.
2 Jankowiak, Fisher, 'A cross-cultural perspective on romantic love', *Ethology*, 31, no. 2.
3 Berlin, *The Crooked Timber of Humanity*, ch. 1.
4 Sutherland, *Irrationality*.
5 Lewis, *Allegory of Love*; de Rougemont, *Passion and Society*.
6 Jackson, *Sociology*, vol. 27, no. 2.
7 Friedan, *Beyond Gender*.
8 Nussbaum, *Love's Knowledge*, ch. 1.
9 Freud, 'Female Sexuality', Standard Edition (SE) 21.
10 Greer, *Slipshod Sybils*, ch. 4.
11 Morris, *The Discovery of the Individual*, Church History Outlines 5, 1972.
12 For example, psychology, sociology, ethology, biology and their various combinations.
13 For a fuller description, see ch. 1.

14 For example, Midgely, *Beast and Man*; Rose, Kamin, Lewontin, *Not in Our Genes*.

15 Person, *Love and Fateful Encounters*, 2, v; 'Final Thoughts'.

16 For example; de Beauvoir, *The Second Sex*; Firestone, *The Dialectic of Sex*; Greer, *The Female Eunuch*; Tweedie, *In the Name of Love*.

17 Burton; 'Love-Melancholy' is 'The Third Partition' of *The Anatomy of Melancholy*.

Chapter 1: A First Look Round

1 Burton [Prologue, 17], III, 2, i.

2 Pascal, *Pensées*, sect. 2.

3 Fisher, *Anatomy of Love*, ch. 2; Lawick-Goodall, *In the Shadow of Man*, ch. 7.

4 Forster, *Maurice*, ch. 44.

5 Shakespeare, *The Merchant of Venice*, 2.7.

6 Shaw, *Getting Married*, Preface.

7 Jackson [Prologue, 6].

8 La Rochefoucauld, *Maximes*, no. 136.

9 Stone, *The Family, Sex and Marriage in England*, part III, ch. 5; part IV, ch. 7.

10 Walster, 'Passionate Love', in *Theories of Attraction and Love*, ed. Murstein.

11 Berscheid, 'Some Comments on Love's Anatomy', in *The Psychology of Love*, ed. Sternberg, Barnes.

12 Comer, *Wedlocked Women*; Giddens, *The Transformation of Intimacy*.

13 Douglas, Atwell, *Love, Intimacy and Sex*, ch. 5; Giddens, [1, 12], chs 4, 5, 7.

14 *Shorter Oxford English Dictionary*.

15 De Botton, *Essays in Love*, ch. II, 13.

16 De Rougemont, *Love in the Western World*, I, 1, ii.

17 Cervantes, *Don Quixote*, part I, ch. 1.

18 Gillingham, 'Love, Marriage and Politics in the Twelfth Century', *Forum for Modern Language Studies*, vol. 25, no. 4, 1989.

19 Pound, 'Homage to Sextus Propertius'.

20 Eysenck, *Sex and Personality*, chs 3, 7.

21 Beck, Beck-Gernsheim, *The Normal Chaos of Love*, ch. 2.

22 In Morrison and Motion's *Contemporary British Poetry* there are only four poems out of seventy which take a romantic or idealistic view of love, and eight more which wrestle with difficult or mature love. In Adcock's *Twentieth-Century Women Poets* there are even fewer.

23 Amis, M., *The Rachel Papers*, 'Eleven-ten'.

24 *The Works of Sir Thomas Malory*, 'The Tale of King Arthur', bk 4.

25 Jackson, [Prologue, 6].

26 Burton [Prologue, 17], III, 1, i.

27 Shakespeare, *Much Ado about Nothing*, 4, 1.

28 Sternberg, 'Triangulating love', in *The Psychology of Love*, ed. Sternberg, Barnes.

29 Lee, 'Love-Styles', [1, 28].

30 Shakespeare, *Twelfth Night*, 2, 4.

31 Ackerman, *Natural History of Love*, V, ii.

32 Austen, *Sense and Sensibility*; *Mansfield Park*; *Persuasion*.

33 Brontë, C., *Villette*, ch. 61.

34 Virgil, *Georgics*, 4; Homer, *Odyssey*.

35 Flaubert, *Madame Bovary*, 1, 6.

36 'Helen of Kirconnel', *Oxford Book of Ballads*.

37 Shakespeare, [1, 27], 1, 1.

38 Moschus, 'Idyll VI', trans. Chapman.

39 Eysenck, [1, 20], ch. 7.

40 Amis, K., *The Old Devils*, ch. 9, ii.

41 Hardy, *The Life of Thomas Hardy*, 1, 1.
42 Dronke, *Medieval Latin and the Rise of the European Love-Lyric*.
43 Pound, Stock, *Love Poems of Ancient Egypt*.
44 Homer, *Iliad*, bk 3.
45 Taylor, *Palladian*, ch. 10.
46 Sappho, no. V, in *Sappho of Lesbos*, ed. and trans. du Quesne.
47 Theocritus, 'Idyll XI', trans. E. B. Browning.
48 Meleager, 'O Gentle Ships', trans. Lang.
49 Catullus, 'My sweetest love', trans. Campion.
50 Virgil, 'The Loves of Dido and Aeneas', trans. Fanshawe.
51 See, for example, Ovid, *Ars Amatoria*.
52 Propertius, 'When thou must home', trans. Campion.
53 Petronius, *Medieval Latin Lyrics*, ed. and trans. Waddell.
54 Doody, *The True Story of the Novel*.
55 Longus, *Daphnis and Chloë*, trans. Turner.
56 See, for example, 'A Wife's Lament', in *A Choice of Anglo-Saxon Verse*, ed. Hamer.
57 Homer [1, 44].
58 Reynolds, 'Social Mentalities and . . . medieval scepticism', *Royal Historical Society*, 6th series, vol. 1, 1991.
59 Morris [Prologue, 11]
60 Johnson, *The Psychology of Romantic Love*, IV, 15.
61 De Rougemont [Prologue, 5], II, 10.
62 Zeldin, *An Intimate History of Humanity*, ch. 5.
63 Stone [1, 9] part IV, ch. 7.
64 Gillingham [1, 18].
65 *The Paston Letters* (years 1468–9).
66 Stone [1, 9], part 1, ch. 1.
67 Keats, *Letters*; to Benjamin Bailey, 22.11.1817.
68 Zeldin [1, 63], ch. 18.
69 Bayley, *The Characters of Love*, ch. 2.
70 Hughes-Hallett, *Cleopatra*, II, 5.

71 De Rougemont [Prologue, 5], I, 1.

72 Shakespeare, *Antony and Cleopatra*, 4, 15.

73 Barnes, *Nightwood*, ch. 3.

74 Dollimore, *Death, Desire and Loss in Western Culture*.

75 Shakespeare, *As You Like It*; Fielding, *Tom Jones*; Tolstoy, *Anna Karenina*; Forster, *A Room with a View*.

76 Fisher [1, 3].

77 For example, Jackson [Prologue, 6].

78 Craib, *Sociology*, vol. 29, 1.

79 'The Song of Solomon', (OT, 1611).

80 See for example J. Ledoux, *The Emotional Brain*.

81 Mandler, *Mind and Body*, II, 'The Organic Tradition'.

82 Tuby, 'Psychological Aspects of Eros', *Guild of Pastoral Psychology*, no. 242. In Jungian terms, the hidden archetype of the Shadow, representing all we hate about ourselves, emerges and begins to destroy the image of the beloved.

83 Roth, *Portnoy's Complaint*, 'Cunt Crazy'.

84 Bacon, *The Advancement of Learning*, 'The Second Book'.

85 See ch. 7.

86 However, if the memory is too disturbing it may be repressed and 'forgotten'.

87 Hutchinson, *Memoirs of the Life of Colonel Hutchinson*, 'The Life of John Hutchinson'.

88 Von Hattingberg, *Rilke and Benvenuta*; Blanch, *The Wilder Shores of Love*, 'Isabella Burton'; Sullivan, *By Heart*.

89 Malory [1, 24], 'The Book of Sir Tristram', XIV; Lodge, *Small World*, V, 1.

90 Burton [Prologue, 17], 'Democritus Junior to the Reader'.

91 Barthes, *Mythologies*, 'Myth Today'.

92 Pinker, *How the Mind Works*.

93 Richard Dawkins talking to Bryan Magee, 29.1.92, Radio 3.

94 Luhmann, *Love as Passion*, Preface.

95 For further discussion of 'love-scripts' see Ch. 7.
96 Shakespeare, *The Winter's Tale*, 4, 4.

Chapter 2: The Symptoms of Happy Love

1 Winterson, *The Passion*, 'The Queen of Spades'.
2 Brown, *Analyzing Love*, ch. 3, iii.
3 Pound [1, 19].
4 Turgenev, *First Love*, ch. 7.
5 Anon, 'Western Wind', *Oxford Book of English Verse*.
6 Nabokov, *Lolita*, 1, 3.
7 Hazlitt, *Liber Amoris*, 'Perfect Love'.
8 Barthes, *A Lover's Discourse*, 'Special Days'.
9 Burton [Prologue, 17], III, 2, iii.
10 Brontë, A., *The Tenant of Wildfell Hall*, ch. 51.
11 Tolstoy [1, 76], part 4, ch. 15.
12 Austen, *Love and Freindship* [*sic*], Letter 6.
13 Donne, 'Elegie XVI'.
14 Nin, *The Four-Chambered Heart*, part I.
15 De Botton [1, 15], ch. XVII, 6; ch. XV, 4.
16 Carlyle, *Sartor Resartus*, bk II, ch. 5.
17 See ch. 7.
18 Poe, 'To Helen'.
19 James, *A Tempting Shore*, ch. 1.
20 Tolstoy [1, 76], part 1, ch. 9.
21 Shakespeare [1, 96], 4, 4.
22 See ch. 7.
23 Beerbohm, *Zuleika Dobson*, ch. 8.
24 [1, 79].
25 Scovell, 'A Wife'.
26 Plato, *Symposium*, sect. 107d.
27 Housman, *A Shropshire Lad*, no. 17.

28 De Botton [1, 15], ch. 1, 8.

29 Murdoch, *The Black Prince*, 'Bradley Pearson's Story', Part Two.

30 Plato [2, 26], 190b–192e.

31 Colette, *Claudine in Paris*, ch. 14.

32 See ch. 9.

33 See ch. 7.

34 Pasternak, *Dr Zhivago*, part II, 14, vii.

35 Ortega y Gasset, *On Love*; Fromm, *The Art of Loving*.

36 Lawrence, *Women in Love*, ch. 13.

37 See, for example, Sartre, *The Transcendence of the Ego*.

38 *A Celtic Miscellany*, no. 46, ed. Jackson.

39 Peacock, *Nightmare Abbey*, ch. 14.

40 Douglas, Atwell [1, 13], ch. 5.

41 Plato, *Phaedrus*, sect. 252.

42 Austen, *Pride and Prejudice*, ch. 25.

43 Gibbons, *Cold Comfort Farm*, ch. 2.

44 Dickens, *David Copperfield*, ch. 26.

45 Barnes [1, 73], ch. 2.

46 Freud, 'Civilization and its Discontents', SE 21.

47 Brontë, E., *Wuthering Heights*, ch. 9.

48 Lawrence [2, 36], ch. 23.

49 Lawrence [2, 36], ch. 19.

50 Singer, *The Nature of Love*, vol. 2, Introduction; III, 9.

51 Auden, 'Lay your sleeping head'.

52 Nin [2, 14], Part I.

53 Winterson [2, 1], 'The Queen of Spades'.

54 Barthes [2, 8], 'The Unknowable'.

55 Brewer, *Symbolic Stories*; ch. 1. Many sociologists would disagree, preferring to see the origin of myth, legend and fairy-tale embedded in the patriarchal power politics of whichever culture created them.

56 Spenser, *The Faerie Queen*, bk. 3; Tennyson, 'The Lady of Shalott'.

57 'Clerk Saunders', *Oxford Book of Ballads*.

58 For prolific illustration of meandering boundaries, see *The Routledge Anthology of Cross-Gendered Verse*.

59 Colette [2, 31], chs 14, 16.

60 Goethe, *The Sufferings of Young Werther*, First Book.

61 Holden, *Laughter, the Best Medicine?*

62 Hazlitt, 'On Wit and Humour', *Lectures on the English Comic Writers*.

63 Beerbohm [2, 23].

64 Catullus, 'Dear Ipsitilla', trans. J. Michie.

65 Anon, *Making Love*, ed. Bold.

66 Sterne, *Tristram Shandy*, vol. 1, ch. 1.

67 Lawrence, *Lady Chatterley's Lover*, ch. 12.

68 Nin [2, 14], part II.

69 Anon, *Pan Book of Limericks*, ed. Untermeyer.

70 Fielding, *Jonathan Wild the Great*, bk. III, ch. 7

Chapter 3: Sex By and Large

1 For a discussion of these difficult borderlands, see ch. 9.

2 Chaucer, 'The Parlement of Foules'.

3 Ruehl, 'Sexual Theory and Practice', in *Sex and Love*, ed. Cartledge, Ryan.

4 Sterne [2, 66], vol. 9, ch. 3.

5 Kinsey, *Sexual Behaviour in the Human Male*, chs. 9, 10, 20, etc.

6 Rubin, *Intimate Strangers*, ch. 9.

7 Byatt, *Possession*, ch. 14.

8 Freud, 'The Transformations of Puberty', SE 7.

9 Kinsey [3, 5], ch. 21.

10 Kinsey [3, 5], *Sexual Behaviour in the Human Female*; Masters, Johnson, *Human Sexual Response, Human Sexual Inadequacy, Heterosexuality* (with Kolodny); Hite, *The Hite Report, Women and Love, The Hite Report on the Family*.

11 Reisman, Eichal, *Kinsey, Sex and Fraud*; Faust, *Women, Sex and Pornography*.

12 Masters, Johnson, Kolodny, *Heterosexuality*, ch. 15.

13 Hite, *The Hite Report; Women and Love*.

14 Wellings et al., *Sexual Behaviour in Britain*.

15 Michael et al., *Sex in America*.

16 Greer [Prologue 16], 'Body: sex'.

17 Freud, *Three Essays on the Theory of Sexuality*, SE 7; see also Phillips, *Terrors and Experts*, ch. 5.

18 Masters, Johnson, Kolodny [3, 10], ch. 3.

19 Lacqueur, *Making Sex*, Preface, chs 1, 6.

20 Foucault, *The History of Sexuality*, vol. 1.

21 Maslow, *Towards a Psychology of Being*, V, 11; *Motivation and Personality*, ch. 5.

22 Morris, *The Naked Ape*, ch. 3.

23 But see McDermott, *Current Anthropology*, 8.96, arguing that such artefacts are women's representations of their own bodies.

24 For a full account, see Warner, *Alone of All her Sex*, ch. 5.

25 Paglia, *Sexual Personae*, ch. 1.

26 Freud [2, 46], SE 21; also SE 9.

27 Jung, 'On Psychical Energy', *Collected Works* (CW) 8.

28 Wellings et al. [3, 14], ch. 2.

29 Freud, 'Jensen's "Gravida" etc.', SE 9; also SE 21.

30 Greer [Prologue, 16], 'Sex'.

31 Weeks, *Sex, Politics and Society*, ch. 1.

32 Laslett *et al., Bastardy*.

33 Hale, *The Civilization of Europe in the Renaissance*, ch. 17.

34 Graves, *The White Goddess*, ch. 22.

35 [2, 57], 'The Demon Lover', *OBB*.
36 Freud, 'The Interpretation of Dreams', SE 5.
37 Piercy, 'Vegetable Love', in *Available Light*.
38 Freud, 'New Introductory Lectures', SE 22.
39 Gibbons [2, 43], ch. 11.
40 Miller, *Tropic of Cancer*, sect. 13.
41 Roth [1, 83], 'The Most Prevalent Form of Degradation'.
42 White, *The Beautiful Room is Empty*, ch. 9.
43 Redgrove, Shuttle, *The Wise Wound*, ch. 5.
44 Browne, *Religio Medici*, 'The Second Part'.
45 Posner, *Sex and Reason*, Introduction, Conclusion.
46 Giddens [1, 12], Introduction.
47 *Sex Madonna*, by Madonna.
48 Freud, 'Group Psychology and the Analysis of the Ego', SE 18.
49 Freud, Preface to 4th ed. of *Three Essays in Sexuality*, interpreted Bettelheim, in *Freud and Man's Soul*, III.
50 Pope, *Essay on Man*, Epistle 2.
51 Jong, *Serenissima*, ch. 11.

Chapter 4: Sex, Women and Men

1 Lacqueur [3, 19].
2 For a full account, see Warner [3, 24], ch. 5.
3 Chaucer, 'Wife of Bath's Prologue', *Canterbury Tales*.
4 Aubrey, 'Sir Francis Bacon', *Brief Lives*.
5 Marcus, *The Other Victorians*, ch. 1, part 3.
6 Krafft-Ebing, qu. Wilson, *The Great Sex Divide*, ch. 8
7 Anon, 'The Ballad of Eskimo Nell', in *Making Love*, ed. Bold.
8 Marcus [4, 5], ch. 1, part III; ch. 3, parts II, III; ch. 4, part I.

9 Freud [3, 17]

10 Kinsey [3, 10], II, 9.

11 Osborne, *Inadmissible Evidence*, Act 2.

12 Fisher [1, 3], ch. 4.

13 *The Life of St Teresa of Avila*, trans. Cohen, ch. 20.

14 Rossetti, C., 'Goblin Market'. Some argue this is a children's fairy-tale, or an allegory of religious or creative experience; see Greer [Prologue, 10], ch. 11.

15 For example, *Deep Down*, ed. Chester.

16 Dworkin, *Mercy*, ch. 5.

17 Jong, *Fear of Flying*, ch. 5.

18 Pym, *The Sweet Dove Died*, ch. 2.

19 Freud [3, 38].

20 Joyce, *Ulysses*, Molly's soliloquy.

21 Kinsey [3, 10], II, 5.

22 Michael et al., [3, 15], ch. 6.

23 Wellings et al., [3, 14], ch. 6.

24 Paglia [3, 25], ch. 6.

25 Joyce [4, 20].

26 Taylor, *A Game of Hide and Seek*, part I, 3.

27 Dworkin, *Intercourse*.

28 Michael et al., [3, 15], ch. 5.

29 In *Tomorrow's Women* (Demos, Paper 26), Wilkinson and Howard see the Pill as the most important of all twentieth-century influences on women.

30 Giddens [1, 12], ch. 4.

31 O'Kelly, 'Onward Virgin Soldiers', *Observer*, 26.6.94; also Radio 4, *Sunday*, 31.7.94.

32 Austen [2, 42]; Byron, *Childe Harold's Pilgrimage*; Charlotte Brontë, *Jane Eyre*; Emily Brontë [2, 47].

33 According to *The Author* (CVII, no. 1, 1996) there was a substantial fall in the number of romantic novels issued by public libraries between 1993 and 1995.

34 Nin [2, 14], part 1.
35 Friday, *My Secret Garden*, chs 3, 5.
36 Leroy, *Pleasure*, ch. 10.
37 Segal, 'Sensual Uncertainty', [3, 3]; Leroy [4, 36], chs 10, 11.
38 Kundera, *The Unbearable Lightness of Being*, III, 7.
39 Miller [3, 40], sect. 7.
40 Wilson [4, 6], ch. 2.
41 Leroy [4, 36], ch. 10.
42 Kinsey [3, 10], II, 6.
43 Nicholson, *Men and Women*, ch. 7.
44 Masters and Johnson, Kolodny [3, 10].
45 Cleland, *Fanny Hill*, 'The First Letter'.
46 Lawrence [2, 67], ch. 14.
47 Sullerot, *Women on Love*, Introduction.
48 Leroy [4, 36], ch. 13.
49 Joyce [4, 20].
50 Lawrence [2, 67], ch. 15.
51 Kinsey [3, 10], II, 9.
52 Greer [Prologue, 16], 'Body; sex'.
53 Keen, *The Passionate Life*, ch. 10.
54 Hite, *Women and Love*, II, 5; see also Dickson, *The Mirror Within*; Faust [3, 11].
55 Michael et al. [3, 15], ch. 7.
56 Michael et al. [3, 15], ch. 5.
57 See, for example, Friday, *My Secret Garden*; Reyes, *Lucie's Long Voyage*; Perriam, *Sin City*; Lunch, *Paradoxia*; see also Chester [4, 15].
58 Kundera [4, 38], III, 8.
59 Michael et al. [3, 15], ch. 7.
60 Roth [1, 83], 'Whacking Off'.
61 Ackerman [1, 31], 3, iii.
62 Miller [3, 40]; *Tropic of Capricorn*.

63 Amis, M. [1, 23], 'Twenty-past'.

64 Kundera [4, 38], II, 15.

65 Hudson, Jacot, *The Way Men Think*, ch. 7.

66 For example, Masters, Johnson, Kodolny [3, 10], ch. 3, agree; Cook, McHenry, *Sexual Attraction*, ch. 1, disagree.

67 Miller [3, 40], sect. 8.

68 Augustine, *City of God*, XlV, 16; Aquinas, ref. by Lewis, *Allegory of Love*, ch. 1.

69 Anon, [2, 5], no. 14.

70 Ovid, 'Elegy VII', bk 3, trans. Marlowe.

71 Augustine [4, 68], XIV, ch. 17.

72 Milton, *Paradise Lost*, bk 4.

73 Lawrence [2, 36], ch. 7.

74 Benjamin, *Bonds of Love*, ch. 2; see also my ch. 9.

75 See also Wrangham, Peterson, *Demonic Males*.

76 Kinsey [3, 9], III, 17.

77 Freud [2, 46], SE 21.

78 Woolf, *Between the Acts*, last section.

79 For a fuller discussion, see ch. 5.

80 Greenstein, *The Fragile Male*, ch. 3.

81 Giddens [1, 12], ch. 7.

82 Stoller, *Sexual Excitement*, II, 3–9; Leroy [4, 36], ch. 11.

83 Ronsard, 'Song', *Lyrics of Ronsard*, trans. C. Graves.

84 Lawrence [2, 36], ch. 13.

85 Pietropinto and Simenaur, *The Male Myth*, ch. 3; Holloway, 'Heterosexual Sex', [3, 3].

86 Bettelheim, *The Uses of Enchantment*, part 2, 'The Animal-Groom Cycle'. The 'animal-groom' tales reflect the male's fear that his maleness may be innately repellent.

87 Barrows, *Mayflower Madam*, ch. 3.

88 Masters and Johnson [3, 10], ch. 1.

89 Leroy [4, 36], ch. 11.

90 Phillips [3, 17], ch. 5.

91 Qu. Marcus [4, 5], ch. 3, v.
92 Updike, *Brazil*, sect. xxv.
93 Ignatieff, 'Homo Sexualis', *London Review of Books*, 3.82.
94 White [3, 42], ch. 4.
95 French, *Beyond Power*, ch. 7, vi.

Chapter 5: Gender

1 Stoller, *Sex and Gender*, I, 5.
2 Berk, *The Gender Factory*, ch. 7.
3 MacInnes, *The End of Masculinity*, ch. 1.
4 Oakley, *Subject Women*, II, 4.
5 Engels, *The Origin of the Family*, ch. 2.
6 Millett, *Sexual Politics*, I, 2.
7 Sarsby, *Romantic Love and Society*, ch. 7; Wellings et al., [3, 14], ch. 2.
8 Wilkinson, Howard [4, 29], ch. 3.
9 Vance, 'Pleasure and Danger', in *Pleasure and Danger*, ed. Vance.
10 Sterne [2, 66], IX, 31.
11 Duncombe, Marsden, 'Can Men Love?', *Romance Revisited*, ed. Pearce, Stacey.
12 Tweedie, *Eating Children*, ch. 7.
13 Greer [Prologue, 16], 'Soul: Stereotype'.
14 Hardy, 'I need not go'.
15 Jack, *Silencing the Self*, chs. 1, 2, et al.
16 Gulbar, Gulbenkian, *The Madwoman in the Attic*.
17 Stoller [5, 1].
18 Astell, 'Reflections on Marriage', in *The First English Feminist*, ed. Hill.
19 Herodotus, *History*, bk 4.
20 Homer [1, 44] bks 3, 6.

21 See, for example, Kleinbaum, *War against the Amazons*.

22 Graves, *The Greek Myths*, vols 1 and 2; authorities cited are Pindar, Herodotus, Strabo, Diodorus, Plutarch, Justinus.

23 Holmes, 'Women Warriors', in *New Scientist*, 8.2.97.

24 Dronke, *Women Writers of the Middle Ages*.

25 Bogin, *The Women Troubadours*.

26 Greer [Prologue, 10], 'Prologue'.

27 Cavendish, M., Duchess of Newcastle, *Philosophical and Physical Opinions* (1685). The Duchess caught the admiring fancy of Charles Lamb (*Essays of Elia*, 'Mackery End') and of Woolf (*Common Reader* 1, 'The Duchess of Newcastle').

28 Hufton, *The Prospect before Her*, ch. 11.

29 Pilkington, 'The Wish', *Poetry by Englishwomen*, ed. Pritchard.

30 Anon, in *Eighteenth-Century Women Poets*, ed. Lonsdale.

31 Gausson, *A Woman of Wit and Wisdom*, ch. 7.

32 Woolf, 'Four Figures', *The Second Common Reader*.

33 Showalter, *Sexual Anarchy*, chs 1, 5; Hammond, *Love between Men*, ch. 5.

34 Dunton, *Petticoat Government*; Dunton was also the author of a long proto-feminist poem, *The Feminiad*.

35 Sophocles, *Tereus*, Fragment 583, trans. Murray, *Oxford History of the Classical World*.

36 Chaucer is said to have based her on the traditional figure of the 'Shrew' – but his creation comes over with gleeful admiration.

37 Paglia, *Sex, Art and American Culture*, Cancelled Preface.

38 Formaini, *Men, the Darker Continent*.

39 Heywood, *Simply Forever*, ch. 2.

40 Shakespeare, *The Taming of the Shrew*, 3, 20

41 Aristotle, *The Generation of Animals*, bk. IV, vi.

42 Augustine, *Contra Mendacium*, bk. VII, x; St Paul, 1 Corinthians xi. And see the attitudes of Milton in *Paradise Lost*.

43 Wordsworth, 'Lucy' poems, no. 4.

44 Ibsen, *A Doll's House*, Acts I and III.

45 Tannen, *You Just Don't Understand*, ch. 10.

46 For a formidable list of women's continuing disadvantages, see the *Human Development Report*, for the United Nations Development Programme, 1995; see also *Britain 99* from the Office for National Statistics.

47 Wilkinson, Howard [4, 29], ch. 3

48 Wilkinson, Mulgan, *Freedom's Children* (Demos Paper 17), 'The Fracturing of British Values'.

49 Kraemer, 'Siring or Fathering', 'Men's Health Matters' conference, Westminster, 7. 1995.

50 Lee, 'Love', in *I Can't Stay Long*.

51 Paglia [3, 25], ch. 1.

52 Formaini [5, 38].

53 Bradshaw, *Creating Love*, Prologue.

54 Oakley [5, 4].

55 Miller, *Plain Girl*, ch. 6.

56 Craib [1, 78].

57 Phillips [3, 17].

58 Woolf, *Orlando*, ch. 6.

59 See chs 3, 4.

60 Fisher [1, 3], ch. 15.

61 Fisher [1, 3], ch. 10; for striking anecdotal evidence, see Souter, *Independent on Sunday*, 9.10.94.

62 Money, Ehrhardt, *Man and Woman*, chs 7, 8.

63 Miles, *The Rites of Man*, II, 6; IV, 12.

64 Oakley [5, 4], II, 3; and see Wilkinson, Howard [4, 29], ch. 3.

65 Sapolsky, *The Trouble with Testosterone*.

66 Nicholson,[4, 43], ch. 8.

67 Money, Tucker, *Sexual Signatures*, ch. 3.

68 De Beauvoir [Prologue, 16], Conclusion.

69 Phillips [3, 17], Preface.

70 Money, Tucker [5, 67], ch. 4.

71 Montaigne, *Essays*, 'Love'.

72 Dickens, *Little Dorrit*, ch. 31.

73 Lewis, 'Mummy, Matron and the Maids', in *Manful Assertions*, ed. Roper, Tosh.

74 Holloway [4, 85].

75 Horney, *Feminine Psychology*; and see, for example, Benjamin [4, 74], Chs. 1, 4, et al.

76 Winnicott, *The Child, the Family, and the Outside World*; Stern, *The First Relationship*.

77 All my references to the 'mother' include any 'prime carer'. If the early and regular prime carer should be the father, or anyone else, the infant's attachment will be to that figure.

78 Stoller [5, 1], Conclusion.

79 De Beauvoir [Prologue, 16], Conclusion.

80 Eliot, *Middlemarch*, ch. 4.

81 Benjamin [4, 74], ch. 3.

82 See ch. 9.

83 Hite, *The Hite Report on the Family*, ch. 6.

84 Burgess, *Father Reclaimed*. The 'father' does not have to be the real father. For children brought up only by their mothers, substitute 'fathers' will often be found among male relatives, teachers, or their mothers' lovers and friends.

85 Radway, *Reading the Romance*, Introduction, ch. 4.

86 Chodorow, *Feminism and Psychoanalytic Theory*, chs 2, 3.

87 Hudson, Jacot [4, 65], ch. 3.

88 Hudson, Jacot [4, 65], Introduction, ch. 4.

89 Paglia [3, 25], chs 1, 6.
90 As Kinsey noted, and the authors of *Sex in America* confirm (ch. 9), statistics on this matter are extremely complex. However, when asked the direct question in the US, by the authors of the latter work, 1.4 per cent of women and 2.8 per cent of men defined themselves as positively homosexual.
91 Fisher [1, 3], ch. 8.
92 Keen [4, 53], ch. 10.
93 Person [Prologue, 15], 4, xi.
94 Person [Prologue, 15], 4, xi.
95 Cancian, *Love in America*, ch. 11.
96 Firestone [Prologue, 16], ch. 6.
97 Person [Prologue, 15], 4, xi.
98 Plato, *Republic*, bk 5.
99 Nicholson [4, 43], Introduction; MacInnes [5, 3], ch. 1.
100 Eysenck [1, 20], ch. 2; see also Maccoby, Jacklin, *The Psychology of Sex Differences*.
101 Maslow [3, 21], ch. 12.

Chapter 6: Attractions, Provocations, Inducements

1 Greer, *Sex and Destiny*, ch. 8.
2 Pope, 'Sober Advice to the Young Gentlemen about Town'.
3 Dion, 'Physical Attractiveness', *Journal of Personality and Social Psychology*, no. 24, 1972.
4 Cook, McHenry [4, 66], chs 2, 3.
5 Jong [4, 17], ch. 5.
6 Walster [1, 10].
7 Buss, 'Love-Acts' [1, 28].
8 Braine, *Room at the Top*, ch. 4.

9 Cook, McHenry [4, 66], ch. 4.

10 Osborne, *Inadmissible Evidence*, Act II.

11 Masters, Johnson [3, 10], chs 15, 16.

12 Mimnermus, 'Youth and Age', trans. Symons.

13 Wellings et al., [3, 14], ch. 3.

14 Jung, 'The Love-Problem of the Student', CW10.

15 Joyce [4, 20].

16 Morris [3, 22], 'Sex'.

17 Barrows [4, 87], ch. 9.

18 Pietropinto, Simenaur, *Beyond the Male Myth*, ch. 7.

19 Jolly, *Evolution of Primate Behaviour*, II, 12.

20 Paglia [3, 25], ch. 1.

21 Morris [3, 22], ch. 2.

22 Shakespeare, *The Tempest*, 1, 2.

23 Oakley [5, 4].

24 Juvenal, 'VIth Satire', trans. Dryden.

25 Warner [3, 24], ch. 5, note 7.

26 Wilson, Nias, *Love's Mysteries*, ch. 2.

27 Wellings et al., [3, 14], ch. 7.

28 Morris, *Intimate Behaviour*, ch. 2.

29 Yalom, *A History of the Breast*.

30 Morris [6, 28].

31 Verlaine, 'Foursome', trans. Elliott.

32 Freeman, C., consultant psychiatrist, qu. *Independent Magazine*, 17.6.95.

33 Tertullian, 'On Female Dress', qu. Smith, 'Patum Peperium', *Misogynies*.

34 Burton [Prologue, 17], III, 2, ii.

35 Hardy, *The Return of the Native*, bk. IV, 3.

36 Fisher [1, 3], ch. 1.

37 Ackerman [1, 31], IV, 10.

38 Taylor [1, 45], ch. 8.

39 Fisher [1, 3], ch. 2.

40 Shakespeare [1, 72], 2, 5.
41 Knapp, *Music, Archetype and the Writer*, Introduction.
42 Jong [4, 17], ch. 12.
43 Ackerman [1, 31], III, 5.
44 Fowles, *The French Lieutenant's Woman*, ch. 17.
45 Festinger, *A Theory of Cognitive Dissonance*.
46 Shakespeare [1, 30], 5, I.
47 Thibaut, Kelley, *The Social Psychology of Groups*.
48 Luchins, 'Primary-recency', in *The Order of Presentation in Persuasion*, ed. Hovland.
49 Wells, P., Russell R., *Animal Behaviour*, no. 47, 1994; no. 50, 1995.
50 Goode, *The Family*, ch. 4.
51 Lewis, *Loving and Loathing*, ch. 1.
52 Plato [2, 41].
53 Tomalin, *The Invisible Woman*, ch. 6.
54 Helen (charles), '(Not) Compromising,' and F. K. Simmonds, 'Love in Black and White', both in Pearce, Stacey [5, 11].
55 Berscheid, Walster, *Interpersonal Attraction*, ch. 3; Goode [6, 50].
56 Longus [1, 55], bk 1.
57 Fisher [1, 3], ch. 2.
58 Woolf, *The Waves*, sect. 3.
59 Aronson et al., 'The effect of a pratfall', *Psychonomic Science*, 4, 1966.
60 Jong [4, 17], ch. 7.
61 Hazlitt [2, 7], 'Letter Vll'.
62 Fisher [1, 3], ch. 3.
63 De Rougemont [Prologue, 5], I, 11.
64 Wilson, Nias [6, 26], ch. 4.
65 Alberoni, *Falling in Love*, ch. 10.
66 Maslow, *The Further Reaches of Human Nature*, ch. 9.

67 Alberoni [6, 65], chs 1, 12.

68 Burton [Prologue, 17], III, 2, ii.

69 Engels [5, 5], ch. 2.

70 Stone [1, 9], part IV, ch. 7.

71 Tweedie [Prologue, 16], ch. 5.

72 Burton [Prologue, 17], III, 2, v.

73 'Lord Thomas and Fair Annet', 'The Great Silkie', 'Childe Maurice'; 'Hynd Horn', 'Hynd Etin', 'Brown Adam', in *OBB*.

74 [1, 65].

75 Sarsby [5,7], ch. 2.

76 Shakespeare [1, 72]; Austen [1, 32]; Hardy, *Jude the Obscure*.

77 Manning, *An Introduction to Animal Behaviour*, ch. 5.

78 Shakespeare [1, 27]; Congreve, *The Way of the World*.

79 Shakespeare, *Troilus and Cressida*, 1, 2.

80 Sargant, *Battle for the Mind*.

81 Shakespeare [5, 40], 5, 2.

82 Morgan, *Women and Sexuality in the Novels of Thomas Hardy*, ch. 2.

83 Burton [Prologue, 17], III, 2, iv.

84 Chaucer [4, 3].

85 See ch. 7.

Chapter 7: What Happens, and Why?

1 Forster [1, 4], ch. 34.

2 Lodge [1, 89], part IV, 1.

3 For a full analysis see Brehm, in Sternberg, Barnes [1, 28].

4 Barthes [2, 8], 'How Blue the Sky Was'.

5 Pearce, Stacey, 'The Heart of the Matter', in Pearce, Stacey [5, 11].

6 Lindholm, *Charisma*; see Freud, Beyond the Pleasure Principle, SE 18. And see my ch. 11.

7 Person, [Prologue, 15], 1, ii.

8 Phenylethylamine; Fisher [1, 3], ch. 2.

9 Plato [2, 41], sect. 251.

10 Fisher [1, 3], ch. 2.

11 Fisher [1, 3] ch. 2, note 36.

12 Walster [1, 10].

13 Lorenz, *King Solomon's Ring*.

14 *Isaiah* XVIX: 15, OT (1611).

15 Those idealogically opposed to Bowlby's views surely must have misread his work – or not read it at all. Cited here, 'Attachment', vol. 1 of *Attachment and Loss* (3 vols).

16 Morris, *The Human Zoo*, ch. 5.

17 See, for example, Burns's poems to Jeannie; John Clare's 'A Secret Love'; Byron's canto CXXVII in *Don Juan*; Dickens's *Great Expectations*; Hardy's Poems of 1912–13; Bellow's *Humboldt's Gift*, sect. 7.

18 Person [Prologue, 15], 2, iv.

19 Freud [3, 48].

20 Freud [2, 46].

21 Murdoch, *The Book and the Brotherhood*, part 2.

22 Fromm [2, 35], 'The Theory of Love', 2.

23 Leviticus XVI: 21, OT (1611).

24 Goodison, 'Really Being in Love', [3, 3].

25 Shakespeare, *A Midsummer Night's Dream*, 5, 1.

26 Pasternak [2, 34], II, 12, vii.

27 Freud, 'On the Universal Tendency to Debasement etc.', SE 11.

28 Morrison, *Jazz*, sect. 1, sect. 4.

29 De Rougemont [Prologue, 5], 1, i.

30 Singer [2, 50], vol. 3, III, x; and see Alberoni [6, 65], ch. 5.

31 Money, *Love-maps*.

32 Freud [3, 48].

33 Jung, *Man and his Symbols*, part 1.

34 For the time being, Jung's work is much out of fashion (in Greer's estimate, 'mumbo-jumbo'). But the archetypes of *animus* and *anima* accord uncannily well with the experience of falling in love.

35 Lamb, 'Witches and other Night Fears', *Essays of Elia*.

36 Murdoch, *A Severed Head*, chs. 25, 27.

37 Such aspects of the *anima* can be perversely adored, as by Swinburne and the 'Decadents'; see Praz, *The Romantic Agony*.

38 Kundera [4, 38], IV, 21.

39 Graves [3, 34], ch. 27.

40 Raine, 'Poetry and the Frontiers of Consciousness', *Guild of Pastoral Psychology*, no. 220.

41 Graves [3, 34], ch. 25.

42 Greer [Prologue, 10], ch. 1.

43 Ronsard, 'Madrigal', trans. C. Graves.

44 Plato [2, 41], sect. 255.

45 Proust, *Remembrance of Things Past*, 'Within a Budding Grove', Part 2, Seascape.

46 For a less psychological slant, see Langford, 'Snuglet Puglet . . .', Pearce, Stacey [5, 11].

47 Updike [4, 92], sect. i.

48 Singer [2, 50], vol. 2, II, 5.

49 De Rougemont [Prologue, 5], V, 8.

50 Lasch, *The Minimal Self*, V, 5.

51 Freud [3, 8].

52 Mitchell, *Women; the Longest Revolution*, lll, v.

53 Branden, *The Psychology of Romantic Love*, ch. 3, ii.

54 Shakespeare [1, 75], 5, 2.
55 Updike [4, 92], 'The Beach'.
56 Bakhtin, *The Dialogic Imagination*.
57 Skinner, *About Behaviorism*.
58 Calderwood, 'Romantic Love and Radical Intimacy', unpublished Ph. D. thesis, Univ. of Essex, 1984.
59 Masters, Johnson, Kolodny [3, 10], ch. 7.
60 Plato [2, 41], sect. 253.
61 Proust [7, 45].
62 Singer [2, 50], vol. 3, III, 10; Conclusion.
63 Lessing, 'The Habit of Loving'.
64 See ch. 10.
65 Sternberg [1, 28].
66 Nin [2, 14], part 1.
67 Shakespeare [1, 72], 5, 2.
68 Fisher estimates about 3 per cent; [1, 3], ch. 7.
69 Fisher [1, 3], ch. 8.
70 Grass, *The Flounder*, 'The Fourth Month'.
71 Morris [3, 22], ch. 2.
72 Durkheim, *Suicide*.
73 Goode [6, 50], ch. 2.
74 Giddens [1, 12], ch. 4.
75 Richards, *The Sceptical Feminist*, ch. 5.
76 Slater, *The Pursuit of Loneliness*, ch. 4.
77 Goodison [7, 24].
78 Jackson [Prologue, 6], 27, 2.
79 Fromm [2, 35], ch. 2.
80 Plato [2, 26], 190b–193e.
81 Qu. Bowie, *Lacan*, ch. 3.
82 Johnson [1, 60], part IV, 19; and Introduction.
83 Bellow, *More Die of Heartbreak*, sect. 1.

Chapter 8: Trouble

1 Alberoni [6, 65], ch. 16.
2 Jung [3, 27], 'Marriage as a Psychological Relationship', CW17.
3 Murdoch [7, 21], part 2, 'Midwinter'.
4 Wellings et al. [3, 14], ch. 3.
5 Noddings, *Women and Evil*.
6 *Deuteronomy*, XXII: 21, OT (1611).
7 Warner notes ([3, 24], IV, 15) that the Gnostics of the second century assumed that Christ and Mary Magdalen were married.
8 Warner [3, 24], chs 1, 3.
9 1 *Corinthians*, NT (1611).
10 Augustine, *Confessions*, bk 8.
11 Augustine, *Soliloquies*, i. 25.
12 Brown, *The Body and Society*, ch. 13.
13 Anon, 'The Pearl', ed. Morris (Early English Text Society).
14 Warner [3, 24], Epilogue.
15 Collins, qu. Greer [Prologue, 16], 'Body: Sex'.
16 Wagner, *Eros Revived*.
17 Blake, *Gnomic Verses*, x.
18 Hardy, 'Candour in English Fiction', *New Review*, January 1890.
19 Weeks [3, 31], ch. 2.
20 Larkin, 'Annus Mirabilis'.
21 Rubin, 'Thinking Sex', in Vance [5, 9].
22 See work (quoted elsewhere in this book) by Faust; Dickson; Masters, Johnson and Kolodny; Hite.
23 Jong [4, 17], ch. 5.
24 Amis, K., *Jake's Thing*, ch. 25.
25 Michael et al. [3, 15], ch. 6.

26 Hite [3, 10], 'Orgasm', and Appendices.

27 Leroy [4, 36], ch. 1.

28 Chaucer [4, 3].

29 Person [Prologue, 15], 4, xi.

30 Masters, Johnson, Kolodny [3, 10], ch. 7.

31 Michael et al. [3, 15], ch. 6.

32 Hardy, 'Poems of 1912–13'.

33 Dworkin [4, 16], ch. 5.

34 Qu. Marcus [4, 5], ch. 3, part iv.

35 Roth [1, 83], 'Cunt Crazy'.

36 Giddens [1, 12], ch. 2.

37 Pietropinto, Simenaur [6, 18], ch. 7.

38 Homer [1, 44]; Boccaccio, *Filostrato*; Henryson, *The Testament of Cresseid*; Chaucer, *Troilus and Criseyde*; Shakespeare [6, 79].

39 Austen, *Persuasion*, ch. 23.

40 Baker and Bellis, *Animal Behaviour*, vol. 40, part 5, 1990.

41 'Wulf and Eadwacer', *A Choice of Anglo-Saxon Verse*, ed. Hamer.

42 Chaucer, 'The Clerk's Tale', *Canterbury Tales*.

43 Austen [8, 39], ch. 23.

44 Jong [4, 17], ch. 5.

45 Fisher [1, 3], chs 4–7.

46 Jacobus, 'The Difference of View', in *Women Writing about Women*, ed. Jacobus.

47 Miller [3, 40], sect. 3.

48 Bellow, *Herzog*, sect. 6.

49 Heywood [5, 39], ch. 2.

50 George Saville, Marguis of Halifax, *Advice to a Daughter*.

51 Wellings et al. [3, 14], ch. 2.

52 Wellings et al. [3, 14], ch. 5.

53 Holloway [4, 85].

54 Jong [4, 17], ch. 8.

55 Duncombe, Marsden, [5, 11].

56 De Beauvoir [Prologue, 16], IV, 1.

57 Anon, 'The Wanderer', *A Choice of Anglo-Saxon Verse*, ed. Hamer.

58 Duncombe and Marsden, *Sociology*, vol. 27, 2.

59 Jack [5, 15], 2, ii.

60 Shaywitz et al., *Nature*, vol. 373, 2.95.

61 Hite [4, 54], I, (2); see also Formaini [5, 38].

62 Duncombe and Marsden [8, 58].

63 Rubin [3, 6], ch. 7.

64 Nin [2, 14], part 1.

65 Craib [1, 78].

66 The London Helpline Centre for Men estimates that at least 5 per cent of the male population are attacked by the women they live with, but the *1996 British Crime Survey* finds only 0.3 per cent of men actually *report* such attacks.

67 Chaucer [4, 3].

68 Burton [Prologue, 17], III, 2, ii.

69 Miles [5, 63], IV, 12. Research by the Industrial Society (J. James, *Sex at Work*) reports that 54 per cent of women are sexually harassed at their place of work.

70 Eysenck [1, 20], ch. 7.

71 Ibsen, *A Doll's House*, III.

72 Showalter, 'Towards a Feminist Poetics', in Jacobus [8, 46].

73 Formaini [5, 38], ch. 14.

74 Grass [7, 70], 'The First Month'.

75 Carter, *The Sadeian Woman*, ch. 2.

76 According to the *1996 British Crime Survey* 1 per cent of all women reported domestic violence by their partners — but the figure *un*reported is thought to be much higher.

77 Fisher [1, 3], ch. 15.

78 Shakespeare, *King Lear*, 4, 5.
79 'Edward, Edward', *Oxford Book of Ballads*; Goethe, *Faust*, part 2.
80 Roth [1, 83], 'Cunt Crazy'.
81 Hite [4, 54], I; Conclusion.
82 Also Gordon, *The Shadow Man*; Secunda, *Women and their Fathers*.
83 Barstow, *Witchcraze*, Introduction; ch. 1; Cohn, *Europe's Inner Demons*, ch. 12.
84 Mitchell [7, 52], l, iii.
85 Horney [5, 75], ch. 2.
86 Lawrence [2, 36], ch. 16.
87 Kraemer, 'The Origins of Fatherhood', *Family Process*, vol. 30, 1991.
88 Astell, 'An Essay in Defence of the Female Sex' [5, 18].
89 Amis, M., 'Let Me Count the Times', in *Naked Graffiti*, ed. Jones.
90 Lawrence [2, 36], Preface; ch. 31.
91 Cohen, *Being a Man*, ch. 2.
92 Redgrove and Shuttle [3, 43], Afterword.
93 Brontë, C., letter to Ellen Nussey, 15.12.1852.
94 Clare, *All in the Mind*, Radio 4, 30.10.91.
95 Freeman, C. [6, 32]; Kraemer, [5, 49]; Report by the Institute of Environment and Health, for the Medical Research Council, 7.95; see also *British Medical Journal*, January, 1997.
96 McLoughlin, *The Demographic Revolution*, ch. 2.
97 Segal, *Slow Motion*, ch. 10.
98 Amis, M., *The Information*, l, i.
99 Bly, *Iron John*.
100 Beck, Beck-Gersheim [1, 21], ch. 5.
101 Greenstein [4, 80], ch. 12.

102 MacInnes [5, 3], ch. 8.
103 Forster, *A Passage to India*, chs 23, 14.

Chapter 9: Agonies

1 Lessing, *Love Again*, sect. 34.
2 De Rougemont [Prologue, 5]; Johnson [1, 60].
3 Homer [1, 34]; Shakespeare, [1, 27]; García Márquez, *Love in the Time of Cholera*.
4 Malory, [1, 24] 'Sir Tristram de Lyones'; Shakespeare [1, 72]; Tolstoy [1, 75]; Lawrence [2, 36].
5 Person [Prologue, 15], 3, viii.
6 Money, Tucker [5, 70], ch. 6.
7 Lewis, *The Four Loves*, ch. 5.
8 Barnes, [1, 73], ch. 7.
9 Jung compared this experience with that of children, when the parental archetypes fade and the magical omnipotence of the parents vanishes (*The Development of Personality*, CW17).
10 Shakespeare, sonnet 147 (ed. Wells et al.).
11 Homer [1, 34], bk 3.
12 Barthes [2, 8], 'The Ghost Ship'.
13 Forster [1, 4], ch. 33.
14 Homer [1, 34], bk 18. (This may have been no more than an old Greek custom, but it would be unreasonable to assume that Homer was not describing genuine grief.)
15 Brontë, E. [2, 47], ch. 16.
16 Murdoch [7, 36], ch. 19.
17 Shakespeare [1, 75], 4, 1.
18 Shakespeare, *Hamlet*; Goethe [2, 60]; Lawrence [2, 36].
19 Tolstoy [1, 76], VI, 31.
20 Phillips [Prologue, 1], ch. 7.

21 Phillips [Prologue, 1], ch. 13.
22 Anon, in *Medieval Lovers*, ed. Crossley-Holland.
23 Sappho, no. IX [1, 46], ed. and trans. du Quesne.
24 Tolstoy [1, 75], VII, 23.
25 Fisher [1, 3], ch. 8.
26 Phillips, 'Getting Even', *London Review of Books*, 19.9.96.
27 Ibid.
28 Plato [2, 41], sect. 230.
29 Malory, [1, 24], 'Lancelot and Elaine'.
30 Wack, *Lovesickness in the Middle Ages*.
31 Bartlett, 'There is a Desert Here', in *A Lifetime of Dying*.
32 Norwood, *Women Who Love Too Much*, Preface.
33 Giddens [1, 12], ch. 6.
34 Goodison [7, 24].
35 Freud [7, 6].
36 Keen [4, 53], ch. 3.
37 Norwood [9, 32], ch. 7.
38 Fisher [1, 3], ch. 8.
39 Fisher [1, 3], ch. 3; see also report of 'Sex and Love Addicts Anonymous', *Independent*, 12.2.91.
40 French [4, 95], ch. 7, vi.
41 De Rougemont [Prologue, 5], IV, 13.
42 Proust [7, 45].

Chapter 10: Love Tomorrow

1 Lewis [9, 7], Introduction.
2 Lawrence [2, 36], ch. 19.
3 Person [Prologue, 15], 3, vi.
4 Jong [4, 17], ch. 18.
5 Lee [5, 50].
6 Aristotle, *Nichomachean Ethics*, VIII; Plato [2, 41]; Bacon,

'Of Friendship', *Essays*; Browne [3, 44]; Wollstonecraft, *A Vindication of Women*.

7   Johnson [1, 60], ch. 19.

8   Tweedie [Prologue, 16], ch. 8.

9   White [3, 42], ch. 4.

10 Cline, *Women, Celibacy and Passion*.

11 Bacon, 'Of Love', *Essays*.

12 Firestone [Prologue, 16], ch. 7.

13 Sterne [2, 66], VIII, 28.

14 Burton [Prologue, 17], III, 2, iii.

15 Greer [Prologue, 16], 'Love: Obsession'.

16 Amis, K. [8, 24], ch. 28.

17 Pietropinto, Simenaur [6, 18], ch. 8.

18 Stone [1, 9], ch. 7, iv.

19 Johnson [1, 60], ch. 19.

20 Shakespeare, *Othello*, 1, 3.

21 Miller [3, 40], sect. 8.

22 Murdoch [2, 29].

23 Bellow [7, 83], sect. 5.

24 Auden, *The Sea and the Mirror*, sect. 1, 'Prospero to Ariel'.

25 Giddens [1, 12], ch. 9.

26 Self, 'The End of the Relationship', in *Naked Graffiti*.

27 Giddens [1, 12], chs 4, 6, 7, 9, 10 et al.

28 Ovid, 'Baucis and Philemon', *Metamorphoses*, trans. Dryden.

29 Bly [8, 99].

30 Vogelsang, 'The Relevance of the God-image', *Guild of Pastoral Psychology*, no. 252.

31 Redgrove, Shuttle [3, 43], II, 1, iv.

32 Lerner, *The Creation of Patriarchy*, ch. 1.

33 But there is disagreement. In *Form in Indigenous Art* and elsewhere, Ucko argues that there was never a goddess

and that she is an invention of the last three thousand years; see also McDermott [3, 23].

34 See Briffaut, *The Mothers*; Chadwick, *The Mycenean World*; Graves, *The White Goddess* (but beware); Gimbutas, *The Gods and Goddesses of Old Europe*; Campbell, *The Masks of God*.

35 Lerner [10, 32], ch. 7.

36 Freud [Prologue, 9].

37 Hughes, *Shakespeare and the Goddess of Complete Being*.

38 Paglia [3, 25], ch. 2.

39 Heilbrun, *Towards Androgyny*, Introduction, et al.

40 Keen [4, 53], ch. 8.

41 Richards [7, 75], ch. 7.

42 De Beauvoir [Prologue, 16], Conclusion.

43 Cancian [5, 95], ch. 1.

44 Kibberd, 'Bloom the Liberator', *Times Literary Supplement*, 3.1.92.

45 Atwood, *The Edible Woman*, part I, 2.

46 Hudson, Jacot [4, 65], Introduction.

47 Tysoe, 'The Personality and Social Psychology Bulletin', qu. *Independent on Sunday*, 13.8.95.

48 Lindholm [7, 6], and see Freud [3, 46].

49 Sullerot, *Women on Love*, ch. 7.

50 Meredith, 'Modern Love', sonnet xlviii.

51 Benjamin [4, 74], chs 2, 4, 5, 6.

52 Dickson [4, 54], ch. 13.

53 Badinter, *Man/Woman*, part II, 3.

54 See also Dinnerstein, *The Mermaid and the Minotaur*; Chodorow, *The Reproduction of Mothering*.

55 Benjamin [4, 74], ch. 3.

56 Kraemer [5, 49].

57 Benjamin [4, 74], ch. 3.

58 Zeldin [1, 62], ch. 18.

59 Johnson [1, 60], Introduction.
60 Wilkinson, Mulgan [5, 48], 'Renegotiating relations'.
61 Calderwood [7, 58].
62 Branden [7, 53], ch. 4.
63 Goodison [7, 24].
64 Alberoni [6, 65], ch. 17.
65 Person [Prologue, 15], 5, xiii.
66 Giddens [1, 12], ch. 1.
67 Tweedie, [Prologue, 16] 'Ten Years On'; Cancian [5, 95]; Walter, *The New Feminism*.
68 Faludi, *Backlash*.
69 At the US Republican Convention in 1992, Pat Robertson described feminism as a 'socialist, anti-family movement, that encourages women to leave their husbands, kill their children, practise witchcraft, destroy capitalism, and become lesbians'.
70 Shakespeare [6, 79], 2, 2.
71 Person [Prologue, 15], ch. 2, v, and 'Final Thoughts'.
72 Lawrence [2, 36], ch. 30.
73 Tennyson, 'In Memoriam'.
74 Barthes [2, 8], 'The Intractable'.
75 Estes, *Women who Run with Wolves*, ch. 5.
76 Chaucer [4, 3].
77 Keen [4, 53], ch. 10.

Permission Acknowledgements

Permission to quote copyright material is gratefully acknowledged, as follows:

Fleur Adcock: 'Against Coupling' from *Selected Poems*, 1983, by permission of the Oxford University Press.

Kingsley Amis: extract from *Jake's Thing*, Hutchinson.

Martin Amis: extract from *The Rachel Papers*, Jonathan Cape.

Margaret Atwood: lines from 'Siren Song', from *Poems 1965–1995*, Little, Brown (Virago).

W. H. Auden: lines from 'In Sickness and in Health', 'Lullaby', 'In Memory of Sigmund Freud', 'The Sea and the Mirror', *Selected Poems*, Faber and Faber Ltd.

Roland Barthes: extract from *A Lover's Discourse*, translated R. Howard, first published as *Fragments d'un Discours Amoureux* by Editions du Seuil, by permission of the estate of Roland Barthes, Jonathan Cape.

Elizabeth Bartlett: lines from 'There is a desert here', from *A Lifetime of Dying*, Peterloo Poets, © Elizabeth Bartlett.

Max Beerbohm: extract from *Zuleika Dobson*, Heinemann.

Robert Bridges: lines from 'Eros', *Political Works*, 1936, by permission of the Oxford University Press.

John Boardman, et al., eds.: lines from Sophocles' *Tereus*, *The Oxford History of the Classical World*, 1986, by permission of the Oxford University Press.

Poems, by permission of The Society of Authors as the Literary Representative of the Estate of A. E. Housman.

K. H. Jackson: lines from 'Reconciliation', from *A Celtic Miscellany*, translated by K. H. Jackson, 1951, Routledge.

Erica Jong: extracts from *Fear of Flying*, Secker and Warburg; from *Serenissima*, Chatto and Windus.

Milan Kundera: extracts from *The Unbearable Lightness of Being*, translated by M. H. Heim, Faber and Faber Ltd.

Philip Larkin: lines from 'Annus Mirabilis' and 'Wild Oats', *Collected Poems*, Faber and Faber Ltd.

D. H. Lawrence: extracts from *Women in Love*, Lawrence Pollinger Ltd and the Estate of Frieda Lawrence Ravagli.

Doris Lessing: extract from 'The Habit of Loving' in *The Habit of Loving*. Copyright 1954, Doris Lessing. Reprinted here by kind permission of Jonathan Clowes Ltd, London, on behalf of Doris Lessing.

Henry Miller: extracts from *Tropic of Cancer*, reproduced with permission of Curtis Brown Ltd., London, on behalf of the Estate of Henry Miller. Copyright the Estate of Henry Miller.

Harold Monro: 'The Vixen Woman', *Collected Poems of Harold Monro*, by permission of Gerald Duckworth and Co Ltd.

Toni Morrison: extract from *Jazz*, reprinted by permission of International Creative Management, Inc. © 1992, Alfred A. Knopf Inc.

Iris Murdoch: extracts from *The Book and the Brotherhood*, *The Black Prince*, *A Severed Head*, Chatto and Windus.

Grace Nichols: lines from 'I go to meet him', from *I Is a Long-Married Women*, Karnak House.

Anais Nin: extracts from *The Four-Chambered Heart*, Peter Owen Ltd, London.

Camille Paglia: extracts from *Sexual Personae*, Random House Inc., © Yale University.

Boris Pasternak: extracts from *Dr Zhivago*, first published in Great Britain by Collins and Harvill, 1958. This paperback edition first published by the Harvill Press in 1996. 0 Giangiacomo Feltrinelli, 1958. 0 in the English translation William Collins and Sons and Co. Ltd., 1958. Reproduced by permission of the Harvill Press.

Petronius Arbiter: lines from 'Ah God', from *Medieval Latin Lyrics*, edited and translated by Helen Waddell, Constable Publishers.

Marge Piercy: 'Vegetable Love', from *Available Light*, Don Condon Associates.

Sylvia Plath: lines from 'Spinster', from *Collected Poems*, Faber and Faber Ltd.

Peter Porter: lines from 'Sex and the Over-Forties', in *Collected Poems* (1983), by permission of the Oxford University Press.

Marcel Proust: extracts from *Remembrance of Things Past*, translated C. K. Scott Moncrieff, Chatto and Windus.

Philip Roth: extracts from *Portnoy's Complaint*, Jonathan Cape.

Sappho: lines from *Sappho of Lesbos*, edited and translated by Terence Du Quesne, Prebendal Publications.

Will Self: extract from 'The End of the Relationship', in *Naked Graffiti*, Bloomsbury.

Lawrence Stone: extract from *The Family, Sex and Marriage in England 1500–1800*, Weidenfeld and Nicolson.

Elizabeth Taylor: extract from *Palladian*, Little, Brown (Virago Press).

William Trevor: extract from *Lovers of their Time*, reprinted by permission of the Peters Fraser Dunlop Group Ltd.

John Updike: extract from *Brazil*, Alfred K. Knopf Inc.

Paul Verlaine: 'Foursome', from *Paul Verlaine: Femmes/Hommes: Women/Men*, translated by Alistair Elliot, published by Anvil Press Poetry, 1979.

Permission Acknowledgements

Helen Waddell: from *Medieval Latin Lyrics*, Constable Publishers.

Alice Walker: lines from 'Did this Happen to your Mother?', from *Her Blue Body*, Wendy Weil Agency.

Jeanette Winterson: extract from *The Passion*, Bloomsbury Publishing.

Virginia Woolf: extracts from *Between the Acts*, *Orlando* and *The Waves*, by permission of The Society of Authors as the Literary Representative of the Estate of Virginia Woolf.

W. B. Yeats: lines from 'Crazy Jane Talks to the Bishop', in 'Words for Music Perhaps', from *Collected Poems*, with acknowledgement to A. P. Watt on behalf of Michael B. Yeats.

Select Bibliography

(With very few exceptions, this contains critical, analytical and academic works only; references to the authors and titles of anthologies, poetry, novels and plays quoted in the text will be found in the Index.)

Ackerman, D. *A Natural History of Love*, Random House NY, 1994.

Alberoni, F. *Falling in Love*, Random House NY, 1983.

Augustine, St, of Hippo, *The Works of St Augustine*, trans. and ed. Dods, Clark (Edinburgh), 1886. Separately, *The Confessions*, Penguin Classics, 1971; *City of God*, Dent, 1945; etc.

Badinter, E. *Man / Woman*, Collins / Harvill, 1989.

Barthes, R. *Mythologies*, Cape, 1972.

——*A Lover's Discourse*, Cape, 1979.

Bayley, J. *The Characters of Love*, Constable, 1960.

Beauvoir, S. de. *The Second Sex*, Cape, 1953.

Beck U., Beck-Gernsheim, E. *The Normal Chaos of Love*, Polity Press, 1995.

Benjamin, J. *The Bonds of Love*, Pantheon NY, 1988.

Berk, S. F. *The Gender Factory*, Plenum Press NY, 1985.

Berlin, I. *The Crooked Timber of Humanity*, Murray, 1990.

Berscheid, E., Walster, E. H. *Interpersonal Attraction*, Addison-Wesley, Mass., 2nd edition, 1978.

Bly, R. *Iron John*, Addison-Wesley-Longman, 1990.

Bowie, M. *Lacan*, HarperCollins, 1991.

Bowlby, J. *Attachment and Loss* (3 vols.), Hogarth, 1969–80.

Bradshaw, J. *Creating Love*, Piatkus, 1992.

Branden, N. *The Psychology of Romantic Love*, Tarcher, L.A., 1980.

Brown, P. *The Body and Society*, Faber & Faber, 1989.

Brown, R. *Analysing Love*, Cambridge UP, 1987.

Burton, R. *The Anatomy of Melancholy* (1621), Oxford UP, 1971.

Butler, J. *Gender Trouble*, Routledge, 1990.

Calderwood, D. I. 'Romantic Love and Radical Intimacy', unpublished Ph.D. thesis, University of Essex, 1984.

Cancian, F. M. *Love in America*, Cambridge UP, 1987.

Cartledge, S., Ryan, J. (eds) *Sex and Love*, Women's Press, 1983.

Chaucer, G. *The Works of Geoffrey Chaucer*, ed. F. N. Robinson, 2nd ed., Oxford UP, 1974.

Chodorow, N. *The Reproduction of Mothering*, Univ. of California Press, 1978.

Cohen, D. *Being a Man*, Routledge, 1990.

Cook, M., McHenry R. *Sexual Attraction*, Pergamon, 1978.

Craib, I. 'Some Comments on the Sociology of the Emotions', *Sociology*, vol. 29, 1, 1995.

Dawkins, R. *The Selfish Gene*, Longman, 1976.

De Beauvoir, S. *The Second Sex*, Cape, 1953.

Dickson, A. *The Mirror Within*, Quartet, 1985.

Doody, M. A. *The True Story of the Novel*, HarperCollins, 1997.

Douglas, J. D., Atwell, F. C. *Love, Intimacy and Sex*, Sage Publications, 1988.

Dronke, P. *Medieval Latin and the Rise of the European Love-Lyric*, Clarendon Press, 2nd ed., 1968.

——*Women Writers of the Middle Ages*, Cambridge UP, 1984.

Duncombe, J., Marsden, D. 'Love and Intimacy', *Sociology*, vol. 27, ii, 1993.

Engels, F. *The Origin of the Family* (1884), Penguin, 1985, etc.

Eysenck, H. J. *Sex and Personality*, Open Books, 1976.

Faludi, S. *Backlash*, Chatto and Windus, 1992.

Festinger, L. *A Theory of Cognitive Dissonance*, Tavistock Publications, 1962.

Firestone, S. *The Dialectic of Sex*, Cape, 1971.

Fisher, H. *Anatomy of Love*, Norton, 1992.

Formaini, H. *Men, the Darker Continent*, Heineman, 1990.

Foucault, M. *The History of Sexuality* (3 vols.), Penguin, 1979–91.

French, M. *Beyond Power*, Cape, 1986.

Freud, S. *The Works of Sigmund Freud*, ed. Strachey J. et al., Hogarth, 1953–80; see also *The Penguin Freud Library*.

Friday, N. *My Secret Garden*, Quartet, 1975.

Friedan, B. *The Feminine Mystique*, Gollancz, 1963.

——*Beyond Gender*, ed. O' Farrell, Johns Hopkins UP, 1997.

Fromm, E. *The Art of Loving*, Allen and Unwin, 1957.

Giddens, A. *The Transformation of Intimacy*, Polity Press, 1992.

Gilbert, S. M., Gubar S. *The Madwoman in the Attic*, Yale UP, 1979.

Gilligan, C. *In a Different Voice*, Harvard UP, 1982.

Gillingham, J. 'Love, Marriage and Politics in the Twelfth Century', *Forum for Modern Language Studies*, vol. 25, no. 4, 1989.

Goode, W. J. *The Family*, Prentice-Hall NY, 1982.

Graves, R. *The White Goddess*, Faber and Faber, 1961.

——*The Greek Myths* (2 vols.), Penguin, 1962.

Greenstein, B. *The Fragile Male*, Boxtree, 1993.

Greer, G. *The Female Eunuch*, McGibbon and Kee, 1970.

——*Sex and Destiny*, Secker and Warburg, 1984.

——*Daddy, we hardly knew you*, Hamish Hamilton, 1989.

——*Slipshod Sybils*, Viking, 1995.

Hagstrum, J. H. *Sex and Sensibility . . . from Milton to Mozart*, University of Chicago Press, 1980.

Hale, J. *The Civilization of Europe in the Renaissance*, Time-Life Books, 1965.

Hammond, P. *Love between Men*, Macmillan, 1996.

Hazlitt, W. *Liber Amoris* (1823), Hogarth, 1985; etc.

Heilbrun, C. G. *Towards Androgyny*, Gollancz, 1973.

Hite, S. *The Hite Report*, Macmillan, 1977.

——*Women and Love*, Viking, 1988.

——*The Hite Report on the Family*, Bloomsbury, 1994

Horney, K. *Feminine Psychology*, Routledge, Kegan Paul, 1967.

Hudson, L., Jacot, B. *The Way Men Think*, Yale UP, 1991.

Hufton, O. H. *The Prospect Before Her*, HarperCollins, 1995.

Jack, D. C. *Silencing the Self*, Harvard UP, 1991.

Jackson, S. 'Even Sociologists Fall in Love', *Sociology*, vol. 27, no. 2, 1993.

Jacobus, M. (ed.) *Women Writing about Women*, Croom Helm, 1979.

Jankowiak, W. (ed.) *Romantic Passion*, University of Columbia Press, 1995.

Johnson, R. A. *The Psychology of Romantic Love*, Routledge, Kegan Paul, 1984.

Jones, V. *Women in the Eighteenth Century*, Routledge, 1990.

Joyce, J. *Ulysses*, Picador, 1997.

Jung, C. G. ed. Read et al., *The Collected Works*, 1953–79, Routledge and Kegan Paul.

——*Man and his Symbols*, Arkana, 1990.

Keen, S. *The Passionate Life*, Gateway, 1983.

——*Fire in the Belly*, Piatkus, 1992.

Kinsey, A. C. et al. *Sexual Behaviour in the Human Male*, Saunders, Philadelphia, 1948.

——*Sexual Behaviour in the Human Female*, Saunders, Philadelphia, 1953.

Kraemer, S. 'The Origins of Fatherhood', *Family Process*, 1991.

——'Siring or Fathering?' Westminster Conference, 'Men's Health Matters', 7. 95.

Lacqueur, T. *Making Sex*, Harvard UP, 1990.

Laski, M. *Ecstasy*, Cresset Press, 1961.

Laslett, P. (ed.) *Bastardy*, Arnold, 1980.

Lawick-Goodall, J. van. *In the Shadow of Man*, Collins, 1971.

Lerner, G. *The Creation of Patriarchy*, Oxford UP, 1986.

Leroy, M. *Pleasure*, HarperCollins, 1993.

Lewis, C. S. *The Allegory of Love*, Oxford UP, 1936.

——*The Four Loves*, Geoffrey Bles, 1960.

Lewis, D. *Loving and Loathing*, Constable, 1985.

Lindholm, C. *Charisma*, Blackwell, 1990.

Lorenz, K. *King Solomon's Ring*, Metheun, 1952.

Luhmann, N. *Love as Passion*, Polity Press, 1986.

Maccoby, E. E., Jacklin, C. N. *The Psychology of Sex Differences*, Oxford UP, 1975.

MacInnes, J. *The End of Masculinity*, Open University Press, 1998.

McLoughlin, J. *The Demographic Revolution*, Faber and Faber, 1991.

Mandler, G. *Mind and Body*, Norton, 1984.

Marcus, S. *The Other Victorians*, Weidenfeld and Nicholson, 1966.

Marcuse, H. *Eros and Civilization*, Routledge, Kegan Paul, 1956.

Maslow, A. H. *Towards a Psychology of Being*, 2nd ed., Van Nostrand, Princeton, 1968.

——*Motivation and Personality*, 2nd ed., Harper Row, 1970.

——*The Further Reaches of Human Nature*, Penguin, 1973.

Masters, W. H., Johnson, V. E. *Human Sexual Response*, Little, Brown 1966.

——*Heterosexuality* (with Kolodny, V. E.), HarperCollins, 1994.

Mellen, S. M. W. *The Evolution of Love*, Freeman, 1981.

Michael, R. T., et al. (eds) *Sex in America*, Little, Brown, 1994.

Midgely, M. *Beast and Man*, Harvester, 1979.

Miles, R. *The Rites of Man*, Grafton, 1991.

Millett, K. *Sexual Politics*, Hart-Davis, 1971.

Mitchell, J. *Women, the Longest Revolution*, Virago, 1984.

Money, J. *Love-maps*, Irvington NY, 1988.

Money J., Ehrhardt, A. A. *Man and Woman*, Johns Hopkins UP, 1973.

Money J., Tucker, P. *Sexual Signatures*, Harrap, 1976.

Morris, C. *The Discovery of the Individual*, Church History Outlines no. 5, Camelot Press, 1972.

Morris, D. *The Naked Ape*, Cape, 1967.

——*The Human Zoo*, ditto, 1969.

——*Intimate Behaviour*, ditto, 1971.

Murstein, B. I. (ed.) *Theories of Attraction and Love*, Springer NY, 1971.

Nicholson, J. *Men and Women*, 2nd. ed., Oxford UP, 1993.

Noddings, N. *Women and Evil*, University of California Press, 1989.

Nussbaum, M. C. *Love's Knowledge*, Oxford UP, 1990.

Oakley, A. *Women Confined*, Robertson, 1980.

——*Subject Women*, ditto, 1981.

Ortega y Gasset, J. *On Love*, Gollancz, 1959.

Paglia, C. *Sexual Personae*, Penguin, 1992.

——*Sex, Art and American Culture*, Viking, 1993.

Paston Letters, The, ed. Warrington J., Dent, 1978; etc.

Pearce, L., Stacey, J. (eds) *Romance Revisited*, Lawrence and Wishart, 1995.

Person, E. S. *Love and Fateful Encounters*, Bloomsbury, 1989.

Phillips, A. *On Flirtation*, Faber and Faber, 1994.

——*Terrors and Experts*, ditto, 1995.

Pietropinto, A., Simenaur, J. *Beyond the Male Myth*, Time Books NY, 1977.

Pinker, S. *How the Mind Works*, Allen Lane, 1998.

Plato, *The Symposium*, Penguin Classics, 1951; etc.

——*Phaedrus*, ditto, 1973; etc.

Posner, R. A. *Sex and Reason*, Harvard UP, 1992.

Radway, J.A. *Reading the Romance*, Verso, 1987.

Redgrove, P., Shuttle, P. *The Wise Wound*, Gollancz, 1978.

Richards, J. R. *The Sceptical Feminist*, Routledge, Kegan Paul, 1986.

Roper, M., Tosh, J. (eds) *Manful Assertions*, Routledge, 1991.

Rose, S., Kamin, L. *Not in our Genes*, Penguin, 1984.

Rougemont, D. de. *Passion and Society*, Faber and Faber, 1940.

——*Love in the Western World*, ditto, 1956.

Rubin, L. B. *Intimate Strangers*, Fontana, 1985.

Sarsby, J. *Romantic Love and Society*, Penguin, 1983.

Scruton, R. *Sexual Desire*, Weidenfeld and Nicholson, 1986.

Segal, L. *Slow Motion*, Virago, 1990.

Shakespeare, W. *The Complete Oxford Shakespeare*, ed. Wells, Taylor et al., Clarendon Press, 1987.

Showalter, E. *Sexual Anarchy*, Bloomsbury, 1991.

Singer, I. *The Nature of Love*, 3 vols., University of Chicago Press, 1987.

Smith, J. *Misogynies*, Faber and Faber, rev. ed. 1993.

Stendhal. *De L'Amour* (1822), Penguin Classics, 1975; etc.

Stern, D. *The Interpersonal World of the Infant*, Basic Books NY, 1985.

Sternberg, R. J., Barnes, M. L. (eds) *The Psychology of Love*, Yale UP, 1988.

Stoller, R. *Sex and Gender*, Hogarth, 1968.

——*Sexual Excitement*, Karnak, 1986.

Stone, L. *The Family, Sex and Marriage in England, 1500–1800*, Weidenfeld and Nicholson, 1977.

Sullerot, E. *Women on Love*, Doubleday NY, 1979.

Tannen, D. *You Just Don't Understand*, Virago, 1992.

Tanner, N. P. *On Becoming Human*, Cambridge UP, 1981.

Tennov, D. *Love and Limerance*, Stein and Day NY, 1979.

Thibaut, J. W., Kelley, H. H. *The Social Psychology of Groups*, Wiley NY, 1959.

Tiger, L. *Men in Groups*, Boyars, 1984.

Tweedie, J. *In the Name of Love*, Cape, 1979.

——*Eating Children*, Viking, 1993.

Vance, C. S. (ed.) *Pleasure and Danger*, Routledge, Kegan Paul, 1984.

Warner, M. *Alone of All her Sex*, Weidenfeld and Nicholson, 1976.

Weeks, J. *Sex, Politics and Society*, 2nd ed., Longman, 1989.

Wellings, K. et al. *Sexual Behaviour in Britain*, Penguin, 1994.

Wilson, G. *The Great Sex Divide*, Peter Owen, 1989.

Wilson, G., Nias, D. *Love's Mysteries*, Open Books, 1976.

Wollstonecraft, M. *A Vindication of the Rights of Women*, Dent, 1992; etc.

I deeply regret that Erica Jong's *What Do Women Want*, and Germaine Greer's *The Complete Woman*, appeared too late for me to benefit from them.

Index

fidelity 245–6
Fielding, Henry 77
'Fire and Ice' (Frost) 94
Fire in the Belly (Keen) 263
first impressions 189
first love 204–5
'First Month, The' (Grass)
   257
Fisher, Helen 246, 325*n*,
   327*n*
Flaubert, Gustav 26
Flounder, The (Grass) 227
Formaini, Heather 150
Forster, E. M.
   Maurice 16, 200, 269
   A Passage to India 265
Foucault, Michel 87–8
Four-Chambered Heart, The
   (Nin) 55, 70, 76–7,
   112, 225, 253
'Foursome' (Verlaine) 182
Fowles, John 187
French, Marilyn 130
French Lieutenant's Woman,
   The (Fowles) 186–7
Freud, Sigmund 5, 9, 12,
   124, 160, 217, 240,
   286, 289
   on falling in love 206
   and idealization 208–9
   on sensation of 'merging'
      68
   on sex 89, 90–91, 93, 235

on sex and love 98–9,
   229–30
on sexual development in
   infants 158
on sexual symbolism 93
on 'vaginal orgasm' 84,
   107
view of mother as
   subordinate 158, 159
on women and sex 102–3
Friday, Nancy 112
Friedan, Betty 7
friendship 281–3
'Frog Prince, The' 71–2
Fromm, Erich 231
Frost, Robert 94

Gaia, goddess 288
Game of Hide and Seek, A
   (Taylor) 110
García Márquez, Gabriel 58
gays *see* homosexuality
gazing 178
gender 131–67, 288
   biological theory for
      determination of
      152–4, 163–4
   bisexuality *see* bisexuality
   cultural argument for
      determination of 132,
      154–7, 164
   defined 132

Index

joy and omnipotence
53–5
lifelong love 58–60
and magic 71–3
'merging' *see* 'merging'
'oceanic' sensation
69–70, 206
and paradox 70–71
pursuit of beloved's
haunts 67
togetherness and
intimacy 63–7
wavering of gender
73–4
'true' love 282
value of 301, 302
variety and range of 23–8
waywardness of 22–3
and women 164, 251–2,
254
and world cultures 3
see also falling in love
Love Again (Lessing) 266
Love and Friendship (Austen)
55
love at first sight 218–19
Love in the Time of Cholera
(García Márquez) 58
love poems 22
'love-maps' 199, 210
'Love-Melancholy' (Burton)
14

Lovers of their Time (Trevor)
46
love-scripts 50, 220, 229
love-songs 185–6
Egyptian 29
'Love's Philosophy' (Shelley)
39
Lowell, Amy 64
'Lucy' (Wordsworth) 147
Ludus 24, 26
lust 96, 222, 230, 236

Macbeth 262
McCarthy, Mary 105
Maccoby, E. E., and Jacklin,
C. N. 153
madness: and love 275,
285–6
Madonna/Whore split
101–2, 238, 244
magic 71–3
make-up 179–80
male bonding 261–2
male domination 256–65,
289
and aggression 257
as gender stereotype 132,
144–6, 251, 255
inability to cope with
image of 262
and patriarchal demands
257–8
role of testosterone in 257

distinguished from lust
96
importance 16
in *Lolita* 53
and rapture 96
role in human creativity
96–7
sexual arousal 87, 114–15,
120, 124, 125
Sexual Behaviour in Britain
(Wellings) 84, 91,
108, 114, 174, 250
Sexual Politics (Millett) 146
sexual revolution 235, 240
sexual scale 82
sexual symbolism 93–4
sexuality: distinction
between sex and 80
Shakespeare, William 9,
156, 213, 282
love at first sight in plays
218
see also individual plays
Shaw, George Bernard 17
'She being Brand'
(Cummings) 119–20
Shelley, P. B. 38–9
'Epipsychidion' 212, 216
'The Indian Serenade' 121
'Love's Philosophy' 39
Showalter, Elaine 142
Singer, Irving 5, 45, 209,
222

'Siren Song' (Atwood)
247–8
Skinner, B. F. 48, 88
'Sleeping Beauty, The' 72
Small World (Lodge) 47, 200
Smart, Elizabeth 47
smell 184–5
social class 190
and love 194–6
sexual attitudes 102
varying of gender
stereotypes 134
'social engineering' 220
'social exchange', theory of
188, 220
social norms 35
socio-biologists 171, 190,
246, 275
Socrates 67
'Song of Solomon, The' 43,
58
'Song of a Young Lady to her
ancient Lover, A' (Earl
of Rochester) 174
Sophocles 142
'Spinster' (Plath) 242
Stanley, Thomas 224
states of mind, preliminary
194–8
Stendhal 201
stereotypes, gender *see*
gender stereotypes
Stern, D. 158

hatred of by men 261
and jealousy 254
and power to conceive and
rear children 260–61
seen as unclean by men
146
and sex *see* sex
as source of sin 259–60
stereotypes of *see* female
stereotypes
as Subject 264, 265
view of love 164, 251
and virginity 109–11
wiles and treacheries of
254–5
Women and Love (Hite) 84,
116, 253
Women in Love (Lawrence)
64, 68, 124, 126, 188,
260, 262, 272, 301
women writers 140, 180
on sex and sexuality
103–6
women's protest 137–43,
148–9
the Amazons 138–9
history 138–42
reasons for long time in
coming 148

speaking up for women by
men 142–3
Woolf, Virginia 141
Between the Acts 124–5
Orlando 151, 156, 292
The Waves 191–2
Wordsworth, William 147
working class 102
and love 195–6
scarcity of writing on love
from 10
World of Love, A (Bowen) 47
Written on the Body
(Winterson) 293
'Wulf and Eadwacer' 245–6
Wuthering Heights (E. Brontë)
68, 269–70

Yeats, W. B. 213
'Crazy Jane Talks with the
Bishop' 236
You Just Don't Understand
(Tannen) 144–5
youth 169, 172, 173–6, 199

Zeldin, Theodore 37, 39,
298
Zeus 247, 257, 260
Zuleika Dobson (Beerbohm)
57, 75